Winnipeg 1912

Winnipeg 1912

JIM BLANCHARD

University of Manitoba Press

University of Manitoba Press
Winnipeg, Manitoba R3T 2M5 Canada
www.umanitoba.ca/uofmpress

Printed in Canada on acid-free paper by Friesens.

Book and cover design by Doowah Design Inc.
Maps by Steven Gaunt

Title page photo: Opening of the Winnipeg Industrial Bureau building, 1912.

Library and Archives Canada Cataloguing in Publication

Blanchard, J. (Jim)
 Winnipeg 1912 : diary of a city / Jim Blanchard.

Includes bibliographical references.
ISBN 0-88755-684-1

1. Winnipeg (Man.)--History--20th century--Chronology.
2. Nineteen twelve--Chronology. I. Title.

FC3396.4.B53 2005   971.27'4302   C2005-905614-2

The University of Manitoba Press gratefully acknowledges the financial support for its publication program provided by the
Government of Canada through the Book Publishing Industry Development Program (BPIDP); the Canada Council for the
Arts; the Manitoba Arts Council; and the Manitoba Department of Culture, Heritage and Tourism.

To the memory of my father,
A.G. Blanchard, 1912-1988

Table of Contents

Winnipeg 1912

Introduction

As a youngster growing up in Brandon, Manitoba, one of the first conclusions I drew about the history of the city was that 1912 was a significant year. I deduced this fact from the dates carved into the pediments and cornerstones of public buildings: there were a lot of 1912s. Later, as a Winnipegger, I made the same observation about my new home. Indeed, in the Wolseley neighbourhood where I live, two major churches—St. Margaret's and Westminster—and Laura Secord School all bear the date 1912. Many other buildings put up in that year still stand as symbols of Winnipeg's emergence as an important Canadian metropolis. Demolishing the old frame and brick buildings in styles transplanted from Ontario, Winnipeggers put up stone and terracotta buildings more in keeping with their ambitions. The Bank of Commerce and the Trust buildings rose above Main Street and the Boyd Building above Portage Avenue. The steel frame of the Grand Trunk's new Fort Garry Hotel went up, although the hotel did not open until 1913. On Notre Dame Avenue, the Street Railway Chambers were under construction and, behind it, the new extension to Robinson's Department Store was completed. Three new public schools, Laura Secord on Wolseley, and St. John's and Kelvin Technical high schools, were all started that year. In the meadows by the Red, several kilometres south of the city, the magnificent Manitoba Agricultural College buildings were taking shape.

The building that best symbolized the confidence and high hopes of the city in 1912 was not yet built, but its magnificent beaux arts design

These welcoming arches expressed the twin themes of Winnipeg in this era, prosperity and progress.

by British architect Frank Simon was chosen in that year. The new Manitoba Legislative Building that, within a few years, dwarfed the old, colonial, Victorian Legislative Building on Kennedy, as well as the new domed parliaments of the upstart provinces to the west, was to be, in the words of Public Works Minister Colin Campbell, "in keeping with the dignity of the enlarged province."[1] According to a local architect, it would be "the most magnificent in Canada." The *Free Press* said that "no loyal citizen of Manitoba will be satisfied with any building not commensurate with the province's importance and dignity."[2]

The question naturally arises, what was going on in 1912 that so much costly construction was taking place or being planned? Certainly, the buildings that survive indicate it was a time of enormous prosperity and optimism. If we look at publications from 1912, we notice the optimistic tone immediately. The Winnipeg-based *Dominion Magazine* had opened the year with the typically boosterish statement that "We Canadians all believe that 1912 will be the greatest year so far, in the history of the City of Winnipeg, of Western Canada and of this Dominion."[3]

At the end of the year, on December 28, 1912, *Town Topics*, a local entertainment and society weekly, struck a similar tone on its front page with a prediction of

> steady growth all along the line, with assurances that these increases will go on—such is Winnipeg's portion. Its future is secure because its people have realized that the future of a city, like the future of a man, is of its own making, and because they have determined to make it all and more than all than the most foreseeing of the pioneer Winnipeggers, dreaming of Winnipeg's destiny, ever imagined.

So spectacular had Winnipeg's development been over the preceding decade that it was attracting attention in the rest of Canada and abroad. A *Chicago Tribune* piece in 1911 had been positively rhapsodic about the growth of the city.

> All roads lead to Winnipeg.... It is a gateway through which all the commerce of the east and west, and the north and south must flow.... It is destined to become one of the greatest distributing and commercial centres of the continent as well as a manufacturing centre of some importance.

The year of 1912 was one in which all the dreams of the founders— people who arrived in the area in the 1860s and 1870s, such as John Christian Schultz and his wife Agnes, James Ashdown, C.V. Alloway, the Drewery brothers—seemed to have become reality. There could no longer be any doubt that the city they had envisaged was a success, well established, turning a profit. It was the third largest city in the Dominion, surpassing the populations of Ontario cities: Winnipeg's population, for example, was equal to those of Ottawa and London, Ontario, combined. She was the second largest English-speaking city, the largest city west of Toronto.

What Winnipeggers did not realize was that the year 1912 also marked the end of this first period of growth—over forty years of sometimes dramatic, but mostly slow, steady expansion. The next period of the city's history was as marked by failure and decline as the early years had been by success and expansion, and it ended in 1939 with the near bankruptcy of the city.

So 1912 is a watershed year, a year of fulfilment and transition, which invites a closer look. This is not an academic history; rather, it is more in the nature of a travel book, an account of a visit to a city long dead, peopled by men and women no longer here to tell their stories. Most of the people who lived in the city in 1912 left very little behind and we know little about them. Those whom we will meet in this book are from among the minority who did leave some evidence of themselves—the city's leading citizens, whose activities were recorded reverently in the newspaper society columns and who left some archival records behind. We will also visit some other groups, such as the people living in the predominantly Jewish neighbourhood north of the CPR tracks, just east of Main Street, of whom we know a good deal because of the careful work of the Jewish Historical Society of Western Canada.

∾∾∾

All good travel books begin with the physical setting. Winnipeg is a city on a plain. Perfectly flat, the land stretches away in all directions to a flat horizon. Within the city, small elevations are given lofty names like Silver Heights and River Heights. The lowest city on the prairies, she sits on what was once the floor of Lake Aggasiz on ground scoured and compressed by the glacier that preceded and gave birth to the lake. The rivers and marshes in and around the city, and the lakes further north, are remnants of this vast, prehistoric sea. During the city's short history, many acres of the ancient marshes have been drained and creeks filled in to provide more dry space on which to farm and build, but a great deal of sogginess remains, providing a breeding ground for Winnipeg's famous mosquitoes. Beneath the topsoil, a solid floor of impenetrable clay ensures that water lingers on the surface. Far below that, a good deal of water lies trapped. In 1912 it was being drawn out through artesian wells to provide the city with water that was hard and clogged pipes with mineral deposits. Many people collected rainwater, in barrels or in reservoirs in their basements, for purposes such as washing

Looking northwest from the corner of Broadway and Kennedy. The old Law Courts
Building stands on the west side of Kennedy, with the Vaughan Street Jail just visible
to the rear. In the foreground are examples of the substantial homes that once lined
Broadway and streets like Kennedy.

one's hair. Winnipeggers soon approved a plan to build an aqueduct to
bring fresh, clear water from Shoal Lake.

If geography forms the character of the people who live in it, this sort
of country—open plains, endless skies, a vast horizon—should have bred
mystics and poets. The Aboriginal peoples who have lived here for millen-
nia have produced their share, perhaps the greatest one known to us being
Louis Riel. Among the whites, poets were, on the whole, still outnumbered by the hard-nosed, the practical, wanting most of all to make good
by taming the land and bending it to their will, although the extravagant
dreams some of them had for their city bordered on poetry.

Most new immigrants to the Winnipeg plain reacted to the geography by turning their backs on it, just as the river-lot farmers had
done. They tried to remake the flat landscape by planting it thickly
with trees, until the city began to resemble an oasis of green in the
pale yellow grassland. The "British-born"—those identified by the
1911 census as having been born in the British Empire, including
Canada—created theatres, hotels, clubs, churches, homes in which
they could live the life they would have lived in the east or in Britain,

For men in 1912, lodges like the Foresters provided recreation and a chance to do useful charity work in the community.

closer to the centres of the Empire of which they were so proud to be a part. The other Europeans who came to the city from Russia and Austria, Hungary and Germany, did the same, transplanting their institutions and with them their buildings and internal environments: almost every church or hall or house was, on the inside, like a little bit of somewhere else. Winnipeg, then, grew up as a city of expatriates, the outpost of many empires—the Canadian, the British, the Russian, and the Austro-Hungarian.

Winnipeg was called the "Bulls-Eye of the Dominion," the centre of the country, a geographic fact held up by the boosters as yet another advantage for their community. But the city's location also contributed to an unresolved identity crisis. As one journalist wrote in 1912, people living west of Winnipeg were considered to be Westerners and those living east were Easterners. He did not go on to answer the obvious question of what that made Winnipeg. Was it a staid, orderly, and respectable eastern city, or at least the colonial outpost of the East, or was it a western city, brash and unconventional? The answer, of course, is that the city was, and still is, a little of both, and this ambivalence results, some people say, in a tendency to introspection and an obsessive need to be reassured by outsiders.

The people who built Winnipeg and made its success their life's goal were overwhelmingly natives of Ontario, and they and the Britons and Americans who shared control of the city with them would probably have said they were building a city on the Eastern model. But the city did not completely lose its frontier–town quality and even the Ontarioans felt free to be more relaxed and less stiff-necked than their relatives back home. As Reverend George Bryce put it, in the West the immigrants from Ontario were "no longer cribbed, cabined and confined" by the limitations of their home province. F.L. Patton, manager of the Dominion Bank in Winnipeg and a member of a wealthy Toronto family, "lived for years in an unpretentious house on Wellington Crescent and was totally unmoved when important customers from the east commented on its flecked paint and windblown hedge."[4] At the same time, as we shall see again and again in our visit to the Winnipeg of 1912, most members of the city's élite were busily recreating the class structures and social consciousness they had left behind in the East.

The city began to branch out from its Red River fur trade roots in 1860 when the first house was built on the prairie just north of Upper Fort Garry. By 1870, 150 people were living in the neighbourhood of present-day Portage and Main in about thirty houses; by 1880 a little over 4000 souls lived in the village that had already declared itself a city. Then came the western land boom of the early 1880s and with it the notoriety and growth anticipated by the early boosters. Attracted by the feverish real estate speculation attending the coming of the railroad, 13,000 people had crowded into the city by 1882. Many left when the bubble burst in the spring of that year, but many others stayed. They believed in the city's potential and guided it through years of unspectacular growth. Then came the decade of spectacular growth, culminating in our year of 1912. The population tripled in that decade, growing from 42,340 in 1901 to 136,035 in 1911. The city claimed the correct figure was actually 166,533, and this latter number is likely closer to the real population if the total includes the seasonal workers who lived in Winnipeg only in the winter and the residents of crowded tenements who were missed by the census takers.

In 1912 Winnipeg was physically about one-quarter its present size. The border between the city and the land around it was indistinct; streets just petered out, turning into lines of surveyor's stakes in the long grass, but its official boundaries were at Smithfield Avenue and Carruthers Avenue in the north and Wilkes Avenue in the south. In its roughly forty years of existence it had spread about ten kilometres north and south along the west bank of the Red River and five kilometres west from the original river lots to a border defined by Kenaston south of the Assiniboine and St. James Street to the north. East of the Red, the city jogged out to take in the suburb of Elmwood, with its northern boundary just beyond Harbison and its southern boundary less than half a kilometre away, near Ness Avenue.

What we now call River Heights and Tuxedo was occupied by farms or covered with scrub oak and bush. Along Portage Avenue the side streets became more and more thinly populated as one approached the western boundary of the city at St. James Street. North of Portage, houses quickly gave place to scattered factories and processing plants, which in turn gave place to open prairie. In the southern part of Winnipeg, the streets in Fort Rouge closest to River Park on the banks of the Red at the end of Osborne Street were slowly filling up, but there were still plenty of vacant lots along Jubilee and Rosedale. Most people lived in the centre of the city, in Fort Rouge close to the Assiniboine River, in the old Hudson's Bay Reserve between Broadway and the Assiniboine, in the West End, in the old district of Point Douglas, and in the crowded and rapidly expanding neighbourhoods north of the CPR tracks.

The environment of the city in which all these people lived was heavily influenced by the technology of the day—the steam train, the electric streetcar, the coal-fired furnace. Twenty-seven different railroad lines entered the city from every point of the compass and dozens of trains passed through every day, belching smoke and cinders. The vast Winnipeg CPR yards were the largest in the Empire controlled by a single company: there were 215 kilometres of sidings with room for 12,000 cars, and 3000 to 4000 men worked there. The Canadian Northern and Grand Trunk Pacific both had major yards and repair facilities in or near the city. About 400 other industrial establishments turned out $50,000,000 worth of products, making Winnipeg the fourth

Main Street shortly after the end of the building boom in 1913 or 1914, showing several
of the new office towers completed in 1912.

industrial city in the Dominion after Montreal, Toronto, and Hamilton.
The factories also created smoky pollution and industrial waste.

Shaking the ground as they rolled over about 160 kilometres of
track, 300 electric streetcars, huge steel and wood vehicles painted
the Winnipeg Electric Street Railway colours of maroon and yellow, rumbled along city streets. Most Winnipeggers still travelled by
streetcar and the extension of streetcar lines was the kiss of life to
new neighbourhoods. The Street Railway Company belonged to Sir
William Mackenzie, who also owned half of the Canadian Northern
Railway. The company also controlled all the street railways in the
surrounding suburbs and sold electricity and gas to Winnipeg homes
and businesses.

In May the *Winnipeg Telegram* summarized letters received in response to an editorial the paper had run about the slowness of the
streetcar service. Everyone, it seems, had ideas for speeding up the
service. Both the mayor and the city comptroller had asked the Street
Railway to put on express cars to run to the suburbs, a service, they
said, most other cities have. One letter complained that cars often
waited a full five minutes at Portage and Main while the conductor

A Hallowe'en party at the Salvation Army's Grace Hospital. In 1912 the Grace took in unwed mothers about to deliver their babies and many of the young women in this picture are likely in the hospital for that reason.

ran to the office to exchange his fare box. Some people felt it would be better to institute a pay-as-you-go system, instead of having the conductor collect from the passengers once they were already on the car. The conductor could then pay attention to whether it was safe to start moving, instead of being caught in the middle of the car in a crowd of passengers.

Winnipeg had fifteen streetcar routes in 1912; six of these— Broadway-St. John's, Fort Rouge-Selkirk, Belt Line, William Avenue, Portage Avenue, and Dufferin Avenue—had cars travelling at fifteen-minute intervals between 6:00 a.m. and 2:00 a.m. The rest of the routes had cars travelling at twenty-minute intervals.

Within a few years this golden age of public transportation ended and the streets were crowded with motor cars. Although there were already some motor cars and trucks on city streets, most traffic was still horse-drawn.

Portage and Main was the heart of the city, surrounded on all sides by stores, offices, apartments, boarding houses, and hotels. The northern limit of the main business section was marked by the Union Bank Tower at William and Main, a landmark that still stands. Many of the other buildings—the McIntyre Block and the Dominion Bank on the west side of Main and the ornate Post Office at McDermot and Main on the east side—are now gone. The broad sidewalks were crowded with people and the atmosphere was charged with energy, hustle, and excitement. The crowds were young and they had things to do, places to go. The business district was inhabited during the day by crowds of lawyers, real estate agents, bank clerks, grain traders, messengers, typists, secretaries, and shop girls. At noon they spilled out onto the sidewalks, emerging from offices that ranged from high-ceilinged chambers that might have been built for a Renaissance prince to small, dark rooms at the end of dim hallways. There were plenty of go-getters in these offices, watching for the main chance that would enable them to join the city's nineteen millionaires in their pantheon of the successful.

Beyond the city boundaries lay a ring of small towns. Of these, only St. Boniface, with a population of 10,000, claimed city status. St. James, or the municipality of Assiniboia, to use its correct name, was undergoing profound changes as developers carved up the old river lots to create suburbs. St. James's leaders seriously discussed whether to join Winnipeg or establish a separate city in 1912; they did neither, postponing making any decision. But most of the real growth that made St. James a city was still in the future, and on the streets feeding into Portage Avenue, there were more vacant lots than houses. The same was true of St. Vital and East and North Kildonan.

In all these suburban areas, lots were sold and resold, subdivisions laid out, maps and pamphlets published, showing streets and boulevards and cosy middle-class homes. The real Winnipeg was only a third the size of the speculator's dream city, very little of which existed beyond the newspaper ads. Many people, Winnipeggers and outside investors, believed in this dream city in 1912 and gambled their savings on suburban house lots. The garden suburbs were eventually built, but not soon enough to save most of the speculators from financial ruin.

~~~

With its preponderance of men—they outnumbered women by about 10,000—and of young people—an amazing eighty-two per cent of the population was under the age of thirty-nine—Winnipeg was still like a frontier community, different in that way at least from eastern cities. The imbalance between men and women made it difficult for men to find a wife, and Winnipeg had a lot of bachelors. Marriageable young women frequently visited the city on what may have been husband-prospecting trips. Crowds of unmarried young men supported the large number of bars in the city, as they did in all western cities. Although bars were much more strictly regulated than they had been a decade earlier, they still bred fights, crime, and other misfortunes. Prostitution was booming in the city in 1912, although the wide-open red light district, with fifty houses around Annabella Street and Sutherland Avenue in Point Douglas, had become an embarrassment to the city. In 1910, Dr. J.G. Shearer, the Toronto secretary of the Moral and Social Reform Department of the Presbyterian Church, had hired detectives to investigate the goings-on in the district and had given a highly damaging interview to the *Toronto Globe*, saying, among other things, "They have the rottenest condition of things in Winnipeg in connection with the question of social vice to be found in any city in Canada."[5] A Royal Commission was set up to examine the problem and it was a major issue in city politics. In January 1912, newly elected Mayor Richard Waugh asked the police to strictly enforce the law in the district and, although it never completely disappeared, it became much smaller and quieter in the years ahead.

Winnipeg was the Canadian city with the greatest proportion of immigrants in its population. A majority of Winnipeggers—about fifty-six per cent—had been born outside Canada and twenty-five per cent were not "British born," as the census of 1911 designated anyone born in the British Isles and other parts of the Empire, including Canada. These people from Europe, Asia, and the United States made Canada the Dominion's most cosmopolitan city. Even Vancouver, with its large Asian population, did not surpass Winnipeg in this regard and none of the other large Canadian cities—Montreal, Toronto, Ottawa, and Hamilton—had more than nine per cent of their population born outside the British Empire.

About half of Winnipeg's non-British-born population came from the western Russian Empire and the eastern Austro-Hungarian Empire, areas now part of Poland, Ukraine, and Russia. Ethnically,

The Winnipeg Industrial Bureau, built in 1912 at Main and Water streets, combined
business displays, an art gallery, and a museum.

they were Germans, Ukrainians, Poles, Russians, and Jews. They had
come to Canada seeking freedom and a better future for their children.
In 1912, most of these people were still struggling to survive, but along
the streets of the North End, churches, synagogues, newspapers, cultural and theatre groups, and schools gave ever-increasing proof of the
energy and determination of these new Canadians.

The close to 9000 Jews were the old timers among them; many Jewish
families were already in their second generation in the city, having arrived
with the first great influx of Jewish settlers into western Canada in the
early 1880s. In 1916, the census of the prairie provinces reported that
4188 of the local Jewish population were native-born Winnipeggers.

The city was also home to approximately 8000 German-speaking
people, and there were 30,000 Ukrainians in the province of Manitoba
but only about 3500 in the city.[6] Another group with no homeland in
Europe, the Poles, were also more numerous in the rural areas than in the
city.[7] There were 6000 Americans. As for the rest, all the continents of
the earth seem to have contributed at least a few people, including Japan,
from whose empire ten people had found their way to Winnipeg.

The flow of new immigration through Winnipeg continued during
1912, as it had done for a decade. There were record-breaking days
during the year, like April 8 when, the *Winnipeg Telegram* reported,
3500 people stepped off the trains. They included 500 people from

The new Post Office Building on Portage Avenue, one of the impressive new public buildings in Winnipeg by 1912. To the right are the offices of the *Manitoba Free Press*.

southern Europe who came on the Grand Trunk and spent their first night in the West in the immigrant hall in the basement of the Union Terminal; another 800 southern Europeans and 500 from Britain arrived on the CPR. No matter where they came from, most of these people passed through the city on the way to taking up land or working further west. Some, however, decided to stay in the city.

~⹀~

This, then, is the city we will explore: a city of immigrants and native-born Canadians, a prosperous, optimistic, and ambitious city. Winnipeg confidently laid claim, with some justification, to the role of metropolis of western Canada: her Grain Exchange and banks provided the commercial facilities necessary for the import and export trade of the whole region; her flour mills, breweries, and slaughterhouses processed the primary products of the prairies; she was the transportation hub for the region; and her surplus capital helped to

For many of Winnipeg's immigrant and working-class families, life was difficult in the city's North End. Crowded, unsanitary conditions like this were a constant concern for the city's health officials.

finance the development of the West. The *Canadian Annual Review* for 1912, for one, was inclined to agree, and, in a special report on Winnipeg, stated:

> Even in 1912, at the end of the period of spectacular growth, and despite the growth of other important centres, this vast country still contributes and must always contribute, in varying degree, to the expansion and riches of Winnipeg.

But it was precisely the growth of other western cities that frustrated Winnipeg's ambitions of consolidating the sort of dominant position that Montreal and Toronto enjoyed in the East. Vancouver, Calgary, Edmonton, Regina, and Saskatoon were all expanding at a faster rate than Winnipeg and laying claim to their hinterlands, which until then had been supplied and financed from Winnipeg. In 1911–12 nearly 145,000 immigrants flowed into western Canada; only 43,477 stayed in Manitoba. Both the city and the Province of Manitoba were aware that their share of new immigration was declining: concern that Manitoba's growth would slow and bring with it an end to the economic boom led to the founding of the Million for Manitoba League with the goal of ensuring that the province had a population

This image, from a 1912 Winnipeg Industrial Bureau brochure, is typical of the boosterism of the period.

of 1,000,000 by 1922. Its members employed the tried and tested methods—pamphlets, talking, promoting—Winnipeg had been using for forty years.

This boosterism took concrete form in the new Winnipeg Industrial Bureau at the corner of Water and Main. The cornerstone had been laid on December 30, 1911, and the building opened just three months later, serving the city as a convention centre, art gallery, and museum, but, most importantly, as a showcase for local firms. The building was lined with display booths where Winnipeg firms could show their wares and the bureau, headed by Charles Roland, turned out informational and promotional pamphlets and reports bragging about Winnipeg and its potential.

But the League's work was of no avail. The long boom was about to end. Soon the coming of war would result in an abrupt end to the flow of British capital and of the new immigrants who had been fuelling Western Canadian growth.

∽JANUARY∽

New Year, Society Life, Theatre

On New Year's Eve, the Royal Alexandra Hotel at Higgins and Main was ablaze with lights, alive with laughter and music. The local newspaper, *Town Topics*, described "the dining room and café being crowded with all kinds of gay little supper parties, a large orchestra enlivening the proceedings. After 12 o clock, the ballroom was thrown open and a jolly dance ensued."

Dancing did not start until midnight because December 31 was a Sunday, and dancing, along with many other things, was forbidden under the 1906 Lord's Day Act. But, when midnight came, the laughing crowd spilled out into the lobby from the Oak Grill and the Dining Room, and hurried up the stairs to the Colonial Ball Room on the second floor. Samuel Barrowclough's orchestra was set up and waiting for the dancers and, as the floor filled up, they put out their cigarettes, finished their New Year's drinks, and began to play.

Samuel Barrowclough was born in England and he had been making music in the city for thirty-one years. His dance band played for most of the big events and celebrations at the Royal Alexandra. He had come to Winnipeg when both he and the city were very young. He had served in the 1885 campaign against Riel, as a bugler in the 90th Winnipeg Rifles, and he was now the leader of the regiment's band and of the Winnipeg city brass band. He had made a good living from music: in 1912 he had his own music store and lived in a comfortable, middle-class home at 813 Balmoral Street.

The Royal Alexandra Hotel, 1912.

The Royal Alexandra was the unrivalled Grand Hotel of Winnipeg from the day her doors opened in July 1906 until 1913, when the Grand Trunk's new Fort Garry Hotel opened on Broadway. In her public rooms, the city's élite entertained with balls and dinners and teas.

The original decision to build a CPR hotel in Winnipeg had been made in 1899 by Thomas Shaughnassy, the new president of the company. It was to be part of a major redevelopment, including a station and office building on the railroad's property at Higgins and Main, and the expansion of the yards a short distance to the west. He hoped that the large, handsome, and expensive building, which he intended to operate on the lines of the Chateau Frontenac in Quebec City, would improve the class of buildings in the neighbourhood.

As an urban renewal project, Shaughnassy's hotel was a spectacular failure: many of the small Victorian hotels and business blocks that the president of the CPR hoped would be swept away were still standing when the Royal Alexandra was demolished in the early 1970s. But in its heyday, it was a symbol of the young city's hopes and pretensions and wealth. Naming it after Edward VII's Queen Alexandra suggested worldliness and style; the Queen was a fashion leader, watched and imitated by millions of women all over the Empire.

More sober on the outside than her sisters, the Empress or the Chateau Frontenac, the Royal Alexandra was as elegant and spacious inside as any of the others. Like all the company's hotels of this period, she bore the mark of Kate Reid, the wife of Hayter Reid, the CPR's superintendent of hotels. Hayter Reid had been, for many years, Superintendent of Indian Affairs in the west and is credited by some with irritating Aboriginal people to the point that they joined with Riel in the rebellion of 1885. Reid masterminded the repression that followed the rebellion, which included the public hanging of eight Cree men in Saskatoon.

Mrs. Reid was the Canadian-born widow of a wealthy New Yorker. She returned home to Canada after her first husband's death and married Reid, her childhood sweetheart. She got her start as a decorator advising Sir William Van Horne, her husband's friend and employer, on the purchase of antiques for his Montreal mansion. She decorated the special royal train that carried the future George V and his wife across Canada in 1901. Then Van Horne put her in charge of decorating the Empress Hotel, the Chateau Frontenac, and the Royal Alexandra in Winnipeg. It was said of her that, "Playing on color harmonies, searching for the right details, matching fabrics and personally choosing the embroidered motifs on the table linen, she came up with a style that managed to be luxurious and domestic at the same time; a style which, in the end, made everyone feel at home."[1]

The manager of the hotel in 1912 was Walter S. Detlor, who lived in the building with his wife and children. By 1912 he had spent over twenty years working for the CPR, learning his trade as chief clerk and accountant at the elegant Place Viger Hotel in Montreal and at the Chateau Frontenac in Quebec. Detlor was the guardian of the hotel's style and a guide for the city's ambitious hostesses, who sometimes thanked him publicly for his advice.

The Royal Alexandra was an immediate success, and this and the crazy growth of the city necessitated a huge expansion project, almost before the plaster was dry in the original building. By 1912 this enlargement of the hotel was nearing completion. There were many new guest rooms, a new, larger, ballroom, and a large banquet room, as well as a number of smaller private dining rooms.

Entering the hotel from Higgins Avenue on New Year's Eve, visitors found themselves in a vestibule with marble steps leading up to the massive L-shaped lobby. This room, with its forest of classical columns, stretched to the southwest corner of the building and then continued along the west side to the billiard room at the rear. Two restaurants, the Oak Grill and the Dining Room, opened onto the lobby. Both rooms were large and exquisitely decorated. The Oak Grill was done in the popular Mission style, with large, square chairs and lamps with stained glass shades. The ceiling was glass and, through it, natural light filtered down from a light shaft in the centre of the hotel. The Dining Room, whose windows looked out onto Higgins Avenue on the south and the station courtyard on the east, was decorated with a series of murals six metres high, depicting scenes of Red River history, painted by Frederick Challoner.

On the second floor were the rooms of the Vice-Regal Suite, with a view across Higgins and south down Main Street. Also on this floor were the Gold Room, a drawing room in which guests could relax and visit, and the Colonial Ball Room, at the other end of the hall, also facing Higgins Avenue.

~~ ~

The Royal Alexandra was the scene of many of the teas, luncheons, balls, and dinners that followed one another in quick succession in Winnipeg in 1912. Social events also took place in other public places and in private homes, but the hotel was the first choice of the city's élite. The ways in which these middle- and upper-middle-class people spent their leisure time emphasized the real gulf between the rich and the not so rich. In addition to simply enjoying themselves, the wealthy often used entertaining as a way to display their wealth, erect social barriers, and reinforce the class structure in Winnipeg. The prosperous families at the top of the social structure watched a little nervously as certain members of other immigrant communities—the Jews in particular—also grew wealthier. There was some interaction with Jews in business matters, but the social world was carefully sealed against them. There were, as well, many newcomers to the city from Ontario and Britain who were potentially acceptable, but who had to be vetted and either welcomed or excluded.

The Oak Grill, off the lobby of the Royal Alexandra, as it looked at New Year in 1912.

In a city of self-made men, where almost everyone with money had worked hard to get it, denying access to the local version of "society" was tricky. This was a common problem that had vexed the ruling classes all over the European world as, enriched by the industrial and commercial expansion of the nineteenth century, the bourgeoisie elbowed their way forward, demanding entry into "society," the exclusive world inhabited by those at the top.

Leaders of local Winnipeg society, such as Mrs. Colin Campbell, the wife of Manitoba's Attorney General, reinforced a system of "door keepers," controlling who was in and who was not, who was invited and who was excluded. Mrs. Campbell was exceedingly proud of having been presented at Court in London and of having been invited to the coronations of both Edward VII and George V, privileges she owed to her husband's position and to her own United Empire Loyalist background. She spoke about these experiences to groups of schoolchildren on occasions like Empire Day and stories about her appeared in newspapers and magazines.

Mrs. Campbell, who was a local Regent in the patriotic and Anglophile Imperial Order of the Daughters of the Empire (IODE), had ensured that Princess Patricia, the Governor General's daughter, was given a life membership in the organization during her visit to the city in July 1912 and she had sent clippings describing the event to Queen

Samuel Barrowclough, whose dance band entertained at many city social events.

Mary's Lady in Waiting and to Princess Christian, the King's sister. She received answering letters from Buckingham Palace assuring her that "The lady in waiting ... is commanded by the Queen to thank her so very much indeed for so kindly sending her majesty the newspaper accounts ... which interested the Queen." Princess Christian wrote that the clippings "interested the Princess greatly." She added that her brother, the Duke of Connaught, the Canadian Governor General, "writes most enthusiastically of Canada, and of all the kindness loyalty and affection he meets there. The Princess remembers well having had the pleasure of receiving Mrs. Campbell at her house in London last summer."

For an ambitious political wife and a United Empire Loyalist, these notes must, on a personal level, have been thrilling to receive. The fact that Mrs. Campbell had them printed in the newspapers shows that they had a broader political and propagandistic purpose: to cement connections with Britain and the Royal Family to and reinforce the established social hierarchies throughout the Empire.

Lieutenant-Governor Douglas Cameron played his role as the local head of official society in Manitoba. He and his wife entertained regularly at Government House, inviting a representative group of provincial and city politicians, mostly Protestant church leaders, and military officers from the Fort Osborne Barracks. From time to time there were larger entertainments, like the garden party the Camerons had in June 1912. The regimental band of the 79th Cameron Highlanders played on the lawn and the Lieutenant-Governor and his wife greeted guests in a marquee hung with Union Jacks. Fairy lights and Japanese lanterns illuminated a scene similar to ones repeated again and again in hundreds of cities throughout the mighty British

Empire and one the Camerons no doubt hoped resembled the garden parties of the faraway King and Queen.

For those who had not grown up in society, it was possible to learn how to entertain and live according to the rules from the dozens of etiquette manuals in print, some of them in many editions. Marion Harland, a popular American etiquette writer from this period, was quite open and frank about her work's being of service to such people:

> Men and women, women in particular, to whom changed circumstances involved the necessity of altered habits of social intercourse, people of humble lineage and rude bringing up, who yet have longings and tastes for gentlehood and for the harmony and beauty that go with really good breeding, these make up the body of our clientele.[2]

To all these people Mrs. Harland offers hope. The manners of the rich are not an impenetrable mystery, but a way of behaving that can be learned. Her books will help with this and she also counsels women to watch closely those hostesses whom they wished to emulate.

The Winnipeg of 1912 had women who guarded the gate to the tiny world of Winnipeg Society and were carefully watched for clues about how to act. The parties given by wealthy hostesses like Mrs. Augustus Nanton and Mrs. George Galt were described in the society columns in the newspapers, so lesser mortals could read about how it was done. Mrs. Hugh Phillips, the wife of a successful Winnipeg lawyer in 1912, recalled many years later: "I remember Mrs. Sutherland—Lady May we called her because she held her head high and was so grand. She had a blue satin drawing room. She told W.F. Alloway to be careful of the chairs: he sat down on one and put his feet up on another."[3]

Mrs. Hugh Sutherland had been in the city since 1878, when she came from Baltimore to marry. In 1912, she presided in relative splendour at 81 Roslyn Road, a house her husband had built only three years before, employing the best materials: red sandstone from Minnesota, mahogany panelling, and red silk damask wall coverings. The Sutherlands entertained lavishly in their beautiful dining room; everything was done properly and no one was allowed to put his feet up on the furniture.

Mrs. George Galt and her husband also entertained on a grand scale. Her husband and his cousin, John Galt, were partners in a large grocery wholesale, which sold, among other things, the firm's popular Blue Ribbon brands. They had come to Winnipeg in the 1880s and were now very comfortable. They were members of the family of Alexander Galt, a Father of Confederation and successful business-man, and they had profited from other family enterprises in western Canada, such as the Galt coal mines in Lethbridge.

In January 1912 the Galts moved from their home on the corner of Broadway and Donald to a beautiful new house at 460 Wellington Crescent. George Galt had designed many features of the house and he made sure it had plenty of room for entertaining. The front hall was seven metres square and had a good oak floor for dancing. The music room was eight metres long and five metres wide. The Galts' daughter, Alice, recalled many years later:

> We entertained at home a great deal. We'd have a sing song or roll back the rugs if we wanted to dance. We had a lot of small parties of about a dozen people or less. We had got our first gramophone in 1908, but if we wanted to dance mother would play....When we were going to have a dance my sisters and I carried most of the furniture up to the third floor to the would-be billiards room so that if people wanted to go up there and sit out they could.[4]

At the end of January, the Galts had two dances—on Wednesday and Friday of the same week—to celebrate Alice's coming out. Young women who were "coming out" were introduced into society at dances organized by their mothers or by a friend and for a year they were celebrated as "buds" of the season. It was during this year that young debutantes often became engaged to be married.

There were 150 guests at each of the Galts' affairs and an orchestra played for them. Everyone sat down to supper after the tenth dance and then continued on for ten more numbers. Because the house was new, the floors were not broken in for dancing and Alice remembered that:

> A new floor is terribly hard to dance on so we danced mostly in the Music Room where we had used talcum powder to help it

along. Next day the hall floor was full of little bits of dirty wax along with the talcum powder. It was a mess. It may have been very grand that night but I spent all next day scraping that darn wax off the floor!

Alice's friend, Marion Boxer, also came out at the dances. About thirty other young women made their debuts that year, so there were many parties to attend. In November Alice's cousins Maryon, nineteen years old, and Evelyn, who was eighteen, made their debut in their father's house at 260 Roslyn Road. *Town Topics* duly reported the young women's rite of passage at

> a brilliant dance given by Mrs. John Galt in honor of the debut of her two daughters, Maryon and Evelyn Galt. The spacious rooms of this lovely home were all beautifully decorated with American Beauty and Killarney roses, shaggy yellow chrysanthemums being used in the dining room. Dancing was carried on in the drawing room and hall, the orchestra playing in a corner of the latter room. Mr. and Mrs. Galt with their two very charming and pretty maidens received their guests at the drawing room entrance.

The fact that other young women also came out at the Galts' dances probably means that their mothers were attempting to reduce the huge cost of the dances by sharing expenses. Girls from wealthier families were also expected to host theatre parties, teas, lunches, and other entertaining during this crucial year.

But the financial and social toll of this kind of socializing had become the subject of social critics. In 1912, Dorothy Canfield Fisher, a writer, educator, activist, and friend of Willa Cather, published her first novel, *The Squirrel Cage*. It dramatized the outcome of middle-class social climbing by following the story of an Ohio middle-class family and their beautiful daughter, Lydia. Lydia's ambitious mother skilfully manages their home with a sharp eye to changing fashions and the likes and dislikes of her social betters. Lydia returns from a year of "finishing" in Europe to have her coming-out dance and her year as a debutante, with all its attendant entertaining. Lydia's mother works hard to ensure that nothing comes in the way of the

The drawing room in the home of Mr. and Mrs. James Ashdown, typical of the formal
settings in which well-off Winnipeggers entertained.

consummation of her ambitions: her daughter's marriage to the son
of one of the town's wealthiest families. It is only a year or so later,
when Lydia's father, a judge, dies penniless that she realizes, to her
horror, that her extravagance has ruined him and contributed to his
death from overwork.

∾∾∾

Perhaps the most basic form of entertaining to be mastered by an
ambitious hostess wishing to prove herself worthy of admission to
"society" was the afternoon tea. Emily Holt, author of the *Encyclopedia
of Etiquette*, praised its usefulness:

> The afternoon tea, or ceremonious at home, has for some years
> enjoyed a popularity that shows no signs of waning…. Such teas
> are given throughout the winter season to introduce young ladies
> to society, to honour special guests, to give a young married
> couple an opportunity to meet their friends and to enable a

hostess in a single afternoon successfully to entertain the whole list of her visiting acquaintances. They are the least expensive and the least exacting functions in the list of social diversions and, considering the many good purposes they serve, the most useful and satisfactory.[5]

We get some insight into the details of an "at home" as practised in Winnipeg from a humorous piece published in *Town Topics* on March 2, 1912. The author, identified only as K.E., injects some humour into her description of how to organize a tea, although she does not question the basic value of the activity. Preparing for a simple tea, which might last from 3:00 p.m. to 6:00 p.m. or 4:00 p.m. to 7:00 p.m., was a great deal of work.

Everything from rearranging the furniture to make more room to decorating the rooms with flowers is discussed by Mrs. Livingstone in her etiquette guide. The society columns always described the flowers chosen by the hostess. In 1912 roses and carnations predominated, but other varieties, more rare and more expensive, are mentioned in descriptions of the parties of wealthier people. In summer, most women would have their own flower gardens, but in the winter they ordered from local florists such as Robert Ormiston, who kept large greenhouses to supply the city. A few homes, like Kilmorie, the Nantons' house, and Government House, had attached conservatories.

The role of servants at an "at home" is spelled out in etiquette books. We can assume most middle-class Winnipeg women at this time could afford only one general servant, who opened the front door, did the behind-the-scenes preparation, and helped the ladies who poured tea. In a 1912 handbook for servants, American writer Anne Springsteed tells the waitress, who in Canada would have been called a parlourmaid, that:

> The simple afternoon tea of a lady who is at home informally is easily arranged by a waitress; but it demands that everything shall be exquisitely dainty.... Two friends of the hostess will be asked to pour, and you must provide a large napkin for each to protect her gown. The waitress is instructed to be watchful of the needs of the ladies who are pouring ... promptly bringing fresh cups and saucers, and being sure that the dishes of cakes, jugs of cream, and

bowls of sugar are replenished whenever necessary. Silver bread trays and cake-baskets and the handsomest china plates may be used for the sandwiches and cakes. Beautiful tall glasses may hold a variety of bonbons and glace fruits. Piles of plates and small napkins find a place on the table, and the waitresses take care that each person entering the dining-room is properly served, and that she is relieved of plate and cup when she has finished.[6]

Once all the preparations were made, the hostess waited for her guests. In *Town Topics*, K.E. says, "The most tiring part of receiving lies in waiting for someone to come. As you have intimated that you are at home for 4 o clock, no one comes before 5 and there you sit bored beyond words...." The hostess stationed herself near the door of the drawing room beside the guest of honour. "At last," K.E. says,

you hear the bell and promptly assume your receiving manner— the stereotyped smile, stereotyped remarks re weather and other inane topics. After a few stiff speeches interspersed with tea, the visitor departs and a repetition is gone through with others. You look in vain for the women who complained about your not having an at home in the first place—they do not come.

Etiquette demanded that guests visit for no longer than fifteen or twenty minutes. Still, K.E. testifies that at the end of the day, you are exhausted and vowing never to do it again. When the newspaper comes out the next day, however, and reports that you received with "that ease and grace for which you are so well known," all your efforts and work of the day before are repaid. With a good review the columnist bestowed a secure status as a member of the "in" group, those who knew the rules of entertaining and could apply them in the effortless way that suggested long familiarity. The writers of society columns, also always women, were, therefore, courted in an attempt to secure just such a positive review: Constance Denholm, the society columnist for the *Telegram*, was frequently named in guest lists of social events of all sizes.

Not everyone was impressed by the formulaic accounts of such events. "Eye Opener" Bob Edwards made fun of them in a February 19, 1910, column in the *Calgary Herald*:

By George, we must get off some society stuff this issue or bust a gut. It is the height of the season and owing to several unfortunate jamborees at the time when the big functions were being pulled off we have not been able to get in our fine work. But better late than never. Last Wednesday night a charming dance was given at the charming residence of the charming Mrs. W. Sloshcum-Kachorker. Old Sloshcum-Kachorker, who had inadvertently got drunk at the Mariaggi that afternoon, was unable to be present, but a pleasant time was had nevertheless. The rooms were tastefully decorated with flowers and ferns. Among those present were: A beautiful gown of blue satin with net trimmings and sage and onion stuffing. A charming white gown of crepe de chine brussels sprouts net over silk, trimmed with old point lace.... It really does not matter who were inside the gowns. Toward the end of this most successful function old Sloshcum-Kachorker came lurching downstairs from an upper chamber looking for a drink and rather spoiled the general effect of the tout ensemble, but on the whole it was a charming affair and the charming hostess was warmly congratulated by her guests.

Let's take a look at just one of the dozens and dozens of afternoon teas that took place in Winnipeg in 1912. The tea on February 20 was duly noted in *Town Topics*:

Mrs. J. Vincent Nutter, the Rosemount, was a tea hostess of Tuesday afternoon. Mrs. Wallace McMillan and Mrs. R.A.C. Manning presided over the tea cups at a table centered with a silver basket filled with pink tulips and lillies of the valley. Mrs. Wm. C. Russell and Mrs. W. Whyte relieved them later. Miss Marquis, Miss Effie Smith, Miss Ruth McDermid and Miss Nora Bell assisted. Among the other guests were: Mrs. Burbidge, Mrs. Gordon Thomson, Mrs. Chown, Mrs. Erb, Mrs. McWilliams, the Misses Gordon, Mrs. C.E. McPherson, Mrs. Fortin, Mrs. Harold Smith, Mrs. McIntosh, Miss Crowe, Mrs. C.M. Scott, Mrs. George Stephen, Mrs. Rutherford, Mrs. Blair, Mrs. Chamberlin, Mrs. P.C. McIntrye, Mrs. Cornell, the Misses Cornell, Mrs. Logan and Mrs. Herbert T. Riley.

The entry is largely a list of names and this is no accident. The people who were invited by Mrs. Nutter gave readers important clues about how well she was doing socially.

Perhaps most significant were the friends she asked to help by pouring tea. They were married to men in jobs similar to her husband's—he worked as an insurance agent with C.H. Enderton, the firm developing the exclusive Crescentwood suburb—and she probably had met them because of this connection. Mrs. Wallace McMillan also lived in apartment 307 in the beautiful Devon Court on Broadway, almost directly across the river from the Rosemount. Mrs. McMillan's husband owned Superior Realty. Mrs. William Russell lived on Kingsway and her husband also worked for C.H. Enderton.

Mrs. W. Whyte, who was also asked to help pour tea, was the daughter-in-law of Sir William Whyte, the recently retired western vice-president of the CPR. Her husband, just twenty-nine years old, worked for yet another real estate firm, W.J. Christie. Inherited wealth meant that the Whytes, although young, could afford a good house in a good neighbourhood, at 66 Kingsway. Young Mrs. Whyte, whose name was Marguerite Marie, was the daughter of W.W. Blair, a successful architect who lived in Armstrong's Point. She had grown up in Chicago where her father practised between 1890 and 1905. She and her husband had been married in 1907, just two years after she came to Winnipeg with her family.

Mrs. R.A.C. Manning was also asked to help. Her husband was a lawyer and a Conservative Party organizer and the Mannings were a well-connected and well-off local family.

Most of Mrs. Nutter's other guests were also the wives of lawyers and managers in various enterprises. The presence of women such as Mrs. P.C. McIntyre, the wife of the postmaster for Winnipeg, and the wife of Captain Gordon Thompson, the private secretary of the Lieutenant-Governor, and Mrs. Herbert T. Riley, wife of one of the successful and wealthy Riley family members, at Mrs. Nutter's tea tells us she was having some success cultivating connections that could benefit her husband's career and her own social ambitions. Mrs. Riley was close in age to Mrs. Nutter and was one of a new generation of women who became social leaders in the city after World War I. We know that she socialized with other young women such as Mrs.

Harold Aikins, the daughter-in-law of James Aikins, a wealthy lawyer and future lieutenant-governor, and Mrs. Whyte, the daughter-in-law of Sir William Whyte.

This was an ambitious guest list for someone like Mrs. Nutter. The Nutters were young in 1912—he was thirty-four—and still making a place for themselves in Winnipeg where they were relative newcomers. He had arrived in the city from Montreal in 1904 and she was a native of Hamilton, who came to Winnipeg when they were married in 1909. Within a few years they moved out of the Rosemount Apartments—by no means a bad address—and into a comfortable

Lady Whyte, one of the formidable, self-made matrons who controlled Winnipeg society.

home in Crescentwood. How successful was she in making inroads in Winnipeg society? We do know that she was invited back at least once, in November, to have tea with Mrs. Whyte, a sign that she was enjoying some success.

⁓⁓⁓

On the first morning of 1912, Winnipeg awoke to twenty-eight degrees below zero. Against the clear, blue skies, plumes of white smoke rose from thousands of chimneys. The brutal cold had gripped the city for two weeks and would continue, the temperature plunging to a low of minus forty-three on January 11.

Outdoor activities were cancelled and equipment was starting to break down: on Friday, January 5, an overhead streetcar cable snapped in the cold, causing a backup of thirty-four southbound cars near St. John's College on Main Street; passenger trains, struggling with frozen equipment, arrived four to seven hours late.

On Monday, January 1, most people were on holiday and a few of them stayed in bed, wondering what to do about the pounding in their heads and making resolutions to never drink again. The *Free Press* published a cartoon of a servant telling his employer, who was in the grip of a terrible hangover, that his coach awaited him. Out on the street a water wagon was waiting at the curb. A few heavy drinkers may have resolved to go to the Gatlin Institute, 147 Hargrave Street, where they could undergo a three-day cure, under the supervision of a physician. A "harmless vegetable remedy" was administered internally with absolutely no hypodermic injections. Cocaine or morphine addicts were also welcome. The manager of the institute, W. Harvey Hamilton, lived in a substantial new house at 100 Arlington, so we can assume that business was good. People wanting to cure the liquor, morphine, or tobacco habits, or who were simply suffering from nerve exhaustion, could also book themselves into the Evans Gold Cure Institute at 226 Vaughan Street. For $120 they would be subjected to the treatment that helped restore Winnipeggers to good health for twenty years.

No one disputed that immense misery was caused by drink. The story of John Shields is typical of hundreds of tragedies related to drinking. Shields had been arrested December 23 for being drunk in public, but was released by the magistrate when he said he did not want to spend Christmas in jail. He was in jail again on New Year's Day, when he became ill. A doctor was called and he told the police to take Shields to the General Hospital, but he died in the police wagon on the way. He was fifty-five. Shields's history is not given in the newspaper, but he was likely part of that large, shifting population of single men who spent the winters in the city and the summers working on railroad gangs or lumber camps or farms. Some of these men saved enough money to go homesteading, or set up a small business. But many, like Shields, drank their summer wages, and, after many summers, finally drank themselves to death.

The *Free Press* and the *Morning Telegram* published papers on New Year's Day, although most businesses were closed. The papers listed plenty of ways to entertain yourself in the city. There was a hockey game at the auditorium rink, which stood on the south side of York Avenue between Fort and Garry. The Winnipeg Victorias defeated

the Montreal New Edinburghs 5
to 2, in one of a series of games that
wound up the following Saturday
with the Victorias capturing the
Allen Cup. The Winnipeg team
included a group of young men—
Colby Fowler, Ollie Turnbull, Herb
Gardner, and Harry Street—who
had learned the game at Alexandra,
a downtown public school, playing
fiercely competitive games against
the nearby private Tuckwell's Boys
Academy.[7] Both teams belonged to
the amateur Interprovincial League,
and there was controversy during
the series about the Montrealer
Jack Ryan, whom many people
judged to be a professional, in
spite of the fact that a letter from
the Amateur Union certified he

The Orpheum Theatre on Fort
Street.

was not. The whole question, no doubt thoroughly chewed over in
hundreds of conversations that week, was discussed fully by Assistant
Sporting Editor Mike Shea in his regular *Free Press* column, "Live
Chat on Sport."

Many people went curling on New Year's Day; all the rinks were
busy: the Strathcona, the Granite, the Civic, and the Assiniboine curling
clubs. A few days later, Premier Roblin inaugurated yet another rink,
the Union Terminal Curling Club, opened to satisfy an ever-increasing
demand for ice. The papers carried the news that a delegation of champion Scottish curlers had landed in Halifax and that they would make
their way to Winnipeg to participate in the bonspiel in February.

If you weren't a sports fan, you might have gone to the theatre,
where you could choose between a melodrama, *Deep Purple*, at the
Walker Theatre, *The Burgler and the Lady* at the Winnipeg Theatre,
or *The Two Orphans* at the Opera House. The Orpheum, a brand-new
theatre on Fort Street, and the Empress both had vaudeville shows.
In the evening the First Baptist Church offered a performance of the

Two theatre ads, one for the vaudeville line-up, including Charlie Chaplin, at the Empress, and one for the Starland movie theatre on Main Street.

Messiah. Winnipeg was an important part of the North American vaudeville circuits. Later in the year, both Charlie Chaplin and W.C. Fields were among the vaudevillians who performed in thew city. Chaplin actually came twice, both times as part of Fred Karno's London Comedy Company, at the Empress. By the time of his second 1912 visit to Winnipeg, Chaplin—still Charles, not Charlie—was well known enough to warrant headliner treatment as the star of a sketch entitled *The Wow Wows.* Fields, who appeared in the summer of 1912 at the Orpheum, received star billing as "The Silent Humorist," but had to share the stage with six other acts, including a "Quintette of Highly Educated Pachyderms."

There were also movie theatres, "cinematograph halls" with names like "Dreamland" and "Starland," which promised patrons "the world at your command in Motion Photography." In 1912, the bill of fare at these early movie theatres included short newsreels along with melodramas with titles such as *Victim of the Mormons.* For more refined tastes, later in the year the Lyceum Theatre presented an "Engagement Extraordinary" with Sarah Bernhardt's film version of *Camille.* Cinema was just beginning to lure the crowds away from the live stages: the fall of 1911 had seen the cancellation of dozens of live travelling shows, including some with big budgets and big stars. In New York City, where movies had already made huge inroads, about 600 movie houses and nickelodeons were in operation and one-third of the live theatres included movies in their programs. Men such as Marcus Leow and William Fox, the movie magnates of the future, operated lines of theatres and made profits in the hundreds of thousands of dollars.

In Winnipeg the first motion pictures were shown in a tent on Main Street in 1899 by John Schuberg and Fred Burrows. By 1912 Schuberg owned a chain of movie houses, including the Bijou and the Province in Winnipeg. There was a

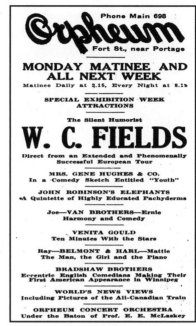

Phone Main 698

Orpheum
Fort St., near Portage

MONDAY MATINEE AND ALL NEXT WEEK
Matinee Daily at 2.15, Every Night at 8.15

SPECIAL EXHIBITION WEEK ATTRACTIONS

The Silent Humorist

W. C. FIELDS
Direct from an Extended and Phenomenally Successful European Tour

MRS. GENE HUGHES & CO.
In a Comedy Sketch Entitled "Youth"

JOHN ROBINSON'S ELEPHANTS
A Quintette of Highly Educated Pachyderms

Joe—VAN BROTHERS—Ernie
Harmony and Comedy

VENITA GOULD
Ten Minutes With the Stars

Ray—BELMONT & HARL—Mattie
The Man, the Girl and the Piano

BRADSHAW BROTHERS
Eccentric English Comedians Making Their First American Appearance in Winnipeg

WORLD'S NEWS VIEWS
Including Pictures of the All-Canadian Train

ORPHEUM CONCERT ORCHESTRA
Under the Baton of Prof. E. E. McLaskey

The line-up at the Orpheum with W.C. Fields as the headliner.

fledgling movie industry in Winnipeg, with companies making promotional films for the railroads. The Starland Company, which also owned the Starland Theatre, made two movies in 1912: one about the Calgary Stampede and another depicting the massive parade at the Odd Fellows Convention in Winnipeg in September.[8]

Movies were an alarming new development for some people. A censor board had been established in Manitoba to ensure that nothing scandalous was shown, and the theatres themselves, some of which were store-front operations, were criticized as being unsafe fire traps, poorly built with only one exit.

∾∾∾

On New Year's Day in Winnipeg, it was a tradition for men to go calling, or "first footing." This was a Scottish custom practised in the days of the Red River Settlement and adopted in Winnipeg by many non-Scots. All over the city, ladies were "at home" and in their parlours the rumble of male voices was heard where, for the rest of the year, only women came to call. Hostesses who normally would offer tea or hot chocolate to their guests, on this day might put out a rum punch or pour a visitor a glass of whisky.

Ruth Harvey, the daughter of C. P. Walker, the owner of the Walker Theatre, gives us a glimpse of her parents' house at 771 Dorchester at New Year around this time:

> From early afternoon until well into the evening all the men in town went on a round of calls. They paid their respects to the crown at the Lieutenant Governor's official reception and then went from house to house of friends where the women were ready with their dining tables spread with sandwiches and cakes and tea and coffee and punch.[9]

She describes a visit from a family friend, Mr. Barley, who sold advertising for the *Free Press* and lived across the river at 30 Furby Street:

> the bell would ring, and when I ran to the door and opened it, Mr. Barley would blow in like a stray brown cocoon on the gust of below-zero air. I would take his beaver coat, his fur cap and gauntlets, and we would settle him in an armchair by the fire with his punch. He would wrap his fingers round the mug to warm them.... He would sniff the punch and smile and sip. Very warming, very fortifying, he would say contentedly.

When the last guest departed into the night, the Walkers turned out the lights and climbed the stairs. The first working day of a busy new year would soon be upon them.

&ESFEBRUARY&ES;

Work, Religion

By 1912, Winnipeg's prominence and unprecedented growth had begun to make it a destination not only for immigrants but for curious visitors of all sorts. In 1909, the city had been able to persuade the members of the British Society for the Advancement of Science to make the long trip to Winnipeg to hold their annual conference. In September 1912, the city hosted a meeting of a different sort when 15,000 Odd Fellows convened in Winnipeg for their annual convention, culminating in a massive, five-kilometre-long parade down Portage Avenue.

One early visitor to Winnipeg who left a fascinating account of the city was Ella Sykes. In 1911, she travelled through western Canada to research *A Home Help in Canada*, her guide for young British women contemplating immigration to Canada. Sykes was no stranger to adventure—a few years before, she had spent two years in Persia and central Asia, accompanying her brother Percy, a British diplomat. Travelling by horse and camel, she became the first European woman to cross the Persian desert. In 1915, she travelled to Kashgar in Chinese Turkestan to help Percy administer a remote British consulate, and she later explored such exotic places as the Takla-Makan Desert and the 4300-metre-high pass of the Karra Dawan.

Even as an indomitable traveller as Ella Sykes marvelled at the speed at which things moved in Winnipeg, a city she described as bright and bustling, full of movement along the immensely wide thoroughfares of Main Street and Portage Avenue, with tramcars constantly running and crowds for ever passing. I notice an almost entire absence of old people, and wondered whether the strenuous life of the Land of Youth was too much for them. Everything here goes hey presto! Here funerals pass at a smart trot, and I could hardly keep up with the brisk pace at which the choirs led the psalms and hymns in the churches.[1]

Sykes found Winnipeg to be a city of hard work, in which she would not have considered looking for work as a waitress.

In all probability I should have been 'fired' the next day, as I heard again and again that English waitresses are looked upon as too slow and are speedily hustled out of their posts by alert Canadians who seem to do their work with lightening speed.[2]

Sykes was not the only writer to warn readers of the hardships and fast pace that awaited them in western Canada. In the 1909 satirical novel *The Letters of a Remittance Man to His Mother*, a young man newly arrived from England is warned by an old-timer not to depend on his classical education and social background: "This is a land of production and to make this land produce one has to work, and consequently a man's worth is estimated by the amount of work he can do."[3]

We get the same sense of hustle and devotion to hard work in a *Winnipeg Tribune* piece of December 18, 1909, written by Russian immigrant Michael Sherbinin, who lived in Winnipeg for the first decade of the twentieth century. Sherbinin comments on all the different nationalities one can see on Main Street, represented in the "hurrying human tide that flows along the street...." He describes a real estate broker as "A fine type of the Canadian businessman of the west. Notice his brisk step and confident air. He is ready to meet any man as an equal in the business field and is not likely to be worsted by anyone he meets."

Sherbinin describes an Italian grocer who is "rapidly making a fortune" and notices two Chinese laundry workers, whom he describes as "industrious and harmless, and ask only to be left alone to work all day and apparently all night too for that matter." A Jewish store

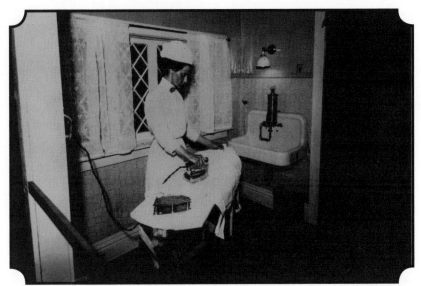

Caring for the elaborate clothes of the period was only one of many jobs a "maid of all work" had to perform.

owner paces "restlessly up and down in front of his store. He has no intention of letting a customer slip through his fingers...." The impression is one of a bustling city with everyone working very hard to make their fortune in the new land.

There was plenty of work in Winnipeg in 1912, more work than people to do it. The actual workforce, according to the 1911 census, was 61,000. In a year with a record number of building permits approved, 10,715 of these workers were employed in the building trades. Carpenters (2778), bricklayers (505), and stonemasons (382) greatly outnumbered concrete workers (20) and structural steel workers (102): the city under construction was predominantly wood and brick. The work turned out by these men can still be seen in the older neighbourhoods all over the city, where solid houses from this era continue to stand straight and true.

There were eighteen women amongst this army of men, five painters and thirteen office staff for construction firms. The names of the five painters are not known, and the story of how they broke into this overwhelmingly male world is sadly lost to us.

It was far more common for women to be employed in domestic service. In private houses in the city, 2281 women worked as maids and cooks, beside about 250 men who earned their living as household servants, gardeners, chauffeurs, and coachmen. Coachmen and grooms still outnumbered chauffeurs, 194 to 58. Hotels and restaurants employed another 2500 people, many of them women. Nine hundred men and women made their living as laundry workers, many of them Chinese men who laboured long hours in dozens of small laundries all over the city. Beginning in 1909, these small laundries had to have a city licence and twenty-eight had been closed because they did not live up to the requirements for light and ventilation and separate living quarters for the workers.

The Winnipeg of 1912 was overwhelmingly a commercial city that extended its influence over the whole prairie region, becoming for a time the metropolis of the west. Commerce employed 15,000 people, the largest single category reported in the census. This army of managers, clerks, accountants, typists, secretaries, and office boys was employed the bank and trust company offices with real estate holdings and mortgages all over the prairies.

The sumptuous, new, western headquarters buildings built by the eastern banks were impressive proof of the importance of Winnipeg for these institutions. In November 1912 the Bank of Commerce opened its massive building on Main Street and the Bank of Montreal's Greek temple neared completion at Portage and Main. One eastern bank, the Union Bank, was moving its national headquarters to Winnipeg from Quebec, on a motion at the bank's annual meeting by Winnipegger R.T. Riley, who, like a number of other local people, was a large shareholder in the bank. Mr. H. Veasey, the accountant at the head office of the Union Bank, arrived in Winnipeg in June with a staff of a score of assistants. By July 1, the general manager, Mr. Balfour, and many more staff had come to settle into their offices in the Union Bank Tower.

About 800 telegraph operators and telephone girls handled the constant flow of information that was the lifeblood of the banks and the grain and real estate businesses. Salesmen who travelled out over the western provinces, keeping small-town commerce connected to the large Winnipeg wholesale houses, numbered 5409 confident, smiling, hand-shaking fellows.

Winnipeg had a growing manufacturing sector in 1912, feverishly promoted by the city. Prospective manufacturers were told they would

Construction workers outside the Manitoba Agricultural College.

enjoy "cheap power, cheap sites, low taxation, a plentiful supply of raw materials, best of labor conditions, unexcelled railroad facilities and the support of the community."[4] Heaton's annual *Commercial Handbook* listed manufacturing opportunities in Winnipeg as being mainly in the area of processing agricultural products. The type of heavy manufacturing in which American cities similar to Winnipeg were involved—farm machinery is a prime example—never really became established in the city. The same favourable freight rates that supported Winnipeg's wholesale businesses discouraged local manufacture of heavy items such as farm machinery, which could be brought in cheaply from Ontario.

About 11,000 people worked in city factories. Women predominated in clothing factories, but everywhere else they were outnumbered by men. One hundred and thirty-six children between the ages of ten and fourteen worked in factories, the two largest groups being twenty-eight children who worked for printers and thirty-four who were office boys. Because the employment of children was a hot political topic in 1912, probably not all child employees were reported to the census takers.

The Manitoba Bridge and Iron Works was one of Winnipeg's larger manufacturers.

There were 4600 people classified as professionals in the city, close to half of them women. Most of these women were working as music teachers, schoolteachers, nurses, and stenographers. There were also twelve doctors and eight dentists, fourteen photographers, fifteen professors, four accountants, and three journalists who were women. This last number was certainly incorrect: all the newspapers and magazines published in the city employed women writers and at least one was edited by a woman.

One group of employees about whom we know a good deal, although they are not separately recorded in the census, are the women who worked in department stores. A study done by the ten-person Civic Committee of the Winnipeg University Women's Club,[5] beginning in November 1913, carefully researched the working conditions of these women in the four largest retail stores in the city in 1912: the Hudson's Bay store on Main, the new Eaton's store on Portage, Jerry Robinson's Department Store on Main just north of Portage Avenue, and Carsley and Company. The four stores together employed between 2400 and 3200 girls and women on staff, depending upon the season.

The study enquired into physical factors that affected well-being, such things as ventilation, heating, light, and flooring materials. They found that none of the Winnipeg stores, except for Eaton's, had a mechanical ventilation system and even there it only moved the air in the basement and on the main floor. For those people posted near the doors, there was sometimes too much fresh air. In one store girls were frequently away for three and four days at a time with severe colds in winter because of cold draughts from the outside coming in through the doors.

Floors, for the most part, were wood, which, although it was very hard to keep clean, was the most comfortable and durable. In Winnipeg, shop girls were not required to stand all day: the Shops Regulation Act required that every female employee should have a chair to sit on when not serving customers. A full hour was given for lunch in all stores in the city. Many people preferred to go out for lunch to get some fresh air, but three of the stores did provide lunch-rooms. One, we may presume it was Eaton's, had a "bright, airy lunch-room, where food is served at cost," and about twenty-five per cent of the staff ate there. Cloakrooms with hooks and small shelves were provided for staff and "Lockers and, in some cases, special rooms are provided for the heads and assistant heads of departments."[6]

Eaton's was unique in North America in having a pension plan for its women employees. Anyone who had worked for Eaton's for fifteen years and had reached the age of forty was eligible for a pension. The pension "ranges from four dollars to eight dollars weekly, and will be paid for life, so long as the pensioner does not marry, does not enter into any employment similar to that which the company gives, and leads a moral life."[7]

What was meant by a moral life provision was not explained.

Hours of work were long and employees worked every day but Sunday. The working day lasted from 8:20 in the morning until 5:30 or 6:00 at night, with an hour for lunch. Three of the stores closed Saturday afternoon in the summer months and Eaton's allowed a half-day off once a week. Beyond these basic hours, one of the stores stayed open on Saturday night, and all stayed open longer hours at Christmas, but they hired extra staff to do so. The committee felt that, given that provincial legislation did not stipulate the number of hours workers should be on the job, the department stores were quite enlightened in what they expected of their staff.

A young Hugh Phillips in his law office.

On the sales floor, the jobs and the pay ranged downward from the sales clerk to the juniors who worked as cashiers, wrappers, and messengers. These latter positions were often held by children or young girls. Although there were no laws against employing children under the age of fourteen, none of the stores did so except for one, which employed the children of customers at Christmas. Young women applying for regular employment were required to bring a signed certificate from their parents stating that they were over fourteen. Young women employees between fourteen and eighteen years of age were required to live at home or with some adult who would be responsible for them.

On the question of pay, the committee was able to report on averages. The salaries ranged from a low of five dollars a week for beginning employees to fifty dollars a week for a few senior women. Most experienced sales clerks were earning between fifteen and eighteen dollars a week. The more junior staff earned between five and eight dollars and waitresses made about seven dollars with free meals. There were a few benefits, such as discounts and an occasional bonus, which augmented these salaries. Eaton's had a minimum wage system that mandated the minimum amount women would earn in each age group. Given the cost of living in Winnipeg at this time, it was thought that a person earning nine dollars a week could probably support themselves and live independently. Many of these employees, then, must have been living with their families or sharing with roommates.

Sharing with other young women was precisely what Ella Sykes suggested in her guidebook for potential British immigrants. Board and room might cost as much as forty-three dollars a month, an amount that would eat up most of a stenographer's wages of forty-five dollars, but a four-bedroom apartment could be rented by four friends for thirty-five dollars each, allowing them to live much more cheaply.

The committee listed the hardships of working in a department store: physical tiredness from standing, bad air, and nervous tension from working with the public. They concluded that these hardships were all part of the job and the only real way they could be alleviated was if shoppers were more appreciative of the work being done for them and showed more patience and kindness.

The committee made two main recommendations at the end of their report: that schools should begin to teach about department store work as part of their commercial courses, to better prepare potential employees; and that the Council of Women should create a list of respectable and clean boarding houses for women employed in stores. As to the widespread belief that women employed in stores were immoral, the committee assured the community that this was not the case and that it was extremely unfair to the women involved.

Another large group of workers who did not show up in the census tables was the floating population of workers who spent summers working on railroad construction or on farms and who were often unemployed in winter. Although in the winter of 1911–12, more men than usual were working in the bush, cutting timber and hauling it to sawmills where it would be transformed into railroad ties or cordwood, by the middle of February, the situation of many seasonal workmen in the city was desperate. Unemployed since the beginning of the cold weather, their savings gone, they had problems feeding themselves and their families. The hopelessness these men felt as they went out every day in search of work was appalling. In his novel *The Letters of a Remittance Man to His Mother*, W.H.P. Jarvis described the monotony and loneliness of life in Winnipeg during the winters. The main character lives in rooms over a Main Street store.

> The one large room we all occupy is over a shop and is heated by
> steam. In one corner there is a small gas stove on which we make
> tea and occasionally cook food when we have it to cook. Jenkins
> and I sit in one room most of the day and when we do go out we
> hurry along the streets to the nearest bar room, where we get
> warm, and leaving that, hurry on to the next, on into the hotels,
> where people stare at us.[8]

Some Winnipeggers showed concern for the terrible problems people ran into in the middle of the winter. At a meeting of concerned citizens in the Great West Life Building in February, a committee was formed to see what might be done about the low wages paid to working people; for example, girls who made three to five dollars per week and labourers who were not earning enough to feed their families.

The constant increases in the cost of living were a perennial problem at the time—in March 1912 the *Labour Gazette* reported that the cost of living price index, based on the cost of thirty selected articles that all families needed, reached its highest point since record keeping began in 1890. The Toronto Board of Trade produced a comprehensive report on the subject at the end of 1912, recommending, among other things, that roads around the city be improved so farmers could bring in their produce for sale directly to consumers.[9] The problem of rising prices became acute during the war; indeed, the growing gap between wages and the cost of essentials has been cited as the major cause of the Winnipeg General Strike of 1919.

During 1912 certain basic items were higher in price: vegetables and feed were higher because of a drought in Ontario; coal cost more because of coal strikes in Alberta, Britain, and the US. One remedy put forward in Winnipeg, and in many other cities in Canada and the US, was to buy food directly from the producer, cutting out the middleman. At the end of September, a public market was held at the Industrial Bureau, organized by the Central Market Committee of the Million for Manitoba League. It was judged very successful. Within the first two hours, cars were lined up along Water Street as women of the first families selected produce.

Thomas Ryckman, editor of *Dominion Magazine*, chaired this committee. In an editorial in the magazine, he argued that a public market would save $3,000,000 a year in food costs. Farmers from

Winnipeg, East Kildonan, Elmwood, St. Vital, Teulon, Stonewall, and Whitemouth had come in, as well as boys from the Knowles School for Boys, which had a large market garden.

A week later *Town Topics* added its vote of approval:

> Unqualified approval is heard on all sides of the operation of the public vegetable market in the industrial hall last week. The gardeners cooperated most heartily and there was an abundance of all kinds of garden produce on hand for all the days that the market was kept open.... The ladies from all over the city went marketing as they do in the eastern cities where a public market is one of the civic institutions.... There is no good reason why a public market cannot be established where the consuming public may purchase their vegetables without paying more than a reasonable profit to the producers.

Town Topics was either not aware of the busy farmers' market at Dufferin and King, or reticent to suggest that the British-born ladies of Winnipeg should go there to rub shoulders with the Jewish customers and the Ukrainian sellers.

~~~

Winnipeggers respected hard work and made a religion out of getting ahead. But, on the whole, they were also motivated by traditional religions. Most Winnipeggers in 1912 would have described themselves as being religious, and they went regularly to their church or synagogue. Many of the city's churches had been expanded continually over the years to accommodate their growing congregations. Westminster Presbyterian Church, which opened its Maryland Street building in June 1912—its third church in less than forty years—had room for 1250 people. There were many more of a similar size and records show that these and many other large places of worship were full every Sunday during the years for two or even three services, as well as hosting a full calendar of social events.

The two largest denominations in Winnipeg were the Anglican and the Presbyterian, both claiming around 30,000 people. Roman Catholics numbered 19,000 and Methodists 15,000. This gave Winnipeg a different religious landscape from Toronto's and those of other Ontario cities where Methodists usually outnumbered Anglicans and Presbyterians. There was, if we relate this religious makeup to culture, greater Scottish influence in Winnipeg than in any other large Canadian city.

The cosmopolitan nature of the city's population is mirrored in their religious life. Winnipeg, for example, had more Lutherans (11,000) than any other city in the Dominion. This number is accounted for by the German and Icelandic communities, as well as Scandinavian-American immigrants from Minnesota and North Dakota. Winnipeg also led the nation in the size of its Greek Orthodox community—3158.

There were other believers reported in the census of 1911: 135 Buddhists, 92 Confucians, and one follower of Mohammed. There were 107 declared agnostics, 4 pagans, 5 Theosophists, and 2 Universalists. The number of people who reported that they followed no religion at all was as large in Winnipeg as in Toronto, 1052 and 1182, respectively, and much larger than in Montreal, which only had 328 such godless folk. In Winnipeg, many people in this category were undoubtedly people dedicated to the tenets of socialism and communism.

Winnipeggers demonstrated their commitment to their churches in a manner very typical for them: by the enormous sums of money they donated for construction and maintenance. In 1910, during four days, the Westminster Church congregation raised a staggering $63,000 for the construction of a new church. At the opening service on June 16, 1912, the collection totalled over $10,000. St. Luke's, the Anglican church on Nassau Street, apparently had no difficulty collecting large sums from its well-off congregation to cover the original church cost of $20,000 in 1904. Over the first ten years, a $5000 organ was added, along with a tower at a cost of $10,000, and a parish hall. Augustus Nanton, who attended the church, paid for the bells and clock for the tower, John Galt funded a mural inside the church, and Lieutenant-Governor Cameron donated the money to pay for the main stained-glass windows.

All this lavishing of money on the churches of the city leaves an impression of a Christian community that was quite worldly. Indeed, an Anglican clergyman, Bishop John Ingham, who was visiting the city in the company of other British churchmen, commented that, at a

The interior of Fort Rouge Methodist Church.

meeting with Archbishop Matheson and some of their Canadian colleagues, "All of us noted the universal domination of dollars and acres. Some of us ventured to question whether our Lord's wide Catholic purpose for the world was not being left out of sight and spiritual loss thereby was not accruing to Winnipeg itself."[10]

The importance of the churches in people's lives was not purely religious. They were also social centres, and, by looking at the parish histories of some churches, we can reconstruct how they filled this role. Clarence McKinnon, the minister of Westminster Church when it was still located on Notre Dame and Hargrave, recalled:

> Large after meetings were held on Sunday night. The social side of life was vigorously organized. Newcomers were met and welcomed. Picnics, socials followed each other in quick succession. Interchurch debates enlivened the winter months, and athletic sports in the summer & many years afterwards & a gentleman, a French Canadian, stopped me on the street to tell me how, when he and his wife were very lonely on their first arrival in the city,

they had strayed into Westminster Church on a Sunday evening and how grateful they were for the happy human fellowship they found there.[11]

His successor, Reverend Christie, wrote of his first winter at the church in 1909

> that it was the heyday of immigration in Winnipeg. Sometimes rooming houses were not too attractive. To linger on the streets on the severe winter evenings was to invite frozen ears. If the church was a mecca for the faithful it was also a welcome refuge for the careless. Indeed on Sunday evenings the entire width of Hargrave Street was black with the stream of people, padding almost noiselessly over the snow, making their way to Knox or Central or First Baptist or Westminster. Groups would be seen, scurrying from one to the other of these over crowded sanctuaries.[12]

The church also played an important role in what might be called the city's "intellectual life." Several Winnipeg clergy—Charles Gordon of St. Stephen's Presbyterian Church, Bertal Heeney of St. Luke's being two—were published authors. Gordon, writing as Ralph Connor, was an internationally known, best-selling novelist. The sermons of some clergy were reprinted as pamphlets and distributed to their congregations, and sermons were reported in the press.

∽MARCH∾

Politics, Dickens

The Victorian brick Legislative Building on Kennedy Street had been the stage setting for Manitoba's political dramas for twenty-eight years by 1912, the year in which plans were unveiled for the enormous building that would replace it. There was no lack of drama during the remaining years of its life: the old building witnessed the tumultuous end of the Roblin government and the disgrace of the man who had been perhaps the province's greatest premier.

But as the members arrived from all over Manitoba for the second session of the province's thirteenth legislature at the end of February, these defeats were still three years in the future. Rodmond Roblin was at the height of his power. During twelve years in government, his seemingly unbeatable party had secured victories for the Tories in three general elections—1903, 1907, and 1910. In each case they had won the popular vote and had never had a majority of less than fifteen members. In the general election of 1914, his last, he again won both the popular vote and an eight-seat majority in the House, in spite of having to face a determined and energized Liberal Party. A year later, after the corruption surrounding the construction of the new Legislative Building became public, Roblin resigned in disgrace and, in the August 1915 election, his party was reduced to five members, although they did receive thirty-three per cent of the votes cast.

Roblin enjoyed a good deal of influence regionally and nationally. His 1908 amendment of the School Act, obliging all schools to fly the

This 1917 photograph shows how the ambitious, new, classical Legislative Building dwarfed its prim Victorian predecessor. By 1917, scandal over construction of the building had swept Rodmond Roblin's government from office.

Union Jack every day, attracted the attention of the British press and he became known as a defender of the British connection. During the 1911 federal election, the reciprocity election, he and his lieutenant, Robert Rogers, had delivered Tory victories when the party had been wiped out elsewhere in the West. He had been offered and had declined a cabinet post in the new Conservative administration of Prime Minister Robert Borden. Rogers went to Ottawa instead.

First elected in 1888 as a Liberal, Roblin was a member of the legislature for twenty-three of the next twenty-seven years, and premier for fourteen years. He had parted company with Thomas Greenway's government in the late 1880s over the issue of the special status of the French language guaranteed in the Manitoba Act. Although Greenway had promised not to tamper with the bilingual legislature and courts, and the dual Catholic and Protestant school system, the Liberals soon moved to abolish both. In 1890 Roblin voted with his fellow disaffected Liberal, Thomas Prendergast, to censure the government for ceasing the publication of legislative documents in French. When the bill to abolish the dual school system came before the legislature, Roblin was one of only eleven members to oppose it and the only English Protestant to do so.

Roblin soon became the leader of the small Conservative opposition in the legislature. In 1899 he stepped aside to allow the popular Hugh John Macdonald, son of Sir John, lead the party to victory. When Macdonald departed for federal politics in the fall of 1900, Roblin took over as premier and held that position with majority governments until his resignation in 1915.

Rodmond Roblin was a progressive in most of his policies, although he is principally remembered now as an outspoken opponent of women's suffrage. Early in his first term as premier, he made a breakthrough on the issue that had thwarted Manitoba politicians for decades—the absence of any real competition for the CPR and the high freight rates they charged as a result. In February 1901 he announced that he had signed an agreement with the Northern Pacific to lease all the lines they controlled in Manitoba—566 kilometres of track—for 999 years. Shortly after, the lines were leased to Canadian Northern, at the time a small railway just setting out on a decade of stupendous expansion. Canadian Northern gave the province control of freight rates in return for provincial guarantees of its construction bonds—the beginning of a fruitful relationship that resulted in lower freight rates for Manitobans and the construction of 2400 kilometres of new railway lines through the province's farming districts.

Roblin created the first publicly owned telephone company in North America, and extended telephone service to rural areas of the province at a time when rural phones in other parts of the country were unknown. He consistently supported the organized farmers in their struggles with the Winnipeg Grain Exchange he had helped to found, and he pursued a temperance policy with respect to regulating the sale of liquor without ever actually banning its sale completely.

He steered a careful course on the issue of French Catholic schools, not wishing to reignite the bitter feud of the 1890s "School Question." Near the end of his tenure, however, with the passage of the "Coldwell Amendments" in 1912, whereby a public school board could take over Catholic schools while retaining Catholic teachers, he made concessions to Catholic parents, which earned him the enmity of many Protestant groups including the Orange Lodge. Roblin was, in short, a politician who had the courage to "do the right thing" for other groups in the province, even when it conflicted with his own interests and background.

Roblin was a successful businessman as well as a successful politician. He had come to the West from Prince Edward County, Ontario, with his wife and baby son in the 1870s and set up a general store in Carman. Like many rural storekeepers, he was soon buying grain and lending money to his fellow settlers. By 1888 his grain business was large enough for him to move permanently to Winnipeg, where he became a grain buyer and a partner in various enterprises, including the Dominion Elevator Company, of which he was the president. After he left politics, he went back to Dominion Elevator as president and also, in partnership with his sons, operated a successful garage and auto dealership called Consolidated Motors, located near Portage and Main.

Rodmond and Adelaide Roblin lived a simple life compared to his peers in the grain industry and in politics. They continued to live in the house they built at 211 Gary Street long after other middle-class families moved to more fashionable neighbourhoods. An incident in early 1912 gives a strong indication of what they were like. There was a huge fire at the Excelsior Auto Works near their house on Gary Street. A number of people who lived upstairs in the Excelsior building had to flee for their lives from the flames. Roblin and his wife invited them to spend the night in their house, and pieces of furniture the people had saved from the fire were stored in Roblin's garage.

Rodmond Roblin was described by one journalist as "having no side to him" and he avoided the kind of social events that were described in the society columns of the papers. He left this sort of activity to his colleagues Robert Rogers and Colin Campbell and their wives.

After the death of his first wife, Adelaide, he remarried and spent part of every year in the southern states. He died while vacationing in Warm Springs, Arkansas, in 1936.

In 1912 Roblin, in the words of the *Canadian Annual Review*, continued to lead the province "with aggressive force, with assured convictions and with success." The year 1912 nevertheless took on the tone of a farewell year for him. A huge banquet was held in April where, before a crowd of 1500, the Tory party honoured him. In May he received official votes of thanks from the civil service and from his own supporters in Dufferin constituency, who told him that Manitoba was now "three times larger than when you assumed the reins of power, more than three times wealthier and with an outlook for the future three times brighter."[1] On his way home from Scotland in December, he stopped in Ottawa where the Governor General knighted him in a simple ceremony attended only by Colin Campbell and Robert Rogers.

Roblin's unbroken success, his aggressive style, and the eventual corruption of his political machine had made him many bitter enemies. John Dafoe, editor of the Liberal *Manitoba Free Press*, was perhaps the most vocal and he poured all the stubborn determination and down-right viciousness he was capable of into his editorial campaign to defeat

Rodmond Roblin in 1912. Premier for eleven years, he was at the peak of his career and hoping to retire.

Roblin. The following poem, which appeared on the editorial page of the *Free Press* on November 4, 1912, is an example.

Reflections of Sir Rhodomontade Robint
When I was a lad of low degree
I always climbed the highest tree
And have never lost my young ambition
To sit aloft in high position ...
Of chivalry I have been cured
By defeats I have endured;
And I find a braggart rudeness
More effective in its crudeness
A noisy rough and tumble fight
Inspires my people with delight
So my knightly sword grows rusty
While I swing my meat axe trusty.

By 1915 Roblin's reputation was ruined, he left the public stage in disgrace, and in that year's election his party was reduced from twenty-eight to five members. His precipitous fall was, to some extent, the result of the departure of his two closest political allies, both of whom had sat with him in Cabinet since 1901. Robert Rogers was elected to the House of Commons in fall 1911, and Colin Campbell, Roblin's logical successor, suffered a stroke in February 1913, from which he never recovered. When Campbell formally resigned from the government in the fall of 1913, Roblin wrote to him that he felt himself to be "entirely alone insofar as the original Cabinet is concerned and as a member of the Legislature.... I wish from the very bottom of my heart that I was out of office at the moment and free from its cares, its worries and its responsibilities."[2]

He never admitted the slightest weakness to his enemies, however, and during the Throne Speech debate in March 1912, he took credit for the state of the province after twelve years of Tory government. The *Manitoba Free Press* reported that

> the premier said that the province of Manitoba was never so prosperous as today. Considering its population and general condition, no part of Canada was so prosperous as Manitoba: there had been an appreciation in real estate values; a large number of industrial concerns were coming to Manitoba; head offices of great financial houses were likewise coming to the province. The government was stronger than ever in the hearts of the people because it was in the van of progressive legislation.[3]

The opening of the annual legislative session was an important event in the Winnipeg year and drew a large crowd. Shortly before 3:00 p.m. on February 22, the new Lieutenant-Governor, D.C. Cameron, left Government House with an escort of military officers, which included Sir Sam Steele and Cameron's own son-in-law, Captain Homer-Dixon, and walked the short distance up the street to the Legislative Building to read the Speech from the Throne.

The clerk's table had been moved and the members' desks pushed back to make room for what was estimated to be the largest crowd ever to witness an opening. R.P. Roblin and his cabinet members sat on the right side of the throne, and Tobias Norris and the Liberals formed a much smaller group to the left. The rest of the chamber and the gallery were crowded with the province's élite, invited guests at one of the major events of the social year. The society columnists took note of the dresses of the political wives and other women so that they could be accurately described in the press.

After the Sergeant at Arms, John McDougall, who had been doing his job for thirty-two years, placed the mace upon the table, Cameron began his first Throne Speech by saying how pleased he was to have been chosen for this important job. The first matter he reported on was the appointment of His Royal Highness Arthur, Duke of Connaught, one of Queen Victoria's sons, as Canada's Governor General. This was the first time a prince of the royal blood had occupied Rideau Hall.

Next, he commented on the extension of Manitoba's boundaries to the 60th parallel—the same as those of her western neighbours, Saskatchewan and Alberta. This extension had been the subject of prolonged, rancorous, and unsuccessful negotiations with the Laurier government. With the installation in the fall of 1911 of a Tory federal government, with Robert Rogers in the Cabinet, the matter had been resolved quickly. On February 27 a bill was introduced in the House of Commons by which Manitoba assumed her present shape.

Cameron announced that the province had reached an agreement for the purchase of the Fort Osborne Barracks, which stood where the west lawn of the Legislative Building now stretches from Broadway to Assiniboine Avenue. Over the succeeding few years, the old barracks buildings were demolished one by one and the magnificent new Legislative Building began to rise.

The Speech referred to two public enquiries: one looking into the operation of the Manitoba telephone system and the other dealing with technical education. Only the latter reported during the current session. The final report on the contentious and embarrassing subject of telephone rates was released after the session was safely over.

One set of amendments—the Coldwell Amendments to the Public Schools Act—created a good deal of controversy. These changes, long asked for by Catholic parents who were struggling to pay public school taxes as well as support parochial schools, were bitterly attacked by the Liberals, who wanted a completely secular and English-language school system. They, and the Orange Lodge, which weighed in on the issue, saw the amendments as an attack on the secular, state-supported school system established under the Laurier/Greenway compromise of 1897. But the 1912 session saw little discussion of the amendments and it was only later that the controversy caused the Tory government to abandon the changes.

A public market for the sale of livestock was to be erected in St. Boniface and the Agricultural College was about to officially move from its Tuxedo buildings to its magnificent new location south of the city on what is now the campus of the University of Manitoba.

The session also passed the Building Trades Protection Act, which mandated that it was the responsibility of employers to ensure that scaffolding, ladders, and machinery were safe for workmen. The inspector appointed to ensure compliance was W.H. Reeve, a founding member of the Winnipeg Trades and Labour Council. He was firm in enforcing the rules and was not afraid to levy fines, and in 1915 he proudly reported that the number of fatalities on building sites had been reduced to only one for the year.

When Lieutenant-Governor Cameron finished speaking, the Speaker took the chair and entertained the single motion that was always introduced at this point to assert the right of the people to govern. Then the house was adjourned until the following Monday.

The purely social side of the opening now commenced. The Speaker, James Johnson of Turtle Mountain constituency, played host to several hundred guests at a reception at the Royal Alexandra. In the evening a smaller, more select group arrived at Government House for a state dinner in honour of the opening. The guests included most of the Conservative cabinet and T.C. (Toby) Norris, the Leader of the Opposition. Several senior judges were there, as well as Robert Fletcher, the Deputy Minister of Education, C.H. Dancer, the Deputy Minister of Public Works, and J.P. Robertson, the Legislative Librarian. Senior clergymen Archbishop Matheson of the Anglican church and Monseigneur Dugas of the Archdiocese of St. Boniface were invited but could not attend, because Lent had begun.

At 9:30, after dinner, Mrs. Cameron entertained the ladies with a concert of songs by Helen Prestwych, the music teacher at Havergal College, accompanied by her pianist sister, Mabel. The next night, Mrs. Colin Campbell, whose husband had now taken over Robert Rogers's former ministry of Public Works, held an "extensive five o'clocker" or afternoon tea for the wives of politicians, mostly Conservative ones, and civil servants. Mrs. Roblin did not do this sort of entertaining;

she and her husband did not enjoy it and the Campbells, who owned a large house, "Inverary" on Roslyn Road, took on the responsibility, as the Rogerses had done before he went to Ottawa. Mrs. Campbell did a good deal of entertaining, but her parties were rarely just for fun and usually had some higher purpose.

Later in March, for example, the Campbells give a musicale for the members of the Tory caucus. Most of these men were batching it in the city, away from the comforts of home. There were, in fact, only four Winnipeg members—Winnipeg North, Winnipeg South, Winnipeg West, and Winnipeg Centre—in the forty-one-member House in spite of the fact that Winnipeg had twenty-five per cent of the registered voters in Manitoba, and nearly forty per cent of its population. All the other MLAs, including Campbell, who represented Morris, and Roblin, whose riding was Dufferin from around his old home in Carman, were from rural seats.

The men from outside Winnipeg must have appreciated Minnie Campbell's taking them in and feeding them, although they may not all have enjoyed the kind of highbrow entertainment she organized for them. The performers were Mr. and Mrs. Hector Chalmers, Mrs. T.R. Ferguson, Mrs. F.W. Ellis, and M. Potvin, who provided an evening of good music. Supper was served around 11:00 at small tables placed throughout the reception rooms, decorated with golden daffodils. The other guests included the Roblins and Hugh John Macdonald, a former premier and leader of the Conservative Party.

~~~

When the House reconvened and the Throne Speech debate began, the atmosphere was rancorous. The Liberals were still smarting from the defeat of the Laurier government the previous autumn. While they had done well further west, where their party controlled the provincial governments and farmers were generally in favour of free trade, eight of the ten seats in Manitoba went to the Tories, although in a couple of ridings the majority had been very small.

The sting of defeat was made worse by the "dirty tricks" that were standard tactics during elections at the time. Every aspect of an election

Solomon Hart Green, Liberal MLA
for North Winnipeg, was one of the
bright, young Liberal members who
made life uncomfortable for the Tories.

was beset with shenanigans, beginning with the registration of new voters to update the voters' lists, a necessary task in a province where new immigrants were still pouring in and many people were transients. The Liberals complained because the clerks who revised the lists in each riding were government appointees and not averse to removing the names of known Liberals. This meant that Liberal party workers and MLAs had to spend time and money to attend the revision hearings in order to lodge complaints and get the names put back on the list.

It was also quite common to charge the workers of the opposite party, under the Contravened Elections Act, with tampering with the voters' lists and have them arrested. The *Free Press* for February 29 reported that during the Throne Speech debate, Hart Green, a Liberal MLA from North Winnipeg, said that, "To make the game easier for the Conservative machine in North Winnipeg, he, the speaker, had been arrested on election day, and of course released without any charge being laid against him." The Liberals also employed this tactic, and the *Winnipeg Tribune* commented on September 21, 1911, at the height of the federal campaign, that "If the battle of warrants between Liberals and Conservatives continues, it is doubtful if there will be any citizen out of jail by the time the polls close, and extra jail accommodation will have to be provided." On October 14, 1912, the *Winnipeg Telegram* reported that, during the federal by-election in Macdonald constituency, several Liberal party workers from Saskatchewan and Ontario were arrested and thrown in jail for engaging in corrupt practices.

The distribution of money and buying of drinks, or "treating," at election time to secure votes was another standard technique all over Canada and would be for many years to come. Giving money, however, was not an absolute guarantee the recipient would vote for you. When Donald Smith lost a federal by-election in 1881 in Selkirk riding, called in the first place because Smith had been convicted of illegal activities during the 1878 election, his riding secretary, the story goes, said: "Donald A., the voters have taken your money and voted against you."

A novel published in 1911, *Love in Manitoba* by Anglican clergyman E. Wharton Gill, described what we may take to be an election scene based on real life. His main character is working in a lumber camp on the eastern slopes of Riding Mountain at the time of an election, likely the provincial election of 1910. There are twelve Ukrainian workers in the camp, referred to by Gill as Galicians, who have visitors the Sunday before election day. The camp boss, Bob Shaw, had said that he would give everyone the day off to vote, but he did not want work disturbed by "heelers," meaning campaign workers.

> Early on the morning of the Sunday before voting-day the Galicians' priest came up accompanied by a very prosperous looking fellow-countryman from Winnipeg.... This gentleman had a prolonged pow-wow with the foreign voters in their own shanty after their spiritual exercises were concluded, and later in the day they had other visitors whom it would only be permissible to call heelers in the heat of a contested election.... Bob Shaw said it was none of his funeral whence came the crisp new $5.00 bills with which the Galicians bought lavish supplies of tobacco and cigarette paper at the camp store, after the last of their visitors had departed.[4]

Hyman Gunn, who worked for the Liberals in North End Winnipeg, gave the following description of vote buying:

> I'll tell you what I have actually seen. Before an election, they'd say, "How many votes do you think you can get?" "Oh, I think I can get about ten." "Alright, here's twenty dollars, two dollars a vote to buy them." They'd go down to the voter and hand them two dollars. "You mark your ballot for so and so." "Alright." He was paid two dollars to mark his ballot.[5]

Liquor was passed out liberally to voters. During the 1913 Gimli by-election, Liberal MLA Hart Green reported finding an outhouse near Chatfield containing two barrels of beer and a sack of whisky bottles, all brought from Winnipeg by Conservative "heelers." A certain Winnipeg hotel owner, accompanied by a provincial police constable, bought rounds of drinks in local bars, encouraging the drinkers to vote Conservative.

As the 1916 Paterson Royal Commission established, much of the money for these activities came from provincial government appropriations. During three by-elections in 1913 and 1914, all of which were won by Roblin's government, substantial amounts—$24,000 in Emerson constituency, $39,000 in Rockwood, and $78,000 in Gimli—were granted from appropriations for road work. A detailed investigation of the pay sheets and other records showed that less than half this money went into building roads. Conservative Party workers submitted inflated and false pay sheets and used the money to pay for transportation to political meetings and to buy whiskey "for the boys." The total amount spent in this way in Gimli, for example, was calculated to be $52,000, or about sixty-five per cent of the $78,000 appropriated for road construction in that constituency.[6]

The 1915 Royal Commission that looked into the cost overruns during the construction of the new Legislative Building documented another time-honoured practice, used in 1913 and 1914: having a contractor inflate the invoices he submitted to the government and pay the difference to the party in power. Thomas Kelly, the main contractor for the Legislative Building and many of the other public buildings erected during Roblin's time, was convicted of falsifying invoices and Kelly did spend time in Stony Mountain Penitentiary. Although Roblin and some of his ministers went to trial, the charges against them were eventually dropped.

Civil servants who were political appointees were expected to campaign for the ruling party during the election, and being in control of government-owned agencies gave the Tories tremendous advantages. An example is the case of F.J. Dixon, an Independent candidate in the 1910 Manitoba election, who discovered, two days before polling day, that the phone number in his committee rooms had been mysteriously changed.[7]

Nellie McClung satirizes the activities of party workers during the 1911 federal election in her delightful short story, "The Elusive

The Conservative committee room for South Winnipeg during the 1911 general election. Cars stand ready to take voters to the polls and political hangers-on speculate about the outcome.

Vote: An Unvarnished Tale of September 21st, 1911."[8] It is the story of John Thomas Green, a rather slow-witted fellow described by McClung as a very good advertisement for votes for women, who was the subject of much attention by the partisans of both parties as the election drew near. He was a known Conservative, so his employer, a Liberal farmer, decided to lock him in the cellar rather than let him be picked up by Tory workers who arrived to drive him to town to vote. The farmer's father, a Tory sympathizer, upset these plans when he whispered to them that John Thomas was in the cellar. He was eventually handed over and taken to town by the Tory workers. He changed hands a couple of times and became increasingly irritated at the political workers who were trying to make sure of his vote. When the ballots were counted, there was one that had "None of yer business" written beside the Conservative candidate's name, and "None of yer business either" beside the Liberal's name. "Some thought the ballot was John Thomas Green's," concluded McClung.

A friendly press was as important in politics in 1912 as it is today. In Winnipeg the *Manitoba Free Press* was the organ of the Liberal Party and the *Telegram* supported the Conservatives. The *Tribune* was owned by R.L. Richardson, who was himself active in politics as an independent with what might be called left liberal attitudes. In the new immigrant communities, the press was not neglected. In 1902 we know that Robert Rogers, then a minister in the Roblin cabinet, offered to put up $5000 to establish a Conservative German-language paper. At the time of the 1911 federal election, the Conservatives owned the German *der Nordwesten* and Liberal MLA Valentine Winkler encouraged Clifford Sifton to buy the paper because "this newspaper has a great influence over our German readers in Manitoba and the Northwest, it being the only paper of importance circulating amongst them, as they are mostly all people from the old country, having no political leanings when they came up here, so they look entirely to the newspaper for information."[9]

For Liberal papers, *Free Press* editor J.W. Dafoe acted as a sort of super-editor, reading and reporting on editorials and keeping editors in line with a quiet word when required.

Once the votes were counted in an election, both parties entered challenges under the Controverted Elections Act. Between 1887 and 1915, there were over 120 such challenges and only two of them were ever fully investigated.

During the Estimates debate in March 1912, the Liberals charged that the bulk of government money that was paid out to contractors went to Conservative Party members. In Portage la Prairie, for example, it was pointed out that $1523.50 had been spent in the previous fiscal year on livery and car hire for the Telephone System. Of this, over ninety per cent went to D.A. Roe and S. Grobb, both of whom were well-known Conservatives.

Colin Campbell was questioned about the practice of paying Department of Public Works grants directly to individuals instead of to municipal councils. He said this was to ensure that councillors would not simply use the money for improvements in their own wards. Asked by C.D. McPherson, the Liberal member for Portage la Prairie, whether these payments usually went to supporters of the government, Campbell answered, "No, it is not the practice." There was general laughter from the Opposition members.

D.A. Ross, Liberal member for Springfield, gave the specific example of $23.62 being paid by Public Works to a well-known Tory, J.J. McLeod, for clearing brush. Ross declared that McLeod had never moved out of his poolroom to do it.

Patronage was the way all parties rewarded their loyal workers and supporters. Colin Campbell's ministerial letter books give us a small glimpse of the patronage system at work. In October 1911, Campbell replaced Robert Rogers as Minister of Public Works and the chief dispenser of patronage for the Manitoba Tories. One of his first letters as minister was to the Honourable James Duff, the Conservative Minister of Agriculture in Toronto. Campbell promised to "get something for your son, if I can get anything available here. I will have great pleasure in offering it to him." He explains he is "just getting into harness."

The next day he wrote to Robert Rogers, who was now the federal Minister of the Interior in the new Borden cabinet.

A dapper Robert Rogers surrounded by the public works for which he had been responsible in Manitoba since 1902. Rogers made sure that the Conservative party benefitted from projects such as these.

> This will introduce you to Mr. S.J. Wood, employed at the Post Office. In 1893, when the patronage was with me, I had much pleasure in getting him a position. Since then he has been slightly promoted, but owing to political proclivities he did not get the advancement to which he was entitled and I trust that during the new era, you may be able to do something for him.[10]

It is not clear whether Campbell's intervention did any good. According the Post Office annual reports, Woods continued to work at the Winnipeg Post Office as a letter carrier at the same salary as before, until the middle of 1913, when he left, perhaps finally receiving his long-awaited reward.

At the end of December 1912, Campbell wrote to Rogers, introducing A.T. Taylor of 204 Maryland, who wanted to have his company's product, not specified in the letter, "prescribed by the Architects ... working for the Federal government." Campbell told Rogers: "I think he has a splendid thing and he is one of our very good friends."[11] "Very good friend" was the code phrase used universally to denote a party supporter.

Prohibition was an important political issue in 1912, as it was for many years before and after, and it was raised during the Throne Speech debate. On February 28, the Liberal member for Birtle, G.H. Malcolm, made a motion to amend the Throne Speech and the government's program to include provision for a referendum on the province-wide banning of liquor sales. The galleries were packed with clergymen and temperance movement leaders. Roblin was not impressed by the show of support for Malcolm's motion, however, and, after stating his belief that prohibition would not achieve the end they had in mind, he moved that debate on the motion cease. His motion was carried twenty to fourteen, with two Tories voting with the Liberals.

Roblin had received a large delegation of 200 members of the Social and Moral Reform Council on February 16, only a few days before the session began. This council had the broad support of temperance groups, the Trades and Labour Congress, and the Grain Growers. The delegation had asked for a referendum on province-wide prohibition but Roblin, as usual, had refused.

Roblin maintained a consistent policy on prohibition throughout his time in power. Because the population was divided on the issue, Canadian politicians usually tried to find a safe middle ground. Hugh John Macdonald went further than most when he was premier and passed a Prohibition Act in June 1900. It was tested and upheld in the courts, but Macdonald had been replaced by Rodmond Roblin, who chose to hold a referendum on the issue before bringing the Act into force. Prohibition was defeated in this vote and most members of the temperance movement never forgave the premier, campaigning against him in every election up to his last in 1914.

Roblin was usually described by his opponents as being in the pocket of the liquor trade, and he did receive support from hotel owners at election time. Nevertheless, he described himself as a temperance man, although, over the years, he pursued a policy that stopped short of complete prohibition. His government took the middle ground, using licensing to control the worst abuses of the liquor trade and leaving the decision on actual prohibition to each municipality—the so-called "local option." As Colin Campbell commented, the Roblin Tories believed "It is better to have a lawful traffic properly controlled than an unlawful traffic uncontrolled." During the Roblin administration, the wide-open saloons of the old Winnipeg were gradually brought under a regulatory regime and the foundations were laid for the strictly regulated liquor trade we know today.

On March 13 the Honourable Hugh Armstrong, Provincial Treasurer, presented his budget for the 1912–1913 year. Armstrong spoke for over an hour, describing the wonderful economic success Manitoba was enjoying and claiming credit for it, something Roblin's governments had been doing for years. While they had been fortunate in being in power during a time of growth and prosperity, Roblin's Tories had not been shy about levying taxes, including a tax on corporations, to balance the books. Armstrong said he was pleased to announce a surplus of $492,000 in the Consolidated Fund, but he then admitted that the Revenue Account had a deficit of $200,000 for the Manitoba Government Telephones and $63,000 for the Manitoba Government Elevators. Armstrong had confidently predicted a surplus for the telephone system the previous year and he spent some time attempting to explain why there wasn't one.

The treasurer could hardly avoid such an explanation, even though the Royal Commission on the Government Telephones was still at work and would not report until the session was over. The telephone system was perhaps the hottest political topic of the moment, a huge controversy having exploded the previous November when a deficit of $150,000 had been announced and a new rate schedule issued to deal with the problem. The Roblin government had approved this schedule in December.

The proposed rates seem modest to the modern reader, but at the time they represented a betrayal of the promises made by Roblin in 1908, when he took over the Bell Telephone system. He had guaranteed that the government would deliver telephone service for as much as fifty per cent less. Three years later, Manitoba Government Telephones were not bringing in enough to meet their expenses and the commissioners who ran the utility proposed raising the rates.

Manitobans had been enjoying a simple yearly subscription with unlimited calls, but the new schedule called for higher rates

Colin Campbell dealing with the endless paperwork that came with the Public Works
portfolio. Within a few months of this photo, Campbell collapsed with an illness from
which he did not recover, and he was forced to resign from Roblin's Cabinet.

and charges for each call made—the "measured service" method of
charging. There was a howl of protest all over the province, led by
powerful groups like the Winnipeg Board of Trade and the Industrial
Bureau, which both appointed committees to look into the rate increases. At the time, Manitobans had more telephones per capita
than any other Canadians and they used the phones more. In 1908,
when the Government Telephones was established, there had been
6000 phones in Winnipeg; by 1912 there were 23,000.[12] Responding
to the complaints of rural Manitobans, the government system had
run wires into rural areas with few subscribers, providing service in
districts where Bell had refused to go because it was unprofitable.
Small municipal phone companies had been linked into the government long-distance system.

So great was the protest that Roblin had tried to defuse the situation
by appointing a Royal Commission: Justice Locke, George Crowe, a
grain merchant and one-time partner of the premier, and R.L. Barry
of Minneapolis.

The principal reason for the telephone system's financial problems, the Royal Commission found, was that no sinking fund had been established for replacements and new equipment, a huge cost because telephone technology was changing so rapidly. In Manitoba the frequent upgrades were charged to the maintenance account, which was rapidly overspent. The large firms, such as AT&T, had adopted the practice of setting aside six per cent a year for replacement of equipment because:

> Improvements in the art of telephony have been numerous, frequent and often radical, and at rapidly recurring intervals it has been necessary to discard, as obsolete, equipment in fair physical condition installed but a few years previously at great cost. The telephone business requires a continuous accession of fresh capital to satisfactorily serve the public.[13]

The Royal Commissioners also mentioned that huge inventories were kept. There were, for example, enough telephone poles to see the system through four construction seasons. The large inventories were a symptom of something the commissioners delicately avoided mentioning: friends of the Conservative Party made money by selling vast numbers of poles and other supplies to the system.

The managers of the telephone system were powerless to avoid the extra expenses that political interference produced. There were, for example, cases where the promise of telephone service was used as an outright bribe to the voters. At the time of the provincial election in 1910, the *Manitoba Free Press*, admittedly not an unbiased observer, reported that "several carloads of poles were unloaded at Woodridge, and it was announced that the work of connecting up Woodridge with the Provincial Government's long distance telephone system would be gone on with immediately after the election."

A number of people from the area were hired with their teams at six dollars per day to move the poles out along the proposed route for the line. After the election, the poles were loaded on flatcars again and taken back to Winnipeg.[14]

But these sorts of political shenanigans were not mentioned by the Royal Commissioners, who laid the blame at the feet of the unfortunate telephone commissioners. These gentlemen resigned with great dignity in June, but not without offering in their self-defence the following sentence in their resignation letter: "... we express the hope and belief that neither your Government nor our successors will be misled by the gross misstatements of fact and the erroneous opinions and conclusions expressed in the Royal Commission Report."[15]

A single commissioner was appointed, the rates rose, and the crisis passed, but not without inflicting its share of damage on the Roblin government. By the end of the year, the newly created Public Utilities Commission had allowed a new schedule of rates that did not employ the measured use principle but collected more from rural and business users.

On March 13, almost exactly halfway through the session, the *Free Press* reported on a private member's bill introduced by Joseph Bernier, the Conservative MLA from St. Boniface. The bill, or, to be more accurate, group of bills, was for the incorporation of a group of companies that would take over the operations of the Winnipeg Street Railway Company. This matter dominated the last half of the session and generated enormous controversy in the City of Winnipeg.

Bernier introduced and sponsored the bills on behalf of a syndicate of businessmen, which included E.B. Reese, an engineer, D.L. Mather, a lumber merchant who had lived in Kenora and moved to the city in 1907, and Robert R. Muir, a Winnipeg grain merchant with interests in several local businesses. Reese, the spokesman for the group, said they were being backed by a group of New York financiers. Many suspected that Sir William Mackenzie, president of the Canadian Northern Railway and the current owner of the Street Railway Company, was behind the scheme and that he hoped to restructure the utility in a way that would be more favourable to "the Company," as the street railway was known in the city.

The company was profitable, earning a surplus after expenses of $474,000 in 1912. It consisted of the Winnipeg streetcar service, which Mackenzie and Mann had owned and operated since 1892, as well as the Winnipeg Selkirk and Lake Winnipeg Railway and the Suburban Rapid Transit Company, electric railways connecting Winnipeg to communities to the north and to Headingley in the west. The boards of all three companies shared the same membership. Augustus Nanton, local hardware wholesaler Morton Morse, Mackenzie and Mann associate Hugh Sutherland, and Sir William Whyte of the CPR sat on the boards and acted as chairs. The company owned an electrical generating station at Pinawa, which produced the electrical current needed to run its cars, and, up to 1912, had been the sole supplier of electricity to Winnipeg customers. It also sold gas for cooking and light and maintained a gasworks and gasholder tank on the bank of the Assiniboine at the foot of Ruby Street. Most cities supplied some of their lighting and cooking needs with such plants, which produced gas by burning coal in a partial vacuum, then purifed it and pumped it to customers through underground gas mains.

In October 1911 the company's monopoly control of electric power had been shattered and it seemed likely that, in the future, profits would shrink. The city had built its own electrical generating plant at Pointe du Bois on the Winnipeg River and, when the current was turned on October 16, 1911, began charging 3.5 cents per kilowatt hour, a fraction of what the company had been charging and a rate that lasted until the 1970s. By December, the company's rates were lowered to match those of the city. In the early months of 1912 the Winnipeg Street Railway Company waged an advertising war to convince the people of Winnipeg that its facilities were a more reliable source of power than the public utility, but it was a losing battle: the company was losing existing customers and in the stampede to electrify homes and buy electrical appliances, thousands of new customers chose the city utility.

There were other irritants between the city and the company. For example, it had recently been proven that electric current was, in certain spots, jumping from the streetcar rails to travel along city-owned cables and water lines and damaging city pipes and equipment. As a result the company had been forced to upgrade the tracks and the copper connectors that joined the rails together. Another problem was the gasification plant and enormous storage tank located in a newly developed middle-class Wolseley neighbourhood, where the city was spending large amounts of money on landscaping and street building and where large, comfortable homes were rising along the streets. The city demanded, before the newly created Public Utilities Commission, that the tank be removed. The company won this battle and the tank stayed in its Ida, later Palmerston, Street location for many years.

The most serious conflict between the city and the company, however, was the lawsuit over whether the street railway had the right to erect poles on city streets to transmit electricity for uses other than

A contemporary cartoonist's view of Premier Roblin as he pilots the ship of state through stormy seas.

powering its cars, and whether it could sell electricity to consumers without invalidating its charter. The case eventually went to the Privy Council in London, Canada's highest court at the time, and the company was victorious. Word of this reverse arrived in the city on February 26, just as the legislative session was beginning.

In spite of the suspicion and bad feeling between the company and the city, they were tied closely together in the operation of the street railway. Under the company's charter, the city received five per cent of the company's gross earnings and had a say in such matters as schedules and fares. The streetcar schedules, so important in a city where private vehicles were still comparatively rare, were debated at council meetings and enshrined in city bylaws. Most important of all was the provision in the charter giving the city the option to purchase the street railway in 1927. If the option was not exercised then, it would come up again every five years.[16]

On March 19, three days after the bills for the incorporation were introduced, City Council held a special meeting. Concern was expressed that, among other things, the sale of the company would result in the negation of the city's option to buy. The next day the city solicitor, Theodore Hunt, appeared before the Private Member's Bills Committee and protested against various clauses in the bills.

Reese countered by claiming that the new company would build thirty new miles of track each year and upgrade the gas and electric distribution systems. The city's fears were confirmed when Reese said that the option to buy would survive, but only for the lines inside city limits. Pointing out that this portion of the system would be valueless without the rest of the conglomerate, Reese argued that the new company and the city should amalgamate their operations and that the company would run the city's new power plant and be the sole distributor of electricity. Reese's strategy was now clear to everyone: the new companies were intended not just to block the growth of the city-owned electric utility, but to literally swallow it up.

A.J. Andrews, another lawyer retained by the city, emphatically rejected this overture, saying that the city had borrowed $5,000,000 and built their own generating station precisely because "the people felt that they could no longer trust to such a private company the working of important public utilities." Andrews listed the many grievances the city had against the company, and said the company had a history of defying city bylaws and now "was asking the legislature to clothe it with the utmost authority to defy the city and public in every way."[17] It is interesting to note that Andrews was not a leftist radical but a member of the Conservative Party who had served in the past as alderman and as mayor. His support for Winnipeg Hydro was based on the belief that public ownership would deliver lower rates—a benefit that business owners wanted as much as the general public.

Both Andrews and the Liberal MLA for West Winnipeg, Thomas Johnson, wanted to know about the relationship between the old and the new companies; would the city simply be dealing with Sir William Mackenzie in a different guise? The next day, March 21, the *Free Press* developed this idea further, claiming to have discovered the hidden agenda in the proposed legislation: "It looks now as if the railway magnates have devised a subtle scheme for immunizing the benefits the city can derive from municipal ownership and at the same time own and operate in perpetuity a system of Winnipeg street traction...."

On the other side of the question, Joseph Bernier, supported by no less a figure than Colin Campbell, Minister of Public Works, argued in favour of the bill, saying that the country needed outside capital in order to grow. A representative of Reese's American investors spoke before the Private Member's Bills Committee and confirmed that investors would not buy into the new company if they knew the city was determined to undercut it and oppose it.

On March 28 Mayor Waugh held a large protest meeting in a Winnipeg theatre. It was decided to protest the bill by a march and demonstration in front of the Legislative Building the following afternoon. Premier Roblin entered the dispute publicly for the first time, in the role of peacemaker and fixer. On Friday he stated in the

Rodmond Roblin addresses a group of striking workers on the steps of the Legislative
Building. It was his style to intervene personally and "fix" problems whenever possible.

legislature that anyone demonstrating in front of the building ran the
risk of having criminal charges laid. But demonstrations, he said, were
unnecessary: if anyone had grievances, they had only to come to him
and he would look after them.

The next day the sponsors of the bill made one last effort to get
the legislation moved on to third reading and passage into law. But
the bill was doomed. In meetings during the next week, Reese and his
group were convinced to withdraw most of the proposed legislation.
For the city, this represented a great victory over their rivals in the
electricity business. Mackenzie and Mann continued to operate the
Street Railway Company until their bankruptcy during World War I
forced them to sell to other investors.

The end of a busy legislative session on April 4 allowed the members to go back to their homes. The previous evening, the Liberals,
frustrated by their inability to influence events, tried to delay the
prorogation of the House by tying up the legislature with a series of
long speeches. They spoke against the estimates for the Government
Elevators and for the Government Telephones and tried to get a response out of the Tories, who sat back to wait the filibuster out. The
premier answered that he agreed the Government Elevators had been

a failure and that his government planned to sell them to the Grain Growers Grain Company. Some of the elevators were, in fact, leased to the Grain Growers later in the year. Roblin said the problems with the Government Telephones, however, were temporary and nothing to worry about. Steps would be taken to improve the management of this enterprise and the current financial difficulties would disappear.

The session closed with the premier firmly in control, as he had been for so many years, having once more steered the Tory ship of state well clear of the political rocks.

≈≈≈

The year 1912 was the centennial of the birth of Charles Dickens and in March, Winnipeg joined in the worldwide celebrations of this important event. Mrs. Colin Campbell hosted a tea in honour of Mrs. Jean Blewett, the vice-president of the Toronto Dickens Fellowship, and an important Canadian poet of the time. The guests included several people who might be expected to appreciate the finer things. In addition to the premier's wife, Mrs. Thomas Hart, whose husband was a Presbyterian minister and a Professor Emeritus at Manitoba College, presided for the first hour at the tea table. Mrs. G.R. Crowe, wife of a wealthy grain trader, and Mrs. Guthrie Perry, another Manitoba College faculty member's wife, took the second hour. The guests included clergy—Reverend Thomas Hart, Reverend Christie, the minister at Westminster Church, and their families. Professor and Mrs. Allan, Mrs. Elizabeth Balch, an American journalist visiting Winnipeg, and Miss Brunstenman, a schoolteacher, were also among the guests. This was not, then, the usual gathering of middle-class businessmen's wives, but a tea for the Winnipeg intelligentsia.

Mrs. Blewett entertained the guests by reciting "Old Fashioned Folk" and "Come Out West," two of her own poems. Mrs. E.M. Counsell, a local stockbroker's wife who was a talented singer, performed, and Miss Henderson played the piano.

Two weeks later, on Saturday, March 16, the local Dickens Fellowship celebrated the centennial by putting on an evening of entertainment in the Convocation Hall of the University of Manitoba. Mrs. Blewett was once again the special guest. Professor A.W. Crawford, in the chair for the evening, welcomed her and said what a pleasure it was to introduce such a well-known Canadian author. She read the poem she had recently recited at the centennial celebration of Dickens's birth in Toronto—it covered most of Dickens's characters and it was received with great applause.

The Fellowship secretary was Gerald Wade, at the time the manager of the *Western Municipal News*, but already evincing the interest in Dickens that later led him to build an impressive library of books and memorabilia about the author. Wade read letters received from Dickens's sole surviving son, who wished them well, and from Sir Luke Fildes R.A., president of the worldwide Dickens Fellowship, who thanked them for their greeting, which had arrived on the day of the centenary, and congratulated them on their progressiveness.

An adaptation of the *Olde Curiosity Shop* was performed. It was written by Hubert Condor, a young Winnipeg man working as a clerk who eventually returned to England and, during the 1920s, became a moderately successful songwriter. The play was acted by a company of enthusiastic young amateurs: E. Cay was a clerk in the office of the Canadian Pacific Steamships; Miss Jean Doran was a stenographer, as were Maud Deverell and Mildred Derby, who may have been her friends. The cast also included a Mr. Youell, one of the three Youell brothers who lived together in Kenilworth Court and worked as clerks for Marshall Wells and Wood Vallance, local hardware wholesalers.

There is no comment in the papers about how the play was received. The Fellowship announced it would have more programs later in the year, including Dickens tea parties and a lecture on the great author by the Reverend Mr. Johnston, the City Librarian.

APRIL

Roslyn Road, the Titanic

In its April 1912 issue, *Dominion Magazine* profiled Mrs. Douglas Cameron, the wife of the newly appointed Lieutenant-Governor. Mrs. Cameron explained that when she and her husband came west in the 1880s, "People did not come to Winnipeg if they had money; they came to make it." Mrs. Cameron said she was interested in music and books and travelling but that, generally, she liked "just what everyone likes." When she moved to Government House, she brought her display cabinets filled "with the pretty things women of taste and means gather around them from all the parts of the world they visit." The article concluded that the Camerons had "the experience, the taste and the wealth to make the place delightful for themselves, knowing they can do everything thoroughly well, and pleasant for all those with whom they come in contact."

The house from which Mrs. Cameron had moved her display cabinets and "pretty things" was 65 Roslyn Road, across the Assiniboine River from Government House. Number 65 was the one of the grandest houses in what was becoming one of Winnipeg's most exclusive neighbourhoods. Roslyn Road was a good address, throughout its length; there was no part of it that was less desirable. Along this green, shady street, called Winnipeg's Rotten Row because of the number of residents who were riders and horse lovers, lived many of the city's wealthiest families. The street was not yet threatened by the encroachment of apartment buildings and less expensive housing that was destroying the exclusiveness of the Hudson's Bay Reserve on the

opposite side of the Assiniboine River. There was a general movement of well-to-do people, such as James Ashdown and George Galt,
out of the reserve and away from Broadway at this time. Over the
past few years they had moved to Roslyn Road, and to Wellington
Crescent, Crescentwood, and Armstrong's Point, all neighbourhoods
that promised more privacy and more spacious grounds than the
reserve.

There had been enormous changes on Roslyn Road since 1900. In
that year there had been only twenty-three houses on the street; in
1912 there were fifty, as well as the Roslyn Apartments on the corner
of Osborne Street. The new construction was not the only change; of
those who lived on Roslyn in 1900, only eight remained and only four
were still in the same house: Leslie Ironside and David Adams, the
coal merchant, were still in their houses at 94 and 90 Roslyn Road,
respectively; the lawyer John Hough still lived in his large home at
the western end of the road, and Mrs. Edward Lemon was still in the
house she had shared with her late husband for twelve years.

A.M. Nanton had moved from number 29 to his estate at 229, and
Heber Archibald, a retired lawyer, had moved from number 15 to his
brick house west of Osborne Street. Beyond these few people, everyone on Roslyn Road had lived there less than twelve years, and
some for a very short time indeed. The Camerons' large brick mansion
at number 65 was the oldest house on Roslyn Road, built by Arthur
Wellington Ross in the 1880s and paid for with profits from his real
estate speculations during the great land boom. Like the Bannatyne
house in Armstrong's Point, it stood for many years as a lonely reminder of this earlier, short-lived era of prosperity in Winnipeg. Ross
had been forced to sell this grand house after his real estate affairs had
faltered and he had declared bankruptcy.

At the extreme eastern terminus of Roslyn, blocking its path east-
ward to Assiniboine, now River Park, stood Number One Roslyn.
This house was occupied by George Killam, a thirty-four-year-old
lawyer who was a partner in the real estate and insurance firm of
Allan, Killam and McKay. He had inherited it from his late father, A.C.
Killam, a lawyer and judge who had left Winnipeg when he was ap-
pointed to the Supreme Court in Ottawa, and who now lay buried in
St. John's Cathedral churchyard.

65 Roslyn Road, built by A.W. Ross in the 1880s, was the home of Lieutenant-Governor Douglas Cameron and his family.

George had been born in Windsor but came to Winnipeg with his parents as a child and was educated at Manitoba College. He was a student in W.R. Allan's firm for four years before being called to the Manitoba Bar in 1903; the next year he became Allan's partner. In 1909 Allan had married George Killam's widowed mother, Minnie Killam. The two men shared a passion for horses; they both loved to ride and were hunters and polo players.

W.R. Allan and his wife lived two doors down the street on the river side, at 15 Roslyn Road. He was forty-eight in 1912 and had been in the city since the 1880s, when so many young Easterners had been drawn to Winnipeg by the stories of the boom and the belief that the future lay in the West. He was a son of the famous Montreal shipping family, the owners of the Allan Lines, and he had been educated at Rugby School in England.

On the south side of the street, to the left of Killam's front gate, was the home of Felix J. Billiarde, Superintendent of Neglected Children in the Attorney General's department. Billiarde was the only resident of the street who was not a businessman, a doctor, or lawyer. An

Englishman who had been in Canada for only nine years, he had begun his working life as a schoolmaster but had found his true vocation in children's aid. Billiarde, one of whose children was adopted, reveals in his annual reports a passionate dedication to the protection of the thousands of children in the city who were living in poverty.

Killam's other neighbours on the river side of Roslyn included William Hicks Gardner, a partner in the firm of Oldfield, Kirby and Gardner, who lived next door to the Allans. Their firm was a real estate and investment company, its success symbolized by the trim, classical building they had erected next to the post office on Portage Avenue. Perhaps one of Gardner's greatest coups was in 1911, assembling the block of land for the construction of the new Hudson's Bay store at the corner of Portage and Vaughan. He was able to acquire the whole block for under one million dollars, keeping the identity of his client secret to prevent a huge escalation in prices.

His firm had many other British clients and, like other Winnipeg companies, they acted as local agents for investors wishing to buy land and buildings in Manitoba and managed the investments once they were made. Gardner was a wealthy man in 1912. He took the first three months of the year off and went on an extended holiday in the Mediterranean, and we get some small idea of his worth from the published reports under the Bank Act, which reveal that he had $55,000 invested in the Merchants Bank of Canada.[1] Gardner was a parishioner of the fashionable St. Luke's Anglican Church on Nassau Street and was the Rector's Warden from 1901 to 1905.

Next door to the Gardners, at 29 Roslyn, lived Captain R.D. MacDonnell, a half-pay British army officer who, since 1893, had lived in Winnipeg as the local agent for the Trust and Loan Company, a large English firm. MacDonnell was Anglo-Irish, the son of the dean of the Anglican Cathedral in Cashel, Tipperary. He was educated at Sandhurst and served in the military as a staff officer with the Indian Army. Like many of his neighbours, MacDonnell was an enthusiastic rider.

The Camerons' house, number 65, was a short distance to the west of Gardner's and MacDonnell's houses. The Camerons were now in residence in Government House, and their home was occupied by their eldest daughter and her husband, Captain Homer-Dixon of Lord Strathcona's Horse, stationed at Fort Osborne Barracks. The

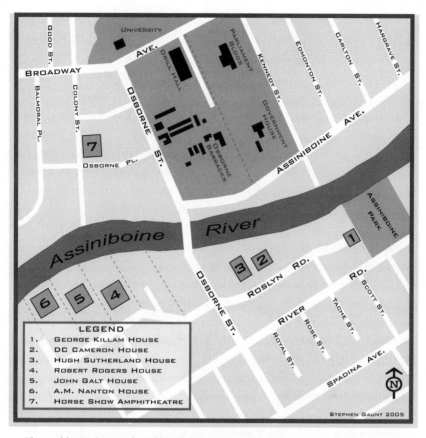

The wealthy Roslyn Road neighbourhood grew up in close proximity to the Legislative Building, Fort Osborne, and the Horse Show Amphitheatre.

Camerons' eldest son, Douglas, married one of Augustus Nanton's daughters in the fall of 1912, and their youngest son was still a student at the Port Hope Academy in Ontario.

The Camerons were from eastern Ontario, where Douglas Cameron was born in 1854 in Prescott County. As a young man he farmed with his father, who, like so many Canadian farmers, went logging and cutting lumber in the winter. This introduction to the lumber business gave Cameron the knowledge he needed to start in the same line when he moved west in 1883. By 1894 he was president of the successful Rat Portage Lumber Company in Rat Portage, later Kenora, Ontario.

By 1912 Cameron was a very wealthy man. Rat Portage Lumber had grown into a large and prosperous business with a mill in Kenora and huge yards in St. Boniface and elsewhere. He was also president of Maple Leaf Mills and a director of the Winnipeg-based Northern Crown Bank. His businesses made Cameron a millionaire and with the money came connections: the Camerons counted Wilfrid Laurier among their personal friends. This and Cameron's service to the Liberal Party—he sat as an MLA in Toronto for two years and tried unsuccessfully to get elected in Winnipeg—led to his appointment as Lieutenant-Governor in the last days of Laurier's regime. He kept the job under Robert Borden's Conservative government, and was knighted in 1913. In 1915 he was in the centre of the events that brought about Premier Roblin's resignation.

Immediately west of the Camerons', at number 81, a large, new house had just been completed in 1909. The construction was closely supervised by the owner, Hugh Sutherland, and the work had been done by Donald Ross of Pratt and Ross, Engineers and Architects.

Ross, the son of A.W. Ross, who had built the Cameron house next door, was thirty-five and a successful engineer who, like his partner, Ralph Pratt, had learned his trade working for the CPR and Canadian Northern Railway. In 1906 they set up their own practice and had already won a number of important contracts, including the construction of the Horse Show Amphitheatre, the largest enclosed arena in Canada. In the year ahead they would work on their most important project to date, the Street Railway Chambers on Notre Dame.

Ross's father, Arthur Wellington Ross, had only recently passed away. He had been a lawyer who came from Ontario to make his fortune. He did indeed make and lose a huge fortune in the great land boom of the early 1880s, leaving behind the huge house on Roslyn Road as a symbol of his success. A.W. Ross had been one of the more notorious speculators in Métis lands, buying, at low prices, land granted to Red River Métis by the government and reselling it for huge profits.

Sutherland spared no expense in the construction of what he knew would be his last home—he was sixty-seven years old in 1912. He imported red sandstone for the walls and decorated the interior with mahogany panelling, silk damask wall coverings, and exquisite plasterwork. The Sutherlands enjoyed entertaining lavishly. An acquaintance later recalled, "Thirty for dinner was nothing unusual with a

The F. Morton Morse house on Wellington Crescent, another area like Roslyn Road, where wealthy Winnipeggers built lavish homes..

floral centre piece, silver and glass & and servants galore."[2] Mrs. May Sutherland was an American by birth, the daughter of the Honorable R.D. Banks of Baltimore. She was known locally as Lady May because "she held her head high and was so grand."[3]

Hugh Sutherland was a newcomer to Roslyn Road, but he had been in the west longer than any of his neighbours, having arrived in Winnipeg in 1874. By that time he had already achieved some success as a contractor and lumber merchant in Oxford County in western Ontario and had enough political influence to be appointed Dominion Superintendent of Public Works in Manitoba and the Northwest, a post he held from 1874 to 1879. He was elected to the House of Commons as a Conservative in 1882, from Donald Smith's old riding of Selkirk.

But he concentrated more of his energy on business than politics, although politics no doubt helped him get the first charter for the Hudson Bay Railway. He tried unsuccessfully for many years to raise the capital to build the railroad and became known as "Hudson Bay Sutherland." He finally sold his charter to Mackenzie and Mann of the Canadian Northern. In 1912 he was still involved with the Canadian Northern Railroad, listed variously as Executive Agent and Chief Executive Officer of the company, with an office in the Union Station building.

Hugh Sutherland was a devoted horseman, with a stable on his property. He rode for exercise in the morning and people later remembered often seeing him and his mount on the Osborne Bridge. The Sutherlands owned fine carriage horses, and his animals were entered in many competitions, including the Winnipeg Horse Show.

West of the Sutherlands lived George Carruthers, aged thirty-seven, the son of a wealthy Eastern family sent west to look after their business dealings. Carruthers Grain was one of the largest grain exporters in Canada and George's father, James, presided over the business in Montreal. In December 1912, the firm moved the first large shipment of export grain over the new Grand Trunk Pacific main line—forty cars of wheat, milled into flour at Maple Leaf Mills in Kenora and shipped to South Africa.

George Carruthers worked from the firm's seventh-floor offices in the Grain Exchange Building, also the headquarters of the family's Standard Elevator line, which allowed them to buy grain directly at thirty-two points out on the prairie. Carruthers was born in Toronto and, after a few years working for the Bank of Toronto to learn something of business, he came to Winnipeg in 1900. He married Clare Wright the year before, and they had a young family of two sons and one daughter. George Carruthers was a well-known athlete when he was young, the captain of the championship Osgoode Hall hockey team and an amateur jockey, riding his father's horses in steeplechase events. Like his neighbours W.R. Allan and George Killam, he was a polo player. He belonged to the newly organized Winnipeg Hunt Club and he was on the board of the Winnipeg Horse Show.

On the south side of Roslyn, east of Osborne Street, lived David Dingwall, at number 52, owner of the largest jewellery store in the city. He was a Scot, born in 1851. R.L. Richardson, the owner and editor of the *Winnipeg Tribune*, lived a few houses further west. He came to the West in 1882 from his home in Lanark County in eastern Ontario to write for the *Manitoba Sun*. When that paper was absorbed by the *Free Press*, Richardson founded the *Winnipeg Tribune*. J.W. Dafoe had this to say about the man who was one of his principal rivals:

> Mr. Richardson divided his attention between journalism and politics. He was elected to the Dominion parliament in 1896,

and thereafter, with the sole exception of the general election of 1911, he contested a constituency at every Dominion election. In addition, he fought two by-elections, all of them, after 1901, unsuccessfully until 1917 when he became Unionist member for Springfield. Mr. Richardson had a considerable gift of humour and his special contributions to his paper, embodied in the reflections and observations of "The Major", gave a good deal of amusement to his readers for a long period. He was also a very effective platform speaker.[4]

Richardson's house was a large one but with five daughters he needed the space.

Next door to Richardson lived D.E. Adams, owner of one of the main coal and wood businesses in the city. Then came Leslie Ironside, a partner in the huge livestock company Gordon Ironside and Fares. He and his partners operated a large slaughterhouse just south of the CPR yards, and, in 1908, had shipped more meat than any other firm in the British Empire. In 1912 they had assets of close to $4,000,000.[5]

At the corner of Roslyn and Osborne Street stood the elegant Roslyn Apartments, home to wealthy young couples starting out in life and to wealthy widows nearing the end of their lives. The widow of A.W. Ross lived in the Roslyn, as did her son Hugh. He left there in January for an extended holiday but never returned; he was one of the Winnipeggers lost in the *Titanic* tragedy.

Across Osborne Street, the character of Roslyn Road changed slightly. The river side was still the more prestigious side of the street, but here the river lots were very much larger, as were some of the homes. Travelling west on Roslyn, one passed the house of Harold Sprague, vice-president and assistant manager of Sprague Lumber, and then came Evergreen Place, a short street running north from Roslyn. On this street were the homes of F.W. Heubach, the Honorable W.E. Montague, and D.L. Mather. Montague was a medical doctor, born in Woodstock and educated at Victoria University in Toronto and the University of Edinburgh. He began practising medicine in 1882 but was soon drawn into politics, serving as Minister of Agriculture and Secretary of State in the last Conservative administrations before Laurier's long reign. In 1905, at the age of forty-seven, he had moved to Winnipeg to join his brother, who had been a businessman in the city since the 1870s. Montague soon re-entered politics and had the misfortune to be in the hot seat as Roblin's Minister of Public Works during the Legislative Building scandal of 1915. D.L. Mather was a lumber merchant who, like Cameron, had become a rich man exploiting the forests in the Lake of the Woods area. In 1907 he and his family had moved to Winnipeg to enjoy the fruits of their labours.

Past Evergreen Place stood four large mansions, built well back from the street, largely hidden on extensive treed lots. Augustus Nanton lived here, next to John Galt and Robert Rogers, the federal Minister of Public Works, and J.S. Hough, a prosperous Winnipeg lawyer.

John Galt was the son of Alexander Galt, one of the Fathers of Confederation. John was born in Montreal in 1856 and educated in schools there and in Gotha in Germany. He started his working life as his father's private secretary but soon left to work for the Bank of Montreal, to learn business principles. Alexander Galt and his family saw the West as a land of opportunity. At the time John settled in Winnipeg in 1882, his sixty-year-old father was travelling across the prairie by wagon, searching for potential business ventures in which to invest. He decided to concentrate his restless energy on developing the coal deposits around what is now Lethbridge, Alberta. He convinced British investors to underwrite the project and, by the time of his death in 1893, the mines were booming, supplying coal to the CPR. Control of the mines passed to Augustus Nanton after 1905, when John Galt's older brother, Elliot, retired. In 1912 Nanton arranged the sale of the mines to the CPR.

John Galt and his cousin, George Galt, founded the grocery wholesale and food processing business that, by 1912, included the famous Blue Ribbon brands of coffee, tea, and spices. Galt's home on Roslyn Road, Greenoch House, a large brick and stone mansion designed by Winnipeg architect J.H. Russell, was a symbol of his success. Galt, who was fifty-four in 1912, lived there with his wife Mabel, who was fifty-six, and their daughters Marion, nineteen, and Evelyn, eighteen, both of whom "came out" in 1912 and were debutantes for the next year. We know something of Galt's affairs from published reports of his investments in banks and insurance companies—$40,000 in the Union Bank and $13,000 in Great West Life. The Galts employed four

George Galt's home on Roslyn Road, Greenoch House.

people to help them run Greenoch House: Mary Henry and Annie Ross, two young Scots women, Nettie Hatt, who was born in Nova Scotia, and Annie Moal, a twelve-year-old girl whose birthplace is given as Manitoba.

On the east side of the Galts' house was the home of Robert Rogers, until the previous autumn the Minister of Public Works in the Roblin government. Rogers was another of the self-made men whose homes lined Roslyn Road. At forty-eight, he had achieved a great deal since coming to the West. He was born in Lakefield in Quebec, the son of a Lieutenant-Colonel. In the years from 1881 to 1900, he amassed a fortune from trading in grain and land and running a general store in Clearwater, Manitoba. After trying unsuccessfully once or twice, Robert Rogers had been elected to the Manitoba Legislature in 1899 and he became Minister of Public Works in the Roblin government in 1900.

Among other things, this meant he was in charge of patronage for the Manitoba Conservatives. He had also been in charge of the federal election campaigns of the Conservatives in western Canada during the decade he sat in the Manitoba House. In recognition of his role in winning the 1911 election, Borden offered him a cabinet post in Ottawa.

In the fall of 1911 Rogers ran federally and was elected for South Winnipeg. He became Minister of Public Works in the first Borden cabinet. He and his wife had been in demand during their Christmas visit to Winnipeg and many dinners were given in their honour.

At the end of Rogers's first session in Ottawa, in April 1912, a journalist made this assessment of the new cabinet minister:

> Some people have been foolish enough to mention Mr. Robert Rogers as an outsider of parts sufficient to make him premier some day. This is a great deal more than he himself would expect, for to give him credit, he has no delusions about his personal size in the scheme of things. He has a ward politician's record which he is satisfied to stand by. He knows that Canada demands a greater outside of respectability in her premiers than it has been his lot to cultivate, and so he takes no chances with the vaulting ambition that o'er leaps itself. There is plenty of work for a politician of his talents and he does that work well. What is more he understands the needs of the west and makes haste to meet them. Although he has been minister of the Interior for only 6 months, he has already given the homesteader all that Mr Frank Oliver [Liberal Minister of the Interior] denied him over the last 8 years.[6]

This analysis of Rogers was wrong in one respect: he did have ambitions and he eventually did run for the federal leadership, at the National Conservative Convention in Winnipeg in 1926. By then his time was past and he came last in the race that saw R.B. Bennett elected.

On the other side of Galt's house was Kilmorie, the home of Augustus Nanton. Of all the young men who came to Winnipeg in the 1880s, Nanton was undoubtedly the most successful. His early life might have been written by Dickens, it was so full of melodrama. He was born in 1860, the son of a promising young lawyer, Augustus Nanton, and Louisa Jarvis, the daughter of the High Sheriff of Toronto and owner of the famous Rosedale estate. Nanton senior came from a wealthy family in England and had been educated at Eton and Oxford, but by the time his eldest son, Augustus, was born he was a hopeless alcoholic. By 1867, drink had killed him, leaving his young wife and four children without money or hope.

The wedding of the son of D.C. Cameron (far left) and the daughter of Augustus Nanton (centre front), on the front steps of the Nanton house, Kilmorie

Louisa Nanton had to survive by teaching French, taking charity from her sister, who was married to Edmund Meredith, a senior bureaucrat in Ottawa, and from Sir Casimir Gzowski, the great engineer, who had been a friend of her father's. This traumatic childhood shaped the young Nanton, turning him into an adult very early. At thirteen he left school and went to work for Pellatt and Osler, a Toronto brokerage house, for $300 per year. He got a second job, sweeping out a grocery store and sleeping under the counter at night. This work brought in another $200 a year.

Young Nanton was able to help his mother with her debts and later he paid for his brother, Herbert, to attend the Royal Military College in Kingston. He never ceased making himself responsible for other people. During the First World War he headed an agency that looked after the needs of Manitoba soldiers' wives and families. He was known to get up in the night and personally drive these women and their children to hospital. When the son of a Winnipeg family was lying severely wounded in a military hospital in England, Nanton anonymously arranged for a telegram to be sent each morning to the parents, reporting on their boy's condition. He was quite embarrassed when it was discovered he was responsible.

The sitting room in the Nantons' home, Kilmorie, on Roslyn Road.

So impressed had the principals of his firm been by this serious, hard-working young man that they made him a partner at the age of twenty-three and sent him to Winnipeg to look after their new western office. In the first year he loaned $50,000 to settlers wanting to buy land and so careful was he that not one of his borrowers defaulted during the first fourteen years of operation. As the years passed, the office expanded and Osler, Hammond and Nanton became agents for real estate developments, for the Galt Coal Company, and various insurance firms. Nanton's personal wealth grew apace and he was appointed to numerous boards, including that of the Canadian Pacific Railroad and to the first Canadian Committee of the Hudson's Bay Company. His reputation was so solid that in 1902 he concluded the sale of 800,000 acres in Saskatchewan, a deal worth several million dollars, solely on the basis of his personal handshake.

Nanton and his second wife, Constance, built Kilmorie in 1900, situating it close to the Assiniboine River on a heavily treed, two-hectare property. Some of her friends had worried that Mrs. Nanton would be lonely, living so far out, but by 1912 Kilmorie was surrounded by the city on all sides. They also built a large stable for Nanton's beloved horses and a gatekeeper's lodge, both of which, with the estate's gateway, still exist.

Kilmorie was home to the Nantons and their six children—a daughter, Georgina, from Augustus Nanton's first marriage, and two more girls and three boys from his second marriage. They employed a cook, four maids, two gardeners, a coachman, and a groom to run the house and attend to the grounds. In 1906 the staff were Fannie Collins, an Irish woman, and three people from England, Clara Chipperfield, Edith Webb, and Frederick Lewis. Charles Beavis was the gardener and he lived in the gatehouse with his wife and son.

On the ground floor of the house were the large public rooms—a library, sitting room, dining room, and music room in which Constance Nanton often hosted concerts for the Women's Musical Club. There were, as well, a laundry, a kitchen, a larder and pantry, and a maid's sitting room and verandah on the main floor. The next floor had six bedrooms and a sitting room with another verandah; accommodations for the servants and a sewing room occupied the top floor. In the basement of the house there was a bowling alley and a billiard room. During the Great War, these downstairs rooms were made available to troops stationed at Fort Osborne Barracks and many nights twenty or thirty young men spent the evening there, finishing up with hot cocoa and sandwiches before going back over the bridge to their beds.

Nanton was well liked in Winnipeg and there can be no better proof of this than the fact that on the day of his funeral in 1925, many businesses closed in the city and many of the streets along which the hearse passed were lined with people.

The last of the four, large, riverside houses overlooking the curve of the Assiniboine River at the extreme western end of Roslyn was the home of J.S. Hough, a successful Winnipeg lawyer.

Also at the western end of Roslyn lived Colin Campbell, the provincial Minister of Public Works, for many years the Attorney General, who had just moved to his new house from Colony Street. Campbell, who was the law partner of Isaac Pitblado, had come to Winnipeg in the 1880s and carved out a successful career in law and politics. By 1912 he was a wealthy man; we know he had $18,000 invested in Great West Life and $84,000 in the Bank of Hamilton. But he was not well. He confided to his wife in April that "I feel tired and feel I need a rest. I was thinking I have worked long enough. It is now 40 years since I started and I feel I cannot go on much longer."[7] Within a year he suffered a massive stroke from which he did not recover, and died in 1913.

His wife, Minnie Campbell, was an important community volunteer in Winnipeg, working tirelessly for Westminster Presbyterian Church, of which she and her husband had been founding members, as well as the IODE, in which she was a Manitoba Regent, and for the YWCA. Mrs. Campbell came from United Empire Loyalist stock, of which she was very proud, and her father was a medical doctor in Palermo, Ontario. She attended Hamilton Female College and taught for a time before coming to Winnipeg. She had a gift for fundraising; when she set out to help the YWCA build its first building in Winnipeg, she called a group of her friends to a luncheon meeting and announced that they were going to put out a single issue women's newspaper. They sold ads worth $6500 and netted $5000 for the building fund.

Next to Campbell lived Captain William Robinson, aged sixty-three. Like Hugh Sutherland, Robinson had arrived in Winnipeg in the 1870s and also had already had experience as a railroad contractor. In Manitoba he contracted to build part of the CPR line from Winnipeg to Lake of the Woods. In 1878 he built his first steamboat and became the first man to offer steam-powered transport on Lake Winnipeg. He was also involved in provisioning and logging on the lake. In 1912, he was still president of the Northwest Navigation Company, a firm in which the Hudson's Bay Company held a large interest. He and his wife had investments totalling $37,000 in the Northern Crown Bank, of which he was the vice-president.

On the south side of Roslyn, several lawyers had built houses. One of these was Robert Maxwell Dennistoun, the son of James Frederick Dennistoun, a prominent Peterborough lawyer and the grandson of Robert Dennistoun, who had been a judge in his native Scotland as well as in Canada. The younger Dennistoun was born in Peterborough in 1864, educated at Queen's University, and called to the Ontario Bar. In 1892 he married Mildred Beck, daughter of the Reverend J.W.R. Beck, Anglican rector of Peterborough. The Dennistouns were very recent arrivals in Winnipeg, having moved to the city in 1908. In Winnipeg, he joined the firm of Machray and Sharpe, an up-and-coming partnership with good prospects. He may have hoped to make his fortune in the expanding economy of Winnipeg and we know that he did make some real estate investments. But, like so many people, including his law partners, he did not become as rich as he had probably dreamed. However, he lived a comfortable like—the fine house they owned in 1912 still stands at 168 Roslyn Road—and he was soon appointed to the bench. He and his wife and children had close to $41,000 invested in various insurance companies and banks.

A retired lawyer, Heber Archibald, who had been one of the founders of the firm now owned by Machray and Sharp, lived next to Dennistoun at number 176, and Dennistoun's partner, Fred Sharp, lived next to Archibald at number 180. Their properties backed onto the courts of the Winnipeg Tennis Club.

Further west, at 218 Roslyn, Walter Moss, vice-president of the Robinson Department Store, lived with his wife and children. Moss, who came to Winnipeg in 1898, married the boss's daughter, Lottie Robinson, and they built the house at 218 Roslyn in 1901. In 1909 they added a wing that included a ballroom and, in 1913, a second wing. The total cost of these renovations was $44,000 (roughly $700,000 in today's dollars); there was clearly money to be made in retail in Winnipeg. The Moss house is the only large Roslyn Road house left standing today.[8]

In April, the residents of Roslyn Road and their friends were touched by a tragedy of international scope. On Monday, April 15, the morning *Telegram* carried a brief report that at 10:25 the previous evening the *Titanic* had struck an iceberg and was sinking in the Atlantic. No further details were available. By the time Winnipeggers read this brief notice, Hugo Ross, his friend Thompson Beattie, Mark Fortune and his son Charles, and another Winnipegger, G.E. Graham, were already drowned or frozen in the cruel North Atlantic.

Ross and the others were part of a small annual exodus of wealthy Winnipegers who were able to escape the prairie winters and travel to warmer climates. Beginning in January, society columns told the less fortunate where the upper middle classes were going. Lawyer R.M. Dennistoun and his wife, the paper reported, had set out for

Bermuda. Their boys had already gone back to school in Port Hope, Ontario. Bermuda was not a common destination for Winnipeggers in 1912; California, on the other hand, lured residents of the city in large numbers. The Northern Pacific Railroad made it easy to get to the sunny south by putting on two through-cars from Winnipeg to Los Angeles every day from January 6 to January 12. Mrs. Thomas Kelly, the wife of the successful builder, was one of those who climbed aboard a California train in early January. A few years later, she and her husband moved permanently to California, after he had served his time in Stony Mountain Penitentiary for his role in the Legislative Building scandal.

While many Winnipeggers went south to enjoy the sun, a few of the city's wealthiest residents travelled overseas, to England, the Mediterranean, and Egypt. The Nantons, for example, went to England, which would allow them to shop for the latest fashions and perhaps buy paintings or antiques for their house.

Egypt was a favourite Edwardian holiday spot. The Thomas Cook Company had been arranging tours of Egypt and the Nile since 1870 and, by 1912, they owned twenty tourist steamers and several luxury hotels. There was a good deal of interest in Egyptian antiquities in 1912, the year the famous bust of Nefertiti was excavated. In his book *Egypt in Transition*, Sidney Low observed that tourists in Egypt usually started out with good intentions and provided themselves with guidebooks and works by archaeologists such as Sir Flinders Petrie, but

> after a time they get mixed up among the dynasties and cartouches. They are rather a jolly lot, who have come from the smoke of London, the chills of Berlin and the winter rigours of Chicago, in a holiday mood, entirely resolved to enjoy themselves. Middle aged gentlemen, exchanging jocularities with the guides; young folks of both sexes, much occupied with one another. Five out of six carry Kodaks and photograph with undiscriminating assiduity.[9]

The real estate millionaire, Mark Fortune, and his wife, three daughters, and son set out from Winnipeg in January for New York en route to Egypt. Their long vacation was to be capped with a special treat: a trip home on the maiden voyage of the new White Star liner

Titanic. One of the Fortune daughters, Alice, met an admirer in Egypt, William Sloper, who was so taken with her that he cancelled his passage on the *Mauretania* and instead bought a first-class ticket on the *Titanic*, so he could travel home in the same ship with her.[10] Both Sloper and Alice Fortune survived the disaster, but their relationship went no further because Alice was engaged to be married.

Mr. and Mrs. Hugh Sutherland also went to Egypt in January, and another wealthy real estate developer, W.H. Gardner, his wife, their son, Teddy, and Gardner's step-daughter, Miss Louise Robertson, who was engaged to be married in the fall, took the train to New York where they would board the *Franconia*, bound for the Mediterranean. They gaily announced that they "will not be back til June." Hugo Ross, yet another Winnipeg real estate man, left with his friend Thomas Beattie for an extended trip that was to include Egypt. They also intended to come home aboard the *Titanic*.

Thompson Beattie and Hugo Ross, travelling with former Winnipegger Thomas McCaffrey, had visited Egypt and cruised the Mediterranean. On a stop in Venice, they met Mark Fortune and his family. Hugo Ross was ill with dysentery during the voyage of the *Titanic* and was last seen on the night of the disaster in his stateroom, still in his pyjamas. Thompson Beattie managed to get into a lifeboat but later died of exposure. His body was found about a month later, still in the lifeboat with two other casualties. He was buried at sea.

Mark Fortune and his nineteen-year-old son Charles helped Mrs. Mary Fortune and their three daughters, Ethel, Mabel, and Alice, into a lifeboat. Mrs. Fortune shouted to her son, a prize-winning athlete and student who would have gone to McGill that fall, to look after his father. Fortune was wearing his Winnipeg buffalo coat, which he always brought along on trips for good luck. The bodies of Mark and Charles Fortune were never found.

George Graham was the manager of the china department at the Winnipeg Eaton's store, who had been in England on a buying trip. His body was found floating in the ocean several days later.

By the Saturday following the disaster—a full week after the sinking—there was still no definite word about the Winnipeg passengers. All social functions had been cancelled and the friends and relatives of the missing people prepared themselves for the worst. Mr. and Mrs. Heber

Hutton and Mr. Charles Allan, who was engaged to be married to Alice Fortune, had left on Tuesday to be in New York to meet Mrs. Fortune and her daughters. Mrs. MacLean arrived in Winnipeg to be with her sister Mrs. A.W. Ross, grief-stricken over the loss of her son Hugo.

A moving concert took place at the Walker Theatre on the evening of Sunday, May 5th. The Royal Alexandra orchestra and the Winnipeg City Band gave the concert to raise money for the families of the *Titanic* orchestra musicians. The band members stated that, "The musicians of Winnipeg have been deeply touched and wish to express their sympathy and admiration in deeds rather than words ... for the members of the *Titanic* orchestra ... who did so much to allay the fears of the survivors and make the last moments of the victims sweeter."[11]

∽ MAY ∾

Railways

Winnipeg was the first and greatest of all the railroad towns that bloomed across western Canada. By 1912 over 4700 people in the city worked for the Canadian Pacific, the Canadian Northern, or the Grand Trunk railroads. Along with the grain business, manufacturing, and construction, the railroads were main engines of growth for the city.

Most of western Canada's railroad towns sprouted in the cinders along the tracks in locations chosen by the rail companies. Winnipeg was different: she made the railroad come to her. As early as the 1860s, Winnipeg's future élite, men like James Ashdown, John Schultz, and the editors of the *Nor'Wester* newspaper, James Ross and William Coldwell, began agitating for a railroad. One of their first manoeuvres, in 1865, was to form an alliance with Sanford Fleming, the Scottish-born engineer who eventually laid out most of the CPR's route across the west, and who achieved lasting fame for developing the system of time zones now used all over the world. Fleming had visited Red River as part of the Hind Expedition and he favoured the idea of a rail link with the east.

The Winnipeg group presented Fleming with a memorandum, which he took to the government of Upper Canada, an early step in the long process of lobbying for and building the CPR. Twenty years later, in October 1885, he watched Donald Smith drive in the last spike of the CPR at Craigelachie in British Columbia.

For Winnipeg, it was important to ensure not only that a railroad was built, but that the main line passed through the city. Once again

The repair and maintenance of the steam engines and rolling stock of the railroads provided Winnipeg with a core of well-paid jobs.

the city founders were successful in shaping events and, after much negotiation, they convinced the railway to divert its main line south from its westerly route and cross the Red River at Winnipeg. They threw so many inducements on the table (including a $200,000 subsidy and payment for the bridge to carry the rails across the Red River) that the cash-strapped CPR could not resist. In 1882 they also passed Bylaw 195, which provided that

> all property now owned or that herinafter may be owned by them [the CPR] within the limits of the City of Winnipeg for railroad purposes or in connection therewith, shall be forever free and exempt from all municipal taxes, rates and levies and assessments of every nature and kind.[1]

In addition to locating the main line through Winnipeg, the CPR also promised to build a 160-kilometre branch line southwest of the city and to erect a passenger station, freight yards, and shops within the city limits. The yards and shops were the most important influence on the early growth of the city. Canadian Pacific steam engines would be torn apart and rebuilt in the city and maintenance of all other sorts would be done there, so Winnipeg was guaranteed a large number of skilled jobs for machinists and tradesmen as well as labouring jobs and all the jobs in-between.

By 1912, not one but four railroads served Winnipeg. The stock-yards and freight-handling facilities had given rise to other industries employing large numbers of people and producing fortunes for the local owners. Along a spur line that ran southwest from the Canadian Pacific yards just west of Arlington, for example, slaughterhouses and meat packing firms had been established. The largest of these was Gordon, Ironside and Fares, a company that shipped at least 50,000 head of cattle for export every year. In 1906 they shipped more animals than any other company in the world.[2]

Dray wagons constantly moved in and out of the yards, hauling freight to and from the huge warehouses that lined the streets to the south. Although Winnipeg's iron grip on the distribution trade had begun to loosen because of adverse decisions by the Board of Railway Commissioners and the steady growth of other prairie cities, in 1912 things were booming. Goods were unloaded in Winnipeg warehouses like those of J.H. Ashdown Hardware or the Galt's Blue Ribbon grocery wholesale, and then shipped out to small stores all over the prairie. Every train that left the city carried commercial travellers who visited the small-town merchants regularly, taking orders and keeping everyone happy.

In addition to the enormous economic significance of the railways in Winnipeg, their payroll and spending for supplies and equipment, the presence of the companies had impacts of other kinds. Steam engines belching out smoke and dropping cinders and ash rumbled over sixty-four kilometres of rail running through many districts of the relatively small city. And there were the bridges that carried the various lines over the Assiniboine and Red rivers. The Louise Bridge on the site of the original CPR Red River Bridge was now a vehicle and pedestrian bridge, and the CP main line crossed the Red a short distance upstream at the extreme east end of Point Douglas. Further south along the Red, the spectacular new Grand Trunk Bridge with its unusual lift section was nearing completion. A little further along, the Canadian Northern Bridge crossed the Red at an angle and carried the CN line into the yards near the

foot of Water Street. Turning at the forks and moving upstream on the Assiniboine, the Grand Trunk and Canadian Northern both had bridges crossing over into Fort Rouge from the yards. Farther west, almost at the boundary of the city, the Canadian Pacific, the Great Northern, and the Canadian Northern all had bridges crossing the river, the former two just west of Omand's Creek, the latter at St. James Street.

The passenger schedules of the railroads brought over a dozen daily trains into the city and local Manitoba trains ran alternate days or twice a week. Each morning between 6:10 and 7:30, four passenger trains—the Prairie Express from Calgary, the Great West Express from Edmonton, the Imperial Limited from Vancouver, and the Soo Line train from the United States—pulled into the Canadian Pacific Station on Higgins Avenue. Departures began at 8:00 a.m. when the Imperial Limited steamed out of the city, bound for Montreal. At 9:40 the Regina Express departed and then there was a lull until 1:15, when the Express train from Toronto came in. At 9:30 in the evening, the westbound Imperial Limited arrived from Montreal and the station was again crowded with passengers stopping in Winnipeg or boarding trains for Vancouver, Calgary, and Edmonton. By midnight, all the westbound trains, including the sleeping car only on Imperial Limited, had left Winnipeg.

The Canadian Northern, the Grand Trunk Pacific, and the Northern Pacific Railroad maintained similar passenger train schedules in and out of the city. Fares were similar for all the railroads. The return fare to Toronto was $41.00, or $48.80 if you took the CPR train to Fort William and then went the rest of the way by steamer. Ticket prices precluded anyone but upper-middle-class people from travelling often.

Carrying passengers, however, was not as profitable as hauling freight. In 1912 the CPR earned a little over thirty-two million dollars from passenger traffic and close to eighty million dollars from freight.[3] The number of freight trains moving into and out of the city far exceeded those carrying people. The most important cargo of all was grain, specifically, wheat, which made up ninety-seven per cent of western grain exports. In the fall and winter, the yards were packed with boxcars full of grain moving east to the Lakehead. Local shippers of other goods complained that their deliveries were being delayed by the grain movement. By 1912 the railroads sought to solve this problem by diverting some of their freight traffic around the city.

The Canadian Pacific yards, the largest in the British Empire, were hemmed in by the city on both the north and south, and the facilities had reached their limit. To relieve the congestion, the CPR built the Bergen cut-off rail line north of the city limits and moved some of its freight handling to new yards in Transcona, where they also constructed a large grain elevator. Although the land under the Transcona yards ultimately proved to be too unstable to support a major freight facility, in 1912 the potential for growth created by these yards, and the massive shops the National Transcontinental Railway was building farther south, created a real estate boom in Transcona.

The Canadian Northern had the same problem of congestion in its Fort Rouge yards, but when, early in 1912, Sir William Mackenzie, president of Canadian Northern, proposed a similar solution—a cut-off running along the bank of the Red River at the south end of Fort Rouge, with a bridge over to St. Boniface—a major controversy erupted.

The *Manitoba Free Press* of February 13 reported that the local residents complained through their spokesman, a lawyer by the name of O'Leary, that the dirt and smoke emitted by a modern locomotive "affect a region extending to probably one third of a mile from the tracks or thereabouts, and the noise caused by it is of such volume and extent as to constitute a violent public nuisance for a distance of at least half a mile from the moving locomotive." The group argued that if the cut-off was built too close to the district's new homes, they would be greatly diminished in value and, to a large extent, spoiled as places of residence. There was also concern over the loss of River Park, through which the rail line would run. The mayor and Board of Control agreed, as did City Council, and a petition with thousands of signatures was presented to the Board of Railway Commissioners.

At a hearing before the board in September, the city's lawyer, Theodore Hunt, said that Winnipeg was cut up into pockets by rail

The Canadian Northern yards behind the newly completed Union Station are visible in
this picture, as is the old CN rail bridge that carried rail traffic across the Red River.

lines and a comprehensive plan was needed before any more lines were
built. The reeve of St. Vital also expressed concern that the proposed
route of the cut-off on the east side of the Red ran within 100 feet of a
new school the municipality had just opened.

The contrast between this protest and the Winnipeg of the 1870s
and 1880s, when nothing was denied the CPR, is a measure of how
diverse the city's economy had become and of how its politics had
matured. Of course, the other controversies the city was having with
Sir William Mackenzie, over his Street Railway Company and the
location of his gasification plant in the new residential area in the city's
west end, did not create an atmosphere conducive to compromise.
New home owners, investing in a middle-class neighbourhood and
building homes, wanted to protect their investments and their peace
and quiet. The city government was inclined to back these taxpayers
and put some limits on the railroad's expansion.

The city received some petitions in favour of the cut-off. At least
some of the signatories to these petitions, which expressed concern that

the railway would move jobs out of Winnipeg, were employees of the Canadian Northern. As soon as the Board of Railway Commissioners' decision came down in December, denying Canadian Northern's application to build the rail line, Mackenzie announced plans to expand his company's freight yards in Portage la Prairie and to divert some freight trains through Morris and Emerson. He also announced that some Canadian Northern staff would be transferred from Winnipeg to these communities.

Competition between the major rail companies had been increasing during the decade before 1912. The CPR was a fabulously successful corporation, producing a surplus of $17.5 million. It had just floated a new stock issue in London, through which it raised two million pounds to finance its expansion. The Canadian Pacific still owned over two million hectares in western Canada, part of the land grant originally given by the government to help finance the railroad. During 1912, 28,600 hectares were sold to new settlers, bringing in close to ten million dollars for the company. However, with the Laurier government's decision to support its two Canadian rivals, the Canadian Northern and the Grand Trunk, known as the Grand Trunk Pacific in western Canada, in its plans to build transcontinental lines, the CPR's dominance had become a thing of the past.

The Canadian Pacific responded by expanding its capacity all across western Canada. In Winnipeg, the yards were extended westward and the Royal Alexandra Hotel was erected and enlarged twice. The company put up a new station and office building adjoining the hotel on Higgins Avenue. By 1912 over 3000 people worked for the CPR, making it the largest single employer in the city.

The line from Winnipeg to the Lakehead was double tracked and the railroad's terminal at Fort William was modernized and enlarged. In the mountains, far to the west, the CPR had recently built the Crowsnest Pass viaduct and the spiral tunnels at Kicking Horse Pass, to speed the movement of its trains over the mountain barrier.

Both the Canadian Pacific's rivals, the Grand Trunk Pacific and the Canadian Northern, were at a very different stage of development. While they were each within three years of completing new transcontinental rail lines, they still carried enormous debt loads and required massive new infusions of capital each year to continue the construction process. The Canadian Northern did produce a surplus of $500,000 in 1912 and sales from its land grants brought in almost $3 million. On the other side of the ledger, the CNR's total interest payments for the year were a chilling $4.6 million.

The Canadian Northern was the creation of Sir William Mackenzie and Sir Donald Mann, who had started their partnership as contractors laying track for the CPR. In the 1890s they began buying up smaller companies and building track to link their acquisitions together. Their first purchase had been the Manitoba Northwestern Railway, which had a charter to build a road from Gladstone to Dauphin and a land grant of 2400 hectares. Rodmond Roblin had given the CN an important boost in 1902 when he took over the Northern Pacific's track and then leased it to Canadian Northern. As part of the deal, he secured for Manitoba the right to set freight rates, with the result that, for the first time, the CPR had real competition in western Canada. Manitoba also agreed to guarantee the CNR's bond issues, which, by 1912, constituted an enormous amount of money.

By 1912 CN was pushing the last section of the transcontinental line that would rival the Canadian Pacific through the mountains of BC, toward the Pacific. The CNR ran through the northern prairies and, all along its line, towns sprang up. Joseph Adams, who travelled from Winnipeg to Edmonton on this railway in 1911, likened the railway to the mythical philosopher's stone, turning base metal into gold wherever it passed.

> The effect was to be noticed in the activity at every stopping place along the line. There were houses newly erected, and others in the course of construction. Barn-like structures advertised themselves in large letters as hotels. Telephone lines stretched from hut to hut, and agricultural implements ... were piled near the stations.[4]

The Canadian Northern had also been expanding its facilities in Winnipeg for several years. The massive Union Station on Main at the end of Broadway was the western headquarters of both the CN and the Grand Trunk Pacific. On the flats behind the station, freight yards were developing on land where J.J. Hill's Northern Pacific had built a roundhouse and yards in the 1890s. The Canadian Northern was also building huge new yards in Fort Rouge, where engine and car repair facilities employed hundreds of people. The streets east of these yards were full of the same kind of small, working men's cottages that surrounded the CPR yards. Here lived the machinists and labourers and the train crews who kept the railway running.

Mackenzie and Mann had always been men in a hurry, knowing that the big profits would begin only after they had a completed transcontinental line. They were anxious to push their line into new territory before their competitors and, as a result, the quality of what they were building was not always the highest. The standard joke about the CNR line was that after a train had passed, the track would flip up and smack the back of the caboose.

The CNR's main rival in the northern prairies was the Grand Trunk Pacific. The Grand Trunk Railway was older than the CPR, dating from Canada's first great railway boom in the 1850s. By the turn of the century, however, the railway was in financial difficulties and without a connection to the west where the coming boom might prove to be its salvation. Like other Canadian railways before it, the Grand Trunk turned to an American, in this case Charles M. Hay, to manage its affairs in a time of crisis.

Charles Hay, first general manager, then president, of the Grand Trunk, prescribed a major expansion as a way out of the company's problems. Like Mackenzie and Mann, he dreamed of duplicating the amazing success of the CPR. Hay went to the government of Wilfrid Laurier in 1903 to ask for backing. At first Laurier's answer was that the country could not support another national railway, but he was eventually won over.

Hay's original plan was to link the Grand Trunk's northern terminus at North Bay with the western division of the railway, to be called the Grand Trunk Pacific, which was to run from Winnipeg to the remote BC port of Prince Rupert. By placing his seaport at Prince Rupert, 640 kilometres closer to Japan than Vancouver, Hay hoped to capture a large share of the Pacific freight business.

Political support came with a price, of course. Once the politicians became involved in the design of the railway, it took on a completely different shape. Instead of beginning at North Bay, the eastern portion of the line was to start at Moncton, New Brunswick, and pass through Quebec City before heading straight west through the largely uninhabited northern forests on its way to Winnipeg. In the end it was agreed that the Government of Canada would build this eastern portion, called the National Transcontinental Railway. When complete, it would be leased to the Grand Trunk on very favourable terms.

In 1912 the Grand Trunk Pacific still faced 800 kilometres of tough mountain construction in order to link Prince Rupert with Winnipeg, and the National Transcontinental railhead was still 560 kilometres east of the city in northern Ontario.

The Grand Trunk Pacific and its sister railroad, the National Transcontinental, were, in many ways, the exact opposite of the Canadian Northern. Construction standards were very high and expense was not spared to build it right the first time. Frederick Talbot, author of the 1912 book *The Making of a Great Canadian Railway,* wrote that the Grand Trunk was considered an example of the superior British engineering that had built the Empire, resulting in "a billiard table track, conducive to fast traveling without the slightest sign of oscillation or vibration."[5]

The Grand Trunk's advertising made much of this difference and of the fact that it resulted in a trip from Winnipeg to Edmonton seven hours faster than the Canadian Northern over a route that was only thirty-two kilometres shorter. Talbot wrote that even the telegraph lines had been strung from poles of a uniform height, instead of hung on trees as the Canadian Northern often did, "so that the line of wires had the peculiarly British methodical appearance."

In Transcona the repair shops that would service the National Transcontinental and the Grand Trunk Pacific were nearing completion in 1912. Here an engine could be taken out of commission for four to six weeks and undergo a complete rebuilding. The shops had a 175-tonne crane for moving engines and every modern machine for train maintenance.

Another example of superior engineering was the new bridge, which was nearing completion in spring of 1912, and soon carried rail traffic over the Red and into Union Station. The bridge was being built by the government-owned National Transcontinental as the western terminus of their road from Winnipeg to Moncton. Resting on piers that extended down to the bedrock beneath the river's muddy bottom, the bridge carried a double track over the Red and onto a viaduct, which, in turn, carried the rails over two streets and other rail lines and into the train sheds at the rear of Union Station. It was equipped with a bascule, a span of the bridge that could be raised like a drawbridge using electric motors and a massive concrete counterweight suspended in a steel tower above the tracks, to keep the navigable western side of the Red River open for shipping.

Another Winnipeg example of the Grand Trunk's lavish style was the Fort Garry Hotel, under construction in 1912, which still stands as a monument to the high standards Charles Hay established for his railroad.

In addition to the construction of the National Transcontinental, the federal government had also extended loan guarantees and subsidies to the Grand Trunk, just as they had done to the Canadian Northern and, much earlier, to the Canadian Pacific. By 1912 the total of subsidies and grants in land and money extended to the three railroads since 1883 was $43.5 million. In return, Canada had 46,760 kilometres of railroad: more rail line per capita than almost any other country in the world. A good deal of it ran through inaccessible and largely uninhabited country that had presented previously undreamt-of difficulties for the builders, but would never generate revenue for the companies.

Neither of the CPR's rivals completed their transcontinental lines before the coming of the war. Suddenly it was impossible to borrow, on the London money markets, the funds needed to complete the ambitious building programs, and bankruptcy followed. Eventually, both railways were taken over by the government and run as Canadian National Railways.

Whatever the cost to the nation as a whole, for Winnipeg the railways, their repair facilities, and staff, as well as the enormous amount of construction they were engaged in on both sides of the city, were an important engine of growth. During the 1912 construction season, 86 kilometres of track were built in Manitoba, 1012 in Saskatchewan, and 643 in Alberta. As well, surveys for the Hudson Bay Railway were being completed and construction was scheduled to begin soon on this long-dreamed-of line. This construction provided jobs for Winnipeggers and a market for city manufacturers and suppliers. Winnipeg builder J.D. McArthur had the contract to build the first part of the Hudson Bay Railway from The Pas to Thicket Portage. He had also sold 100,000 railroad ties to the National Transcontinental from

As western vice-president of the CPR,
Sir William Whyte was in charge
of operations from Winnipeg to the
Pacific.

his timber operations in Manitoba. John Vopni of Winnipeg had the contract to build two large stations for the National Transcontinental, at Transcona and Redditt. The J. McDairmid Company of Winnipeg would be paid $26,000 each for three massive coaling stations for the railroad.[6] These are only a few examples of the benefits to Winnipeg of railroad construction.

In the city, about 4700 people or ten per cent of the population worked for one or another of the railways in the 1911 census year. Wages paid ranged from $1.77 an hour for labourers in the yards to an average of $12.50 an hour for company officers or managers.[7] Senior executives, who undoubtedly owned shares in the companies, earned much more.

As western headquarters for the three railroads, Winnipeg was home to members of the upper levels of management, as well. Sir William Whyte had been western vice-president of the CPR from 1904 until his retirement in 1911. His large home on the Assiniboine, which stood at the junction of River Avenue and Wellington Crescent, testified to the success of this lifelong railroader of relatively humble Scottish origins. Whyte first arrived in Winnipeg in 1886 when the CPR was a young company. By 1912, when he died, he was a leader among the city's élite.

Whyte's successor as vice-president, George Bury, had worked for the CPR all his adult life. He came to Winnipeg in 1908 to work as general manager of Western Lines. Thomas Shaughnassy, the president of the CPR, liked Bury and commented that he had the "driving energy and clear thinking that brought quick promotion."[8] Bury and his family were, like the Whytes, accepted into the Winnipeg élite and their names often appeared in the social columns in accounts of teas, dances, and dinner parties. Bury's son George was a student in the law office of Machray and Sharpe in the new Bank of Commerce Building on Main Street. In 1912 his daughter Mary became the wife of another young lawyer, Humphrey Drummond-Hay, who was just beginning what became a long and successful career with the firm of Pitblado and Hoskin.

In 1912, another Winnipeg railroad millionaire, Alexander Rae Davidson, was celebrating and displaying his great wealth by building a massive home at 10 Ruskin Row. The house was sumptuous, even by 1912 Winnipeg standards, and contained a ballroom and public rooms large enough to entertain dozens of guests. Rae and his brother had made a fortune in railway building in Wisconsin and Michigan, and later sold over 400,000 hectares of land to homesteaders in Alberta and Saskatchewan.

In the newly opened Union Station on Main Street, lesser Canadian Northern officials worked diligently behind the frosted glass doors of their offices, dreaming of one day being as rich as Whyte or the Davidsons. Ranged below them were about 100 Grand Trunk officials along with the many typists, clerks, and office boys who worked with them. Several blocks to the north of the Union Station on Higgins Avenue, in the CPR office building attached to the station on Higgins, Vice-President and General Manager George Bury presided over a similar establishment of about 125 managers, trainmasters, solicitors, and engineers. In addition, some of the management for the Royal Alexandra was located in the CPR office building.

We can get a flavour of what working for the railroad was like through the amusing stories told in a 1925 memoir called *Rail Life: A Book of Yarns* by Alfred Price, written when he had retired from a life of work for the CPR. His father had also been a lifelong railroad man who had worked for the Grand Trunk. Price reveals a good deal about the internal culture of the CPR through his stories, which, while they may not all be literally true, give us a sense of the attitudes of the author and his intended audience—his fellow managers.

A common problem for the managers of these large national corporations was that they had to endure a good many transfers around the country. Price records Jack Switzer, at one time the CPR chief engineer, as saying, "In the last 10 years I have moved 16 times, and now my furniture is so well trained that I have only to open the front door and make the announcement and it all walks out into the street."[9]

As part of the prosperous managerial class of Winnipeg who worked for national firms, the officers housed in the two station buildings brought stability to the city and their social class. They and their wives were part of the social life of the city and we see their names in the society columns. But they also disrupted that stability when their companies inevitably transferred them elsewhere, either to cities like Montreal, or perhaps to smaller regional centres to gain experience.

Away from their families, the railway officers socialized with each other in a sort of joyous adolescent manner. Listen to this description by Price of the trip of a group of western managers to a meeting in Montreal: "nobody thought of retiring until the milkmen were on their rounds in the grey mornings, for, in the words of Frank Peters, why waste time in sleep." The last night before reaching Montreal, they wasted very little time sleeping, going to bed at 3:30 after many hours of drinking. The train pulled into Windsor Station in Montreal at 6:00 a.m., "and the intention of the officers was to sleep until 8 or 9. But Jim Woodman, the Terminal Superintendent, had decreed otherwise, as he considered the occasion should be suitably honoured by giving the western officers a rousing demonstration and a royal welcome." A switch engine slowly passed the newly arrived train, exploding fog signals, called torpedoes. "The noise of the explosions was deafening and the reverberations in the great train shed were something terrific. Then, two Italians with hand organs serenaded the occupants of the train, who made use of some of their choicest selections of profanity, got up, and moved to their hotels, where they hoped to get a little sleep before work began."[10]

Interacting with railway customers was an important part of the duties of these company officers. Price's book contains the following account of a meeting between James Ashdown and William Lanigan, General Freight Superintendent:

> Jimmy, as everyone called Mr. Ashdown behind his back, although a strictly honourable man, was not always the most agreeable of men to do business with, and nothwithstanding that Billy (W.B. Lanigan) understood him perfectly well and knew how to handle him, at times he found it hard to control his celtic temperament, especially when some concession was being insisted upon which Billy thought no one was entitled to.

One day in 1908, Ashdown was in Lanigan's office on the first floor of the CPR office building on Higgins, and the two men were arguing while watching a crew construct a new garden in the station yard. Lanigan said he did not agree with the plans to beautify the grounds and Ashdown asked why. Lanigan replied, "I wanted them to erect a statue of the present Mayor of Winnipeg [Ashdown].... I would have kept a basket of rotten eggs on hand, and whenever I felt as I do now, I'd throw up the window and peg away at him."[11]

Below the company officers, further down the railway hierarchy, were the working men who made the railway run and the foremen who supervised them. There were three large groups of railway workers in 1912. The most highly skilled and highly paid were those employed in the running trades—engineers, firemen, conductors—who worked on the trains and kept them on schedule. These men had fought hard to establish trade unions and, by 1912, while their fight was not over, they had enjoyed some success in having their organizations recognized.

The second group was the shop craft union workers, called the "backbone of the Winnipeg labour movement" by its historian, Doug Smith, in his book *Let Us Rise*.[12] These were the skilled machinists, boilermakers, blacksmiths, and carmen who maintained and overhauled railway equipment. A successful strike by the machinists in 1899 had forced the CPR to recognize their union. But in 1908 the railway provoked a bitter dispute by reversing this earlier decision and refusing to recognize the shop craft unions. At the same time, the company cut wages. With the help of strike breakers, the CPR won this battle.

At the bottom of the ladder were the unskilled maintenance-of-way workers. These men had no trades and they were easily replaced from the vast pool of unskilled labour available in western Canada. Their struggle to have their union, the Brotherhood of Railway Employees, recognized had so far met with failure. During a bitter strike, strike breakers were used and one of the union organizers was shot and killed.

In March 1912, they complained that the company was discriminating against members of the Brotherhood of Railroad Freight Handlers and Railroad Clerks, comprising about 500 employees. The provincial Minister of Labour set up a special board under the Industrial Disputes Investigation Act, with Judge H.A. Robson in the chair, to look into the matter. They found that the railroad had dismissed thirty-seven union members. Of these men, twenty wished to return and they were reinstated. That concession having been won, the union and management returned to their respective corners. Robson concluded, "It does not seem to the undersigned that any good end will be gained by setting forth the controversy at any greater length or by further elaborating this report."[13]

Relations between workers and company officers was, then, at best a sort of hostile truce in 1912. Humour was one way for the relatively powerless labourers to even the score with those who had authority over them. One of Price's stories tells of a general superintendent who was a crank about scientific management and rigid economy. One cold day, this official and a group of other managers were on an inspection tour and they stopped in a switchman's hut to get warm. When they left the switchman asked who the superintendent was and expressed surprise that he seemed so pleasant, considering the stories he had heard. He said, "Why they say he was at the funeral of Tommy Hurdon's poor wife, and when the six pall bearers came out wid the carpse, he raised his right hand and sez Howld on wan minit boys, yiz can get along widout two of yiz."[14]

In the years before 1912, the Winnipeg Trades and Labour Council had succeeded in securing a workmen's compensation plan so that men injured on the job would be compensated without having, as was the case until then, to go to court. Why the plan was needed is illustrated by another Price story that uses dark comedy and exaggeration to demonstrate how workers reacted to their often grim working conditions.

A railway worker had lost all his fingers on the job due to accidents that befell him while manually coupling train cars together. He went to his trainmaster to see if the man would find him another job. "The Trainmaster unfeelingly told him that he knew of nothing he could do except that he might be able to recommend a successor, when the poor chap said, Well boss, there's a fellow over in the blacksmith's shop who has 14 fingers; he might last a little longer than I did."[15]

In December of 1912, Mr. Justice Prendergast awarded $5000 to the widow of a Canadian Northern Railway watchman who was killed in June 1911, when a CN train struck a streetcar at the junction of the two rail lines on Osborne Street. The watchman, who was trying to prevent the collision, was killed when the streetcar tipped over, crushing him. The compensation, small by today's standards, was only awarded after the woman had pursued the matter in the courts.

In the hierarchy of the railway employees, the divisions were marked not only by type of job and pay, but also by ethnic origin. The officers were, for the most part, "British born," which, in the language of the 1911 census, meant anyone born within the British Empire. This category included natives of the British Isles as well as Canadians. There were also a few Americans, who, having proven themselves working

J.T. Arundel, one of the officers of the CPR.

for American roads, were often hired as managers by Canadian railroads. William van Horne, Thomas Shaughnassy, and Hay were the most famous examples. The foremen, roadmasters, and trainmasters usually seem to have been from the same background, as were tradesmen and craftsmen working in the shops.

At the bottom of the hierarchy in the most physically difficult, unskilled jobs were men who could not speak English at all or only very poorly. New arrivals from eastern Europe or Italy took these jobs because they desperately needed work. These men were not usually treated well in terms of pay or working conditions because they were expendable; there were always more new arrivals desperate for work.

The prejudice against these men seems to have been expressed in open and sometimes brutal fashion, as we can deduce from Price's stories, intended to amuse but often having the very different effect of inspiring shock and pity. In one story, a roadmaster in the Winnipeg yards called Pat Barney, was supervising a crew of fifty Galicians who were digging a ditch for a pipeline. General Superintendent J.T. Arundel was passing and

greatly to his amazement saw Pat start at one end and proceed all
the way down the line giving each man a vigorous kick.... Arundel
wanted to know what all the trouble was and Pat gave him the
preposterous answer: Aw, Mr. Arundel, they're an awful, ignorant
squad, they are; sure they don't aven know their own language.[16]

Canada's railroad corporations played an enormous role in the life
of Winnipeg in 1912, just as they had throughout its history. Through
direct employment and by providing work for contractors, the railroads poured millions into the local economy and their employees
contributed to the life of the city in countless ways. Physically, however, the presence of many railway lines as well as yards and buildings
within the city had highly negative effects upon the environment and
Winnipeg paid a high price for the prosperity that came with the presence of the railroads.

⌒JUNE⌒

Horse Show, Weddings

In Winnipeg in 1912, the annual June Horse Show was an event of great importance. The show celebrated the tremendous affection for horses still felt by a population just making the transition to the automobile age and it symbolized the continuing economic importance of the horse, despite the arrival of the motor car. It was also a social event where the city's élite went to see and be seen.

Approximately 6200 horses still clopped and jingled along the streets of the city, hauling freight and fire engines and delivering milk and beer and most other things.[1] They had started their long retreat before the motor cars and trucks that were beginning to fill the streets, but horses were used for many more years, and, briefly, during the First World War, when fuel and parts were scarce, their numbers increased as many businesses again turned to horses to do their heavy work.

The horse population in 1912 was in decline for several reasons, but the most significant was cost. The purchase of horses for work or pleasure was comparable to the cost of a car or truck. A team of choice draught horses could be had for $700, and, of course, one did not necessarily need top-of-the-line animals to deliver freight. A wagon cost $200 or $300 and harness from Eaton's catalogue was about $30. So, for about $1000, a young man could go into business for himself. The original purchase of the horse, however, was only the first expense, as many starry-eyed horsepeople have discovered to their regret. Feed is a cost whether the horse is working or not and accounts for about fifty per cent of the cost of maintaining a stable. In 1912 some people were

Horses, as this 1912 photo shows, were being crowded out by motorized traffic on
Winnipeg's streets.

building new stables in order to comply with new regulations regard-
ing stable cleanliness, and blacksmithing, medical care, hardware, and
harness repair added to the costs. The expense of removing tons of
manure from the streets and burning it was borne by every citizen.

These sorts of expenses meant that horse ownership for personal use
was never as widespread as car ownership soon became. In 1908 the Ford
Motor Company newspaper ads claimed that their cars were twenty-five
per cent cheaper to operate than a horse and rig, and could "cover 5 times
the ground and do 3 times the work." The ads were right: cost and conve-
nience made the onslaught of the motor vehicle unstoppable.

In 1912, however, cost still prevented most people from buying a car.
Although Henry Ford was working hard to remove this impediment
by expanding production and lowering the cost of his simple black
cars—in 1912 he built 75,000 Model Ts, ranging in price from $590
to $900—most automobile companies made products for wealthier
people. Close to three-quarters of cars on the market cost more than
$1600 and half were priced above $2000, putting them out of reach of
most people living in Winnipeg. At the top of the price range, one of
the most expensive cars on the road was the American Locomotive
Company's limousine at $7250 (now more than $100,000).

There were over 2000 registered vehicles in Winnipeg in 1912
and the licence records have preserved the makes of cars and their

owners. Cadillac, priced in the mid-range of $1500 to $2500 (roughly $25,000 to $42,000 in today's dollars), was not the most expensive car but it had a certain cachet, and ads in Winnipeg papers listed the names of local middle-class people who owned one. Packards were in the same price range and were popular with wealthy Winnipeggers, such as W.H. Gardner of Oldfield Kirby and Gardner, and F. Morton Morse, the hardware wholesaler. There were few exotic cars, but Fred Heubach, the real estate developer who was promoting Tuxedo, had a Mercedes Benz, and C.H. Enderton, another developer, of Crescentwood, owned a Rolls Royce. There were lots of Fords, but they were slightly outnumbered by the Canadian McLaughlin cars, the most popular make in Winnipeg.

Automobiles were already bringing familiar problems to city streets. Excessive speed, accidents, and even some fatalities were commented upon in the press. In May *Town Topics* called for additional motorcycle cops to control speeders. Parking was not yet the problem it would become in the 1920s, when the car population exploded, but David Dingwall complained about people parking in front of his Portage Avenue jewellery store and blocking his entrance.

Car thefts were common and some young boys made a hobby of stealing cars and taking them for joyrides. One such young thief boasted that he could start any make of car. He was carrying spark plugs when apprehended—many car owners removed the plugs as a way of thwarting thieves.

The relentless outward spread of the city was another influence favouring the motor truck and car. Draught horses, while ideal for short-distance hauling, became exhausted if they were expected to travel very far, and required rest and feeding. In a city like Winnipeg, therefore, which was growing very quickly and had seen the decentralization of freight yards to Transcona and St. Boniface, and the extension of residential suburbs out along new streetcar lines, the switch to motor power was inevitable. Eaton's, famous for its delivery horses, purchased four trucks in 1912 to deliver to the most distant suburban routes. By 1912 the Hudson's Bay Company was also reducing the number of horses it kept and the company had purchased its first motor trucks.

Horse-drawn cabs, never a huge business in Winnipeg, had virtually been replaced by motorized taxis by 1912, a fact dramatically emphasized by the demolition of the Palace Livery Stables on Smith Street just south of Portage, to make way for the new Palace Auto Livery Garage. The change began in Winnipeg in March 1910, when the Winnipeg Taxicab Company opened with a fleet of brand-new Franklin cars. Shortly afterward, the Taxicab and Auto Livery Company opened for business. In 1912 the J.E. Harrison Auto Taxi and Livery at 363 William had thirty-one cars available for use.

Because the horse cab business had never been very profitable in Winnipeg, the existing cab owners, with one or two exceptions, could not raise the capital to move into motorized cabs. So the horse cab and livery operators, like the colourful Dublin Dan, who had first come to Winnipeg in the 1880s, sold their businesses for what they could get. One exception was Arthur F. Piggott, who bought up many of the downtown livery stables for a song and went into the motor taxi business. Later he became a very successful automobile dealer.

The developing urban environment was not a comfortable one for horses. The advance of paved streets meant that recreational riders had to go farther and farther to find soft footing for their mounts. Draught animals also had difficulty with hard pavement, especially in the winter when ice could result in fatal accidents. When streets were icy, "blacksmith shops are open 24 hours a day, and the unfortunate animals that cannot be sharp shod, or whose owners neglect them, might as well be on skates."[2] The new Hunt Club, which opened in 1912, was located well south of the city next to the new Agricultural College site, but even there paved roads were a problem and the members asked for a bridle path beside the new road leading to the college.

In the cities of the western world, the horse had enjoyed, in the previous half-century, one of its most important and productive periods in the long history of contributing to the human economy. Ironically, it was the great modernizing juggernaut of the nineteenth century, the railroad, that had given the horse this position of importance. While they replaced horses in long-distance transport of people and freight, railroads greatly increased the use of horses in the movement of freight over short distances from the rail yard to its final destination.

This was true in Winnipeg with its large wholesale and warehouse business. Winnipeg's huge building boom, just coming to an end in

The Russell was typical of the expensive cars being purchased by many middle-class Winnipeggers in 1912.

1912, required hundreds of horses for excavations and moving building materials. Companies that owned a large number of horses, like the Street Railway Company, Manitoba Cartage, the Hudson's Bay Company, and Eaton's, had their own stables in the downtown area. In 1909, in an effort to enforce new regulations governing drainage, ventilation, and disposal of manure in stables, city inspectors visited a total of 1434 such buildings. Of these, 55 were livery stables, 146 were private stables with room for five or more animals, and 1233 were lumped in the "other" category, some of which were big enough only for a family's single horse.

At least twenty-three new stables were erected in the city during 1912, built to replace older facilities that did not meet the city's standards. J.D. McArthur, the contractor who, among other projects, was working on the Hudson Bay Railway north of The Pas, put up a building large enough for fifty teams. Many of the other stables were smaller than McArthur's, although still substantial buildings: David Morosnik built a brick stable for thirty-eight horses on Derby Street, Security Storage built a one-and-a-half-storey brick building on McGee to house its sixty horses, and D.E. Adams Coal put up a twelve-horse stable on Stadacona. At least one substantial private stable also went up: W.T. Alexander, the local manager of Great West Permanent Loan, built a one-and-a-half-storey stable behind his new house on Wellington Crescent. There were stalls for eight horses and an apartment up above for a groom.

These buildings were not always popular with people in the neighbourhood. In December 1912, when a livery stable was proposed on the corner of Stella and Schultz, next to Selkirk Park, Parks Board Chairman T. Wilson wrote to City Council, reminding them that "these little breathing spots installed at various places in our city should be protected from everything suggestive of impurity so that the families in the neighborhood can enjoy a mouthful of fresh air in the days to come."[3] W.F. Lee, who owned an apartment building nearby, also protested the construction of the stable because, he said, "it would be injurious to the welfare of my tenants."[4]

Most of the livery stables were concentrated in central Winnipeg, away from residential areas, in a cluster around Portage and Main, moving west to Smith or Donald, or north along Princess and Elgin streets, close to the City Market, and east of Main Street between James and Market streets. The livery business consisted of renting out animals and vehicles on a short- or long-term basis. A stable owner might also operate a board, feed, and sale business, providing accommodation for animals whose owners did not have stables of their own. An example is the Exchange Livery, Feed and Sales Stables at 326 Elgin, where, according to newspaper advertisements, the staff promised to give "Special attention to the outfits of private gentlemen. Our patrons, their horses and rigs will be given the best of attention and care. Up-to-date horse clipping and grooming machines. First-class grooms and attendants. Horseshoeing shop in rear, first class in every respect."

For those who could afford it, the hobby of riding and driving horses was both healthy and highly prestigious. For men like Augustus Nanton, owning fine animals was a way of showing the world that, like all true gentlemen, they knew good horseflesh and that they had enough money to buy the best. As a young man, Robert Riley raised horses for sale to farmers on a large farm he managed at Westbourne. According to his son: "Father was a keen horseman and liked handling them [although] we didn't have any flashy horses in my younger years but my father finished up with the best money could buy."[5] They rode and drove their horses and participated in activities that required good horses, such as playing polo and hunting foxes at the St. Charles Country Club and at a new Hunt Club just built in St. Vital.

These pastimes were the quintessential British aristocratic sports indulged in by élite groups all over the Empire. From the King down,

English gentlemen were expected to know about horses and to participate in equine sports such as fox hunting and polo. Augustus Nanton,
whose stable has survived on Roslyn Crescent, now transformed into
a home, kept five horses in 1912. This stable had space for the animals,
and a carriage house where vehicles and eventually cars were kept.
The many ribbons and trophies that Sir Augustus's animals won in
horse shows were displayed in the stable.

He went riding every morning, quickly making his way out beyond
the edge of the city where he could find unpaved roads. On Sundays
he and his wife drove to nearby St. Luke's Church in his brougham,
pulled by a perfectly matched pair of fine carriage horses. Nanton was
able to employ both a coachman and a groom. Many of the Nantons'
neighbours along Roslyn Road, people such as Hugh Sutherland and
Lieutenant-Governor D.C. Cameron, also kept horses on their property and were seen taking morning rides in the area.

Winnipeg was an important horse market and $7,000,000 had been
spent at her stockyards on horses in 1911, as farmers and townsmen
outfitted themselves with draught animals. Many of these animals
were shipped in by rail from Ontario, but in 1911, for the first time,
shipments from the east declined as western three- and four-year-olds
began to come onto the market in large numbers. So important was
the business that Premier Roblin made it one of his arguments against
reciprocity with the Americans during the 1911 election campaign.
He stated that the twenty-five per cent duty on American horses,
and the health regulations that Manitoba farmers had lobbied hard
to establish, were all that kept inferior animals from Montana from
flooding the market and forcing Manitoba breeders out of business.[6]

For all these reasons, it is no surprise that the Winnipeg Horse Show,
begun in 1906, had, by June 1912, developed into a major local event.
The show was the project of the Horse Show Association, a group that
included many of the city's most influential people. The president in
1912 was Hugh Sutherland; the treasurer was W.A. Machaffie, manager of the Home Bank; the directors included the printer A.B. Stovel,
Augustus Nanton, Lieutenant-Governor D.C. Cameron, and George
Carruthers of Carruthers Grain Company. All the executive members
had stables on their property, or kept horses in the association's stables
across from the Amphitheatre on Colony Street.

Horse shows had evolved from the agricultural fairs at which animals were bought and sold. Those like the one in Winnipeg were still an opportunity for breeders to demonstrate the quality of their stock by participating in judged contests, but they had also developed into social events for high society. The growth of the social aspect reflected the high status attached to horse ownership and the growing importance of breeding horses for pleasure and exercise, now that motorized transport was replacing them in the streets. The aristocratic sport of show jumping was only about forty years old, and the 1912 Stockholm Olympics were the first international competition with a full equestrian program. Riders in Winnipeg and other cities all over Europe and the Americas practised this relatively new sport, participated in at the Olympics by aristocrats and dashing cavalry officers such as the young George S. Patton.

In Canada, the large horse shows in Montreal, Toronto, and Winnipeg were modelled on similar events in England and the US. In Toronto the Horse Show took place in the Armouries in a setting of exclusive social events attended by the Lieutenant-Governor and the city's élite. The wealthier attendees purchased boxes in the arena and there was a good deal of strolling around and visiting other box owners. All this activity and news of what everyone was wearing were recorded in the society pages of *Saturday Night* and the daily papers.

The Winnipeg Horse Show grew steadily in importance and prestige during its first six years. In the beginning, Augustus Nanton and the other promoters of the show had been at pains to distance their event from the seamier world of the racetrack, with its touts and cheats. To this end, they tried to give it a semi-official flavour. For example, in 1908 they asked Chief Justice Dubuc to open the show. He said the Horse Show was a sign of the "growth of culture and refinement" in the city. Newspaper ads assured the public that this was not simply a "race meet." In 1909 a beautiful new Horse Show Amphitheatre, the largest

Horse show entries lined up east of the Horse Show Amphitheatre.

enclosed arena in Canada and the second largest in North America, rose west of the Legislative Building on Colony Street. Designed and built by the local firm of Pratt and Ross, the "Amp" served the city for many decades as a venue for hockey, public skating, and many other events.

By 1912 the Horse Show was firmly established as a horse market and a major social event. The Lieutenant-Governor himself, in addition to being on the organizing executive, was a contestant with animals entered in the show. His entrance at the opening ceremonies made up in energy and confidence what it lacked in dignity. The June 8 issue of *Town Topics* reported that "The big doors were thrown open, the band played God Save the King and the [Cameron's] carriage came into the arena with a good deal of dash."

Cameron used his position to muster a company of the 18th Mounted Rifles, the newest of the local militia regiments, as his escort, and a military band provided the music. Members of the Rifles, in red dress tunics, acted as ushers at the show. Cavalry was glamorous in 1912 and

The interior of the Amphitheatre, decorated for a vegetable show. Notice the boxes around the outside of the show ring.

Town Topics of June 1, 1912, commented on "How much more attractive are the red coats of the soldiers than the dull clothes ... of the ordinary groom one usually sees at a horse show."

Winnipeggers entered their horses in many events. Two of Augustus Nanton's daughters rode or drove and his youngest son, Paul, drove in the pony class. Nanton's carriage horses, Beau Brummel and Beauty of Bath, although described as a little fat, were much admired.

The Lieutenant-Governor entered his carriage horses, Lintoll and Lucky Jim, and they came second in the Duke of Connaught Cup competition for carriage teams. Cameron's daughter, Mrs. Homer-Dixon, was not well enough to compete, having just given birth, but her horse, Lonsdale Maid, placed third in the jumper class.

Hugh Sutherland's team, Sirdar and Senator, were entered in the competition, driven by a professional driver from Chicago; the daughter of A.J. Andrews, an important city lawyer, drove a tandem team in the ring; J.A. Knott, President of Winnipeg Fur, entered a pair in the Duke of Connaught Cup competition.

Della Lemon, whose father, recently deceased, had been a horse dealer in the city, drove in the heavy harness singles and won third prize. For Miss Lemon and other young women, such as the Misses Nanton and Miss Betty Galt, participating in equestrian sports—hunting, jumping, or driving—was a desirable and ladylike pastime. Some women members of the St. Charles Country Club also played polo, a less ladylike pastime. From comments made by the reporters covering the show, one has the impression that the women drivers were as much on display as their horses. Mrs. Elizabeth Balch, a New York journalist visiting the city, wrote in *Town Topics* that one driver "drove splendidly, and looked so well doing it."

The horse show was not just a stage on which to display fine horses; as the first event of the summer season, it was a chance to display new dresses and to gossip. This made the box seats at the side of the ring desirable enough that these seats were auctioned in the lobby of the Royal Alexandra Hotel. S.H. Jones spent the most for a box: $275. On June 8, *Town Topics* printed Elizabeth Balch's full report, in which she explains,

> Next to being in an opera box, nowhere can a woman look better than at a horse show. There is such a wide choice of clothes that run to any extreme, and one feels as if one were more than just seeing the show; one feels part of it.... This being the first of the summer events, the women especially are interested in seeing what each other will wear.

Balch comments at length on the display of expensive dresses—in effect, the display of the wealth of the women and of their husbands or fathers. A little bored by the judging, she was glad to have the new summer dresses to look at. She says that on the first night of the show, "there was a splendid audience.... The boxes were filled and those costumes for which trips to New York and Minneapolis were made—and to our local modistes—were very much in evidence."

In the days leading up to the show, there had been a lot of secrecy about what would be worn. There is in this an element of fun, of a game, but also of a competition to be the best dressed, the most elegant and beautiful. Balch says,

> of course, those who are to wear these latest creations and importations are keeping profound silence; no word is allowed to

escape about them, as half of the delight of being up-to-date, or a
day or two ahead of it, in having the latest things in chiffons and
chapeaux, is springing them upon one's neighbours.

How up-to-date the women of Winnipeg were is a question that
bears some examination. Certainly, they had the opportunity to buy
dresses of the latest Paris designs, or at least the designs of the year
before. Around 1911 and 1912, American wholesalers began going to
Paris to buy the rights to designs created by couturiers such as Paul
Poiret. They then mass-produced dresses for the middle-class market
and shipped them out over North America to be sold in stores like
Eaton's and Hudson's Bay, as well as smaller dress shops. Magazines
such as *Harper's Bazaar* contained patterns and illustrations of the latest clothes, which local dressmakers could copy.

Mrs. Balch was not impressed by the high fashion of the time.

> What will the grandchildren say when they look upon a picture
> of grandmama dressed in a silk frock, the skirt with a puff around
> the bottom, so tight that a step of more than a foot and a half is
> impossible, and a step up demands a waddle, and so short that the
> ankle bone is well seen; the little short waisted jacket with short
> sleeves quite large and almost ill-fitting; and this crowned, almost
> eclipsed, by a hat so large that the shoulders are concealed.

The hobble skirt she complains of was still the height of fashion in
1912, the product of a veritable revolution in style brought about in
1908 by Paul Poiret in Paris. His most important innovation was the
narrow skirt, which gave women, for the first time, a more natural
look. Abandoning the older style corset, which pinched the waist and
contorted the female body to produce the s-shaped, full-hipped look
that had been fashionable for many years, Poiret promoted a longer
corset, which, at first, descended almost to the knee and was lower
in the bust. This produced a straight figure, a more natural look, de-
emphasizing instead of exaggerating curves.

Along with this change came the brassiere, made necessary now by
the changes to the corset, and simpler slips. Gone were the frills and
puffs of the Victorian and early Edwardian dress. The simpler lines

Amphitheatre, 1912.

were in keeping the new attitude of upper- and middle-class women who wanted to be less an ornament and more a participant in society—a voting, working, active citizen.

While it was part of Poiret's revolution, the hobble skirt was still a piece of high-fashion clothing, meant for the wealthy and the idle. Fashion historian Elizabeth Ewing calls the skirt "a hampering line, a fashion which, as in the past, was only for the leisured and privileged and which proclaimed that fact—it was impossible to wear it and demean oneself by being other than decorative."[7]

The hobble skirt made its way into the wardrobes of middle-class women in Winnipeg in the form of copies made under license and sold to dress shops and department stores in North America. It had been modified to allow more freedom of movement by the addition of pleats or side slits. The Hudson's Bay Company catalogue of 1910 offers nothing but narrow skirts in all the dresses and suits available, but they are all pleated—fashionable but practical for middle-class women and working women to wear.

Another fashion phenomenon of the time was the enormous hat, which became more enormous as the skirt became narrower. Poiret struck a blow in this area about this time when he introduced the toque as simple and serviceable headgear for women. Winnipeg brides had begun to wear these smaller hats in 1912.

For those interested in watching the horses, the show included events for draught animals. Teams of delivery horses were shown in the Delivery Class. Harry Lauder, a horse belonging to Allward Brothers, won first prize in this category and horses belonging to Eaton's won second and third prizes. The Old Horse Class—animals from seventeen to twenty-five years old—was a favourite with the crowds and seems to symbolize the sentimental attachment many people felt toward horses. The winner in this class was Billy, a nineteen-year-old who had been well known in Winnipeg before being sold to Colonel Carmen of Regina. Grey Dick, driven by Harry Adams, a veteran firefighter from the south station, was twenty-three years old. *Town Topics* said he had been a fire horse for eighteen years and was

> known to practically everybody in the city who has seen the department turn out, which means the whole population above babes in arms. Dick had broken his leg in a fall a few years before but instead of having him destroyed—the boys at the station couldn't stand the thought of that—they nursed him back to health for over a year.

The horse show was accompanied by numerous "dinner parties preceding each evening's performance and many jolly suppers followed," reported *Town Topics*. The Amphitheatre was decorated more lavishly and expensively than ever before, with the rafters covered in thousands of tree branches and garlands of flowers. The boxes were painted gold and hung with bunting in the club's blue and gold colours. Elizabeth Balch concluded, in a paragraph in *Town Topics* that would have been music to any Winnipegger's ears:

> In looking over the audience on Wednesday night, the onlooker did not need to make comparisons with any other place that would be to the detriment of the city. There is little of the pioneer spirit needed in coming here and the wild and woolly west seems as remote as the expression is old fashioned.

June was also the month for weddings. On Saturday, June 8, the wedding of Miss Alice Elizabeth Fortune to Mr. Charles Holden Allen of Fredericton took place quietly and without celebrations because the Fortune family was still mourning the death of Elizabeth's father and brother in the *Titanic* disaster. Allen was a lawyer, son of Mr. and Mrs. Carleton Allen of Fredericton, and grandson of Chief Justice Sir John Allen, and he practised in Fredericton for some time after the couple was married, before moving to Montreal to work for the Canadian Surety Company.

Charles Allen's brother also married a young woman from Winnipeg, on the following Saturday. Jean Andrews and Kenneth Carleton Allen were married at Holy Trinity Church by Archdeacon Fortin. The bride's father, A.J. Andrews, was a successful local lawyer and the wedding was given considerable attention in the society columns. *Town Topics* reported that "Carriages and motors around 4 o'clock wended their way to Holy Trinity Church which looked very gay with its awning stretched from the church door to the road and the crowds of gaily dressed matrons and maids in their light summer attire."

The guests then went to the Wellington Crescent home of the bride's father.

> Huge marquees were erected and the grounds presented a very animated spectacle, an orchestra playing throughout the afternoon. The bridal party received numerous guests after which the bride entered the marquee, where the mammoth wedding cake reposed on a bed of tulle and flowers. After the cutting of the cake and the usual toasts had been honoured, she left to don her traveling attire....

The couple set out for their honeymoon in St. Andrew's-by-the-Sea on the 6:20 p.m. train. A crowd of friends accompanied them to the station and gave them a merry send-off. The best man and ushers then entertained at a dinner at the Royal Alex, going to the Country Club later.

All the weddings described in the society columns followed much the same format: a church or house wedding followed by a reception in the

The wedding party of Sybil Meyers and Edward Kopstein sees the happy couple off at the CPR station.

bride's home and the departure of the wedding couple by train for their honeymoon. The whole procedure rarely lasted more than two hours. Ukrainians and other immigrants put on longer weddings that involved dancing and more celebration but it was many years before these customs began to migrate to the weddings of the "British born."

The fact that almost all newly married Winnipeggers spent their first night together on the train may have created some very romantic notions, now long forgotten, about train travel.

On September 13, several bachelors who lived together in the house at 142 Mayfair—one of many such houses shared by relatively well-off single men in the south end of the city—entertained at dinner in honour of Miss Maude Matheson, the daughter of Archbishop Matheson, and her fiancé and their housemate, Harold Trenholme. Trenholme, now giving up his bachelor life and his bachelor digs, was in business in the North End. He was partners with John Tymchorak, the owner of the Midland Hotel on Market Street, and their firm was called Trenholme and Tymchorak, Private Bankers, Steamship Agents, Insurance

Brokers, with offices at 856 Main. He is an interesting example of a British-born businessman, the son of a New Brunswick judge, who had formed a partnership with a non-Anglo-Canadian businessman. The couple was married a week later on September 19th. When they returned from their honeymoon in October, they moved into a house on Wellington Crescent.

Wedding guests sometimes continued celebrating after the bride and groom had departed for their honeymoon. After Beatrice Sutherland's wedding in September, the best man and the ushers treated everyone to an evening at the Orpheum, Winnipeg's new vaudeville theatre. The best man and ushers at Jean Andrews's wedding in June entertained the wedding party at the Royal Alexandra after seeing the couple off at the CPR station.

In the fall, two fashionable weddings took place at St. Luke's Church on Nassau Street. On September 5 at 3:00 p.m., the children of two of the most powerful families in the city were united in one of the more lavish ceremonies of the year. Georgina Nanton, eldest daughter of Augustus Nanton, the child of his first marriage, married Douglas Cameron, the Lieutenant-Governor's son. They were married by Archdeacon Fortin, assisted by Canon Goorhies. *Town Topics* reported that

> the church was transformed into a perfect bower of green and white, for in addition to the chancel banked with palms, ferns and white roses, an archway of ferns and Easter lilies connected the guests pews in the centre aisle. Georgina Nanton entered to Lohengrin's wedding march, and was given away by her father. The choir sang O Perfect Love during the ceremony and during the signing of the register Mr. Brabazon Lowther sang Song of Thanksgiving. Two flower girls scattered rose petals in the path of the bride and groom as they left the church.

Among the guests was the bride's grandfather, William Hespeler, for many years the German Consul in Winnipeg, who had been instrumental in organizing the immigration of Mennonite settlers to Manitoba.

The guests drove the short distance to Kilmorie, the Nantons' house on Roslyn Road, and the bride and groom received them in the music room, standing between two Corinthian pillars festooned with ropes of smilax and roses. They stepped outside and had their picture taken with their relatives on the steps of the verandah. Later in the afternoon, the young couple went by train to Montreal, where they boarded the *Mauritania* and sailed for Europe.

On September 21, St. Luke's was the scene of another wedding involving one of the wealthy families who lived on Roslyn Road. Mary Robertson, daughter of Mr. and Mrs. W.H. Gardner, married William Lyon McIntosh at 3:45 in the afternoon. Archbishop Matheson married the couple. The bride's gifts from the groom were a platinum bar pin and a baby grand piano. *Town Topics* described the reception

> at the residence of Mr. and Mrs. Gardner on Roslyn Road where perfect arrangements prevailed for the comfort of the guests. The wedding party received in the drawing room, the bride and groom standing in a bower of flowers. In a marquee on the lawn was set a long table centred with the wedding cake and decorated with lovely bride roses. An orchestra played throughout the reception. The bride's health was proposed by Archbishop Matheson and responded to by the groom in a few well-chosen words.

The couple left on the six o'clock Soo Line train for Lake Placid and New York City, and the best man and ushers entertained at a dinner and theatre party that evening.

∽ JULY ∾

The Exhibition, First Nations

I t was late on the evening of Tuesday, July 9, when the viceregal train rolled into the CPR station in Winnipeg. As the big engine blew off steam, the waiting crowd strained for a first glimpse of the Duke of Connaught and his beautiful daughter, Princess Patricia. When he emerged, white moustache and sunny smile making him almost a caricature of the elegant Edwardian gent, the crowd cheered. The cheering did not stop until the Duke left for the west a week later.

The Duke was in the midst of a prodigious 288,000-kilometre journey that took him to every corner of the Dominion during his first year as Governor General. He had a $12,000 travel budget (over $200,000 today) and every penny must have been spent transporting him over the country's rail lines. Connaught was an outgoing and vigorous man, a professional soldier who had graduated from the Royal Military Academy at Woolwich, the school that trained artillerymen and engineers. He had an engineer's intelligent interest in how things worked, and he charmed Winnipeggers by asking endless questions about their city. It was not his first visit to the province: he had travelled extensively in Canada in 1907. After a long career in the army, which began with a tour of duty in Canada in 1870, he had expected to be appointed Commander in Chief of the British army. He was disappointed, but all the energy he would have poured into that post, he now applied to the job of Governor General of Canada, the senior dominion of the Empire.

It was common for Canadian imperialists, wanting closer ties to Great Britain, to ask that a member of the Royal Family serve as Governor General. The Duke of Connaught, who was Queen Victoria's son, was the only royal ever to serve at Rideau Hall. The Duke was a good ambassador for the British Crown and, during the impending war, he strengthened the bonds of loyalty to the Mother Country as few other viceroys could have done. Speaking to a crowd of over 1000 at a Canadian Club luncheon during his visit to Winnipeg, he said:

> I feel sure that if Canada will be true to herself she will be equally true to the Empire ... Canada for Canadians, but let us hope all Canadians will be ready to respond to the Imperial call, should it ever come, and that they will support the Crown and flag in the future as they have done in the past.[1]

Princess Patricia, who later had a famous Canadian regiment named for her, was twenty-six years old in 1912, a good-looking and charming young woman accompanying her father because her mother was suffering from peritonitis and unable to travel. The Princess was already becoming a very popular member of the household at Rideau Hall, where she entertained at skating parties and costume balls; young women watched her to find out the latest fashions. When she bobbed her hair in imitation of the popular dancer Irene Castle, many Canadian girls followed suit. Patricia left Winnipeggers starry-eyed with admiration.

After a short ceremony, the party started out on the route followed by so many official visitors, from the CPR station to Main Street, then south into the heart of the city. The streets were brightly illuminated and City Hall, where the mayor officially welcomed the Duke, was ablaze, its architecture picked out with strings of white light bulbs. City Council, wanting to publicize the cheap electricity that Winnipeg Hydro now provided, had spent $2000 to light the building. Cheering crowds packed the sidewalks as the people of Winnipeg and thousands of visitors in town for the Industrial Exhibition cheered the Duke and his daughter

The procession, complete with carriage, outriders, and footmen, ended at the front door of Robert Rogers's large, comfortable home on Roslyn

Road, where the Duke and his daughter would stay. It was said that Government House was not large enough to accommodate the Duke and his staff, but it is also possible that Rogers, a minister in the new Tory government, had pulled rank on Lieutenant-Governor Cameron, who was a Liberal.

The next morning the Duke and his daughter emerged from the Rogerses' house at noon and set out to perform their first official duty in Manitoba: opening the exhibition. They rode along Roslyn Road in an open landau, accompanied by mounted troops from Fort Osborne Barracks. They turned at Osborne,

Princess Patricia, daughter of the Duke of Connaught, after whom the famous Canadian regiment was soon to be named.

crossing the newly reconstructed Osborne Bridge, completed only days before, and drove down Broadway and north on Main Street, cheered by crowds of office workers out on their lunch break. The party turned left at Dufferin and continued west to the exhibition grounds on Sinclair. The cheering continued on the north side of the tracks, where

> large numbers of foreign immigrants had gathered before their houses and cheered, many of them, as heartily as those of British birth. Many of the houses along Dufferin ... were nicely decorated and flags, small and large, floated gaily in the breeze while every child that watched the great event carried a flag or banner to honour the Duke and Princess.[2]

Most of the people living on Dufferin, at least those east of McGregor, were Jewish, so they may not have been newly arrived immigrants at all. The Jewish community in Winnipeg was forty years old and many of the young flag wavers were likely born Winnipeggers.

As the Duke's party approached and the word spread through the exhibition grounds, excited fair goers began to crowd around the

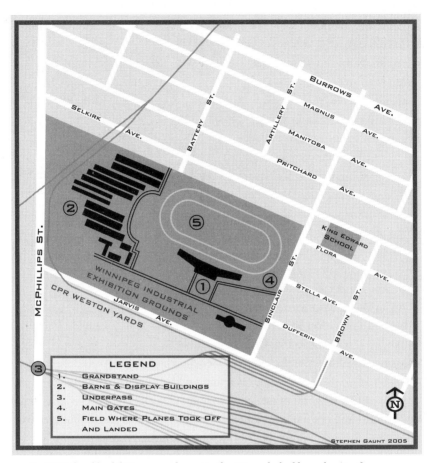

By 1912, the old exhibition grounds next to the CPR yards had been the site of Winnipeg's annual fair for 20 years.

Sinclair Street gate, hoping to get a glimpse of the Governor General. At one o'clock he arrived and was escorted by the exhibition directors to lunch in their official dining hall, located under the grandstand. As the Duke entered the huge, whitewashed room, draped with flags and banners, he was greeted with an enthusiastic roar of welcome from the 300 "representative" guests at the luncheon, the VIPs of Winnipeg. The head table stretched across the southern side of the room and other tables extended out from it at right angles, the usual banquet configuration at the time. The *Manitoba Free Press* recorded that the Duke seemed pleased with the welcome and impressed by the banners and the mountains of flowers on the tables.

Seated at the head table with the Duke were local dignitaries, such as Archbishop Matheson, Chief Justice Howell, and Premier Roblin. After lunch the official party proceeded to the grandstand, where a royal box had been constructed and, after being introduced by the president of the exhibition board, A.A. Gilroy, the Duke officially opened the exhibition. The paper recorded that the crowd stood during the Duke's speech "and cheered heartily at the conclusion."

For the next ten days the exhibition grounds on Sinclair, north of the CPR yards, were crowded with thousands of excited visitors, eager to enjoy the magical environment of a large summer fair with its grandstand performances, sideshows, and horse races. But entertainment was not the primary, official reason for putting on the Canadian Industrial Exhibition, in spite of what anyone in the crowd would have said. The exhibition was a trade fair where manufactured goods, farm produce, and livestock could be displayed and find buyers. During the Victorian era, fairs had also taken on the higher purpose of educating the public by showcasing the amazing advances of modern industry, the progress of modern civilization. These ideas are played out at the great nineteenth-century world's fairs, beginning with the Great Exhibition of 1851 with its Crystal Palace. Many of these large fairs commemorated historical events; the Columbian Exposition in Chicago in 1893 celebrated the 400th anniversary of Columbus's arrival and the St. Louis Fair in 1904 commemorated the Louisiana Purchase. These fairs could also attract enormous publicity and numbers of tourists for the host city. The St. Louis Fair, for example, attracted nearly 20 million visitors over its six-month span. In one single day, the Chicago Fair actually hosted 751,000 visitors.[3]

Winnipeg had wanted to make the 1912 Canadian Industrial Exhibition, as the Winnipeg summer fair was called, a celebration of the Selkirk Centennial, the 100th anniversary of the arrival of the first group of Selkirk Settlers in 1812. A representative committee was formed in 1908 to promote the idea of a Centennial Exposition to showcase the growth and resources of the whole West. Delegations visited the expositions in St. Louis and Portland and, in April 1909, a trainload of Winnipeg leaders travelled all over western Canada to sell the idea of the fair. Delegations went to Ottawa to try to convince Laurier to grant $2.5 million over three years to finance the event.

T AEROPLANE TO FLY IN WINNIPEG. EXHIBITION-1911

Jimmy Ward's biplane soars over the Exhibition in July 1911.

Although the idea gained support from other western cities such as Regina, and organizations such as the Montreal Board of Trade, the T. Eaton Company, and the Grand Trunk Pacific Railway, Laurier could not be convinced to put up any money. The poor relations between Laurier and the Conservative Roblin government likely played a role, although the delegations that spoke to him included many influential Manitoba Liberals. For later historians, the failure to secure federal support for the exposition was a warning sign that the city had over-reached itself and that the long boom was nearing its end.[4]

The exhibition board did the best it could to celebrate the Centennial, even without federal support. Certainly the city's optimism was buoyed up by the visiting Governor General—not the King, as the promoters of the exhibition had wanted, but the King's brother, the Duke of Connaught—who told them that "you are now on a wave of prosperity that nothing in the world can stop." The Duke's week-long visit, while it was not worth two million dollars, was a consolation prize that added a great deal to the fair.

The exhibition grounds were bounded by McPhillips on the west, Sinclair on the east, Jarvis on the south, and Selkirk on the north. They had been in use for over twenty years and the Winnipeg fair had grown to completely fill them. Later in 1912, a bylaw was passed to relocate the exhibition to a much more beautiful location on the land north of Kildonan Park. E.L. Drewery, long-time member of the Parks Board, argued that this site was a better setting for the event, and that Winnipeg was falling behind other cities that had already secured more attractive fair grounds and buildings. Perhaps feeling that the old location next to the CPR had hurt the city's chance to host a great exposition, Winnipeggers voted in favour of the bylaw. But, with the depression of 1913 and the onset of the war, the plan was abandoned. The exhibition grounds on Sinclair were used for many more years, and the Kildonan site was developed instead as a municipal golf course.

If the Industrial Exhibition fell short of world fair status, it was certainly a major regional fair reflecting Winnipeg's importance as a regional metropolis. Special trains put on by the CNR and the CPR brought thousands of visitors to the city from all over Manitoba and Saskatchewan. The railroads cooperated by offering cheaper excursion fares on their regular runs and the Specials offered even lower rates. Some trains had standing room only. Most people from Manitoba made a day trip into the city, arriving in the morning and going home again late the same night, after the fireworks. The regular train to Teulon, for example, normally left the city at 5:40 p.m. but during the exhibition, departure was delayed until 11:00 p.m. to accommodate fair visitors. Anyone wishing to stay over in Winnipeg would find the hotels were full. With luck, they might get a bed in a boarding house or a private home.

Most people came to the exhibition by streetcar, as they had been doing for two decades. In fact, the first official run of the new electric Winnipeg Street Railway had been from City Hall to the exhibition grounds in July 1892. In 1912 streetcar traffic was so heavy that cars were often lined up on Dufferin, waiting to drop passengers, and on Selkirk, waiting to make the trip back downtown. A second route to the rounds, made possible by the new CPR underpass on McPhillips Street, had just been inaugurated. During the busy afternoon period, cars would travel every four minutes from Fort Rouge over the Maryland Bridge, down Sherbrook to Logan and west to McPhillips, and then north to deposit passengers at the west gate of the grounds. People living in the west end were encouraged to take this route to avoid the congestion on Dufferin and Selkirk.

As visitors climbed down from their cars on Sinclair, the first thing that struck them was the noise. If one of the twice-daily grandstand

The crowded grandstand at the Industrial Exhibition Grounds in 1912.

shows was in progress, they heard the "distant rumble of many voices," as the *Free Press* reporter described it. As fair goers stepped up to the ticket booths at the entrance, the sounds of the midway, the calliope of the merry-go-round, the shouts of the pitch men, and the rattle of the amusement rides and the screams of their riders washed over them.

The people pushing excitedly through the gate did not realize that, until Monday, July 16, almost the middle of the fair's run, some of the ticket sellers were defrauding the exhibition. City Comptroller W.H. Evanson, the treasurer for the exhibition as well as the comptroller for the city, had noted discrepancies between the number of visitors and the money taken in. On Monday, the ticket takers were watched; some of them were pocketing tickets and passing them to accomplices who resold them, splitting the money with the dishonest exhibition employees. One man was caught red-handed with over thirty tickets hidden on his person. By the next day, three men were in the cells at the James Street Police Station, waiting to be charged, and the directors of the exposition were promising to "probe the matter to the bottom."

Once inside the Sinclair Street gate, visitors were confronted by the massive bulk of the grandstand with the fenced-in racetrack in front of it. City Council had just spent $10,000 for roofing the central section and to spruce up some of the other buildings on the grounds. The central section, which faced directly north toward the stage and the racetrack beyond, was reserved seating during the exhibition and anyone sitting there had to purchase a special ticket. Seats in the east and west wings of the stands, which angled out from the central area, were free with the price of admission.

If you sat at the top of the stands, you could look out over the back and get a panoramic view of the city and the noisy, dirty CPR yards just across Jarvis Street. The yards and, of course, the heat of the afternoon sun were the reasons that the grandstand turned its back on the city and faced north. Looking north, you would see the whole exhibition spread out before you. On July 11, 1912, a *Free Press* writer described the opening-day scene viewed from the tower on top of the nearby Colonnade Building, a long, low structure that divided the grandstand from the midway:

> Crowds swarmed in and out of the different exhibit buildings and a constant stream of humanity passed in and out of the Midway. In the grand stand the colour blending was magnificent. Women clad in bright colours, little children all in white, and men in dress suits were scattered throughout the stand, while the tall distinguished figure of the Duke of Connaught as he watched the races from the Royal Box could be distinctly seen. The booths and tents as well as practically every building were decorated with flags and coloured bunting. These decorations fluttering in the wind presented a striking appearance.

The space under the huge grandstand was not wasted. There the Exhibition Board of Directors had their offices and their banquet hall, where special luncheons took place every day. The food in this hall was catered by Mrs. G.R. Williams, who, in 1912, celebrated her twenty-second year of providing food at the exhibition. The *Free Press* gave Mrs. Williams the best review possible: "There is a large and competent staff, the food is wholesome and clean and in short, it is every bit like eating at home."

The Women's Christian Temperance Union also operated a large dining hall under the grandstand, donating their time and paying all

The daring Jimmy Ward and his wife. It is easy to see why he was chilled to the bone during his 1912 flight high above the city.

profits over to their cause. This restaurant also met with the approval of the *Free Press* journalist, who said that visitors could not "do better when desiring a good clean meal."

People were attracted to the exhibition partly by the exotic things it could show them, but when it came to food, they wanted some familiar and "clean" home cooking. There had been problems in past years with food poisoning. Although the directors assured visitors that this year food was carefully screened to protect it from flies, and booths selling cold drinks from punch bowls were required to keep the bowls covered at all times, many visitors preferred the home cooking of the dining rooms under the stands.

Horse races took place in front of the stands every afternoon, except for the last day, when a motorcycle race was allowed to churn up the track. The first afternoon had a typical race card; a pace or trot race with fifteen entries and a purse of $2000, the Centennial Futurity with a $1000 prize, a four-furlong dash, and the Mackenzie Cup race.

Scandals over betting and tampering with horses had brought racing into disrepute in the previous few years. All but a few American tracks had closed and many state governments had outlawed racetrack gambling. The new pari-mutual betting system, with its carefully controlled ticket sales and a percentage for the local government, was invented in 1908 but was not widely used as yet. In Winnipeg bookies still took bets, and at the northeast corner of the stands a special enclosure had been set up for the bookies and their clients. In this enclosure, on Monday, July 16, detectives swept down on some racetrack touts, "suspicious characters" from "across the line," who were accused of various shady activities including picking pockets. The scene was described in the *Free Press*:

> The ring was crowded with bettors, and the bookies were doing a flourishing business, when three detectives suddenly entered and rounded up the five men who were crowding around the bookmakers' stands with bundles of the long green in their hands.

"Touts" were racetrack characters who approached their marks with the claim that they had inside information on a "sure thing" and they would place a bet if the mark would supply the money. They would take their percentage whether the tip paid off or not. They were usually also guilty of a variety of other petty crimes and were not welcome.

Other attractions for the grandstand included the afternoon and evening stage shows. On July 11, 1912, the *Free Press* reported that the show opened with a typical vaudeville review. The Murano Brothers performed a classic balancing act: one brother stood on the stage and balanced a ten-metre pole, at the top of which the other brother did various gymnastic feats. The Pederson Brothers did gymnastics on a balancing beam and two troupes of comedy tumblers, the Nelsons and the Davis Family, entertained with perhaps the most ancient of all circus acts. There were two equestrian acts, a young woman called simply Marguerite, whose horse did a low bow to the Duke of Connaught, much to his delight, and the Two Cottrells, who posed and balanced on the backs of galloping steeds.

The Rex Comedy Circus, which "hardly needs an introduction," presented trained dogs and cats and a "wonderful pony which runs at express speed around a revolving table and the bucking mule that sends a whole group of stable men rolling over one another." One of the most popular acts was a British silver band, the Royal Brown Besses of the Barn, whose distinctive sound must have been very sweet in the ears of homesick English immigrants in the crowd.

The most spectacular act at the grandstand was the pilot Jimmy Ward and his Curtis biplane returning to the exhibition for the second year in a row. It had been planned to have two pilots, but Ward's counterpart, George Mestach, a French pilot with a Borel Mathis monoplane, crashed into the fence at the west end of the racetrack on the morning of opening day. Mestach's plane was caught by the powerful winds blowing that day and he was unable to get enough elevation to take off.

Jimmy Ward and his wife were among the first to reach the wreck. Once he was sure his fellow aviator was not hurt, Ward helped the mechanics clear away the hopelessly wrecked plane. He told the *Free Press* that he had also had a very rough flight that morning. Ward complained that the racetrack enclosure "is too small" to take off from and "the fences and tents and booths surrounding it are so close that it is exceedingly difficult to get high enough to clear them." He was able, nevertheless, to become airborne and perform thrilling dives and rolls most of the days of the exhibition without incident, although he continued to be dogged by the prairie winds. Flying an open plane at altitudes of up to 1000 metres was a cold business and when he landed, "Ward was chilled to the bone and hobbled around for several minutes before he got warmed up again."

Flying was less than ten years old in 1912 and there were frequent tragic deaths. Only a week before, at the Boston Aviation Meet, Miss Harriet Quimby, one of the world's first women pilots, was thrown from her plane at a height of 300 metres and killed. She was the fifty-fifth air fatality of 1912.

After the lighter part of the program came the Selkirk Centennial Pageant, which presented an overview of Red River history in a series of mimed tableaux. These scenes are fascinating because of what they show us of the world view of Winnipeggers and western Canadians at the time. The first scene showed an Aboriginal camp by a river. An Aboriginal man appeared at stage right to announce the arrival of La Verendrye: history begins with the arrival of the whites. The French-

Canadian explorers were "well received by the cautious Indians." More fur traders entered and there was a fight over possession of the furs.

The next scene was greeted with cheers from the audience. It showed a Red River cart and, accompanied by the pipes, the arrival of the first highland settlers. The next scene jumped to Fort Garry in 1870 and the audience watched as the "crafty" leader of the rebels, Louis Riel, took control through "long parlayings." In the scene, Riel runs away on hearing of the arrival of Wolseley's troops. The July 11 *Free Press* described the final triumphant scene:

> While the scenery was being changed several bands played patriotic tunes, including the March of the Cameron Men, Rule Britannia and The Maple Leaf Forever. The climactic scene depicts the final victory of the Empire over the rebel Riel. A band of Indians under Riel slaughters an English force and gives itself up to "jubilant triumph". But it is short lived for the relief force comes soon, Riel flees for safety, and peace is once again restored following a battle in which the Indians are defeated.... The final scene gives the rallying of the soldiers of the Empire round the flag and as the cheers break forth on every hand the bands start up the refrain of Rule Britannia. Then comes the perennial number, the Human Flag, old but ever new and refreshing. A magnificent display of fireworks concludes the performance ... first come showers of rockets and other designs in various colours. Then follow a threshing machine on fire, Niagara Falls, Queen Mary's fan, her diamond ring and, at the close, the portrait of the Duke of Connaught ... which is greeted with the greatest enthusiasm, the whole audience rising and joining in the National Anthem.

The pageant, which clearly met with the approval of the crowd, and was reviewed by the Winnipeg-based *Dominion Magazine* as "impressive" for its "realism and historic accuracy," depicts western history as a triumph of the Empire over rebellious Aboriginal people. They are described as "Indians" with no distinction made between Métis, Cree, Ojibway, or other cultures. The theme of retribution delivered by "British" troops after the provocation of a massacre of a small force is a common one in the nineteenth-century history of the Empire and was repeated over and over in India, Africa, and wherever the Union Jack flew.

The Duke of Connaught and Princess Patricia watch the show from their box in the grandstand. Mrs. Cameron is seated to the Duke's right.

The pageant presented the Anglo-Canadian view of western Canadian history as it had been developed in the writing of men like Dr. George Bryce, professor at Winnipeg's Manitoba College, who had written about twenty books on the history of western Canada, including one for the Selkirk Centennial, published in 1912, *The Life of Lord Selkirk: Coloniser of Western Canada.* For Bryce and other Anglo-Canadian historians, the Métis and Louis Riel represented the old Northwest of the wild half-savage *bois-brûlés.* The taming of the Aboriginal people and Métis was an essential step in the opening of the West to progressive British settlers. Bryce may well have been consulted in the writing of the pageant; it conforms, in a simplified form, to his view of what had taken place.

The Selkirk Centennial was also marked by a museum of Red River Settlement artefacts assembled by the Selkirk Association and housed in one of the display buildings on the exhibition grounds. The *Free Press* of July 12 encouraged the public to attend, "even those who have but little knowledge of the history of the Province of Manitoba," to get an "idea of the life and manners of the first settlers."

In the manner of the time, artefacts were not put into a context but were jumbled together in the display cases. A gun used at the Battle of Seven Oaks was placed next to a hammer that had belonged to the famous stonemason Duncan McRae, who built St. Andrew's Church, among many other structures. Two dogsleds from the North, a bell from York Factory, and a copy of the company charter were loaned by the Hudson's Bay Company. A buckle from Lord Selkirk's shoe, a cannon he sent to the settlers, and a bayonet used at the Battle of Inkerman during the Crimean War shared the space with a painting of Sir John Moore at Coruna during the War of 1812. Curiosities, icons of the history of the British Empire, and relics of the Red River Settlement created a patriotic display that showed that Winnipeg was no "Johnny come lately," but a community with a history.

The buildings at the west side of the grounds contained many other displays in addition to the museum. The Arts Building, the Manufacturers Building, and the stables and barns that housed the prize livestock that had been brought to Winnipeg to compete were also visited by fair goers taking a break from the more exciting amusements at the fair or, as happened during a particularly heavy downpour on Tuesday, July 16, to stay dry.

On his second visit to the exhibition, the Duke of Connaught visited the display buildings. The papers reported that he spent more time than most fair goers, asking questions and looking carefully at the booths. He saw the City of Winnipeg exhibit concerning hydroelectric power, the lower rates the city was charging, and the various home appliances that could be operated with electricity. The Dominion government installation showed off the bounty of the prairies and explained the newly established system operated by the Board of Grain Commissioners to protect farmers from abuses at the hands of grain companies.

A wide variety of items representing the skill of Manitoba women at sewing, cooking, and "women's work," or household arts and crafts, was also on display along with the prize ribbons awarded by the judges.

The automotive display was of enormous interest to a general public fascinated by the new technology of the car. Cutting Motor Sales of Toronto had rented one of the booths to display the model line standard for most companies in 1912: two different touring cars, the T55 and T35 Torpedo Touring Cars, and a two-door coupe, the A-30 Roadster. The display reminded the public that the Cutting was the car that World Speed King "Wild Bob" Brennan had driven in the Indianapolis Sweepstakes in May, pushing it to the highest speed attained at the meet until two tires blew out in the 300th mile, causing Wild Bob to "turn turtle" on the track.

Manitoba Gypsum had a large display of the products they manufactured at their plant on St. James Street, using gypsum hauled all the way from Gypsumville, down Lake Manitoba by boat to the rail line at Delta Beach. They gave out a free pamphlet explaining the superiority of their Empire Cement Plaster and "gypsement," and they displayed the plasterboard they sold in eight-by-twelve-inch blocks.

The Sovereign Perfume Company of Toronto was selling one-dollar sample collections of their perfumes and lotions, including the Ideal Orchid Perfume, made from the rare Orchid of Borneo, which, if smoothed on the skin, would give the wearer health and vigour as well as a nice smell. Many of these samplers were carried home to be treasured through the coming year in a bureau drawer and applied on strategic occasions. The Peace Weatherstrip Company, Charles Fawcett, the New Brunswick stove company, and Michael Ert Importing, who brought in the Continental Tires used on all Mercedes cars, were also at the exhibition, and the Duke saw them all. He took special interest in the livestock and commented on the quality of the Clydesdale horses bred in Saskatchewan and western Manitoba. He asked one of the grooms to trot one of the big horses around the ring, and he laughed when the boy answered: "Well, guvnor, I ain't quite used to this game, but I'll try."

For most fair visitors, the midway, with its exotic sideshows offering entertainment slightly more risqué than the fare in front of the grandstand, was much more interesting than the display buildings. In one tent you could see Princess Victoria, the smallest woman in the West, who played tiny musical instruments and sang. In another, a deep sea diver in suit and helmet demonstrated in a well-lighted tank. Mademoiselle Trixie, the fat lady, was paying a return visit to Winnipeg. When a man expressed doubts that her enormous body was real, she invited him to come sit on her lap for three minutes to see for himself. The newspaper reports that "he did not try it."

Mamie the Peerless was an artiste who danced in the style of Loie Fuller, a vaudeville performer who used flowing robes and coloured lights to create beautiful visual effects. Cowboys and cowgirls and Indians in war paint offered "shooting and riding and the hundred and one things that make up a real wild west show."

On every one of the ten days of the fair, a different group was honoured. Manufacturers, Citizens, Farmers, Old Timers, Children, and Commercial Travelers (a fraternal mutual aid society formed by travelling salesmen in 1888) all had their days. There was some kind of special event and, usually, a special lunch in the directors' dining hall. On Citizens' Day, Mayor Waugh declared a half holiday, and on Children's Day, admission to the grounds was reduced to five cents for children and almost everything that might be of interest to children was sold at reduced prices. Americans' Day was perhaps the most low-key day of all, being marked only by a few people wearing American flags in their lapels. Travelers' Day, by contrast, was a virtual extravaganza.

The Travelers started out at their clubrooms on Garry Street and rode around the city in a special "street car parade" accompanied by a brass band. They arrived at the grounds about one p.m. and sat down to lunch in the directors' dining hall. Various toasts were proposed and drunk, a representative of the Brandon Fair, coming up on July 23rd, promised the Travelers "the time of their lives," and Harry Moreton, of the United Commercial Travelers association, spoke about the benefits of membership.

The Commercial Travelers were the largest special group to visit the exhibition and they made the largest impact. They all wore special caps and were equipped with noisemakers, which they used liberally. They each paid one dollar for the ride around the city, the cap, the rattler, the lunch, and a seat in a specially reserved section of the grandstand. "Never will Vaudeville turns have a better or more appreciative audience," commented the *Free Press*. It was noted that "Their cheers could be heard all over the grounds."

As the exhibition rolled along, the Duke of Connaught and Princess Patricia were busy with a full schedule of events, designed to put them in contact with as many Winnipeggers as possible. Each day the Duke lunched with a different group—the Grain Exchange, Industrial Bureau, and so on. These events were accompanied by tours of the floor of the Exchange, of the new Industrial Bureau Building, and many other facilities. Given the building boom in the city, there were plenty of cornerstones to lay and plenty of official openings. He opened the Municipal Hospitals, Children's Hospital, and the Selkirk Municipal Hospital.

The Duke's party at the opening of the new clubhouse at the St. Charles Country Club.

Accompanied by Princess Patricia, he cut the ribbon at the St. Charles Country Club, opening the elegant new clubhouse that would burn down within months. The papers reported on the event, saying that the grounds of the club "are in pretty good shape just now and were raked and swept to make the best appearance possible. To the left as one entered the clubhouse the band of the 79th Highlanders discoursed popular airs, their brilliant uniforms making a vivid splash against the brilliant green foliage." At the door they were met by the president, Sir William Whyte, and the vice-president, Fred Drewry: "Sir William Whyte, in his usual happy manner made a speech of welcome to the royal visitors to which the Duke responded, after which an adjournment was made to the grounds where his Royal Highness drove off a ball from the first tee. The ball, by the way, will be kept among the club's treasures."

About 1000 Boy Scouts camped out at the exhibition grounds, holding a Jamboree. By Friday, July 12, the boys had finished all their contests and it was planned that the Duke of Connaught would present them with prizes. It rained all afternoon, preventing him from doing more than inspecting the scouts and giving the King's Flag to the North Winnipeg Troop, which had the distinction of being the largest in Canada.

The Duke's car passes Main and Bannatyne on the way to the CPR station, where he will depart for the West. A spontaneous parade of Winnipeg drivers gave him a warm send-off.

In his address to the boys, he told them that Lord Baden-Powell, the founder of the Boy Scouts, was a friend of his. He said that the Boy Scout movement was intended to bind the boys of the Empire together, create friendships among them, and develop in them a respect for their elders. He knew that the skills they were learning in scouting would be useful to them in their future lives. He finished his speech by leading the boys in three rousing cheers for the King. Mayor Waugh then called for three cheers for the Duke, and the cheering went on for a full two minutes. There were cheers for the mayor and the Winnipeg troop and then the Duke saluted the boys and walked to his car.

Princess Patricia was given her own welcome in the city. Among other events, on Monday, July 15th, the Women's Canadian Club entertained her at a luncheon in the dining room of the Royal Alexandra. Later, the Manitoba Chapter of the Imperial Order of the Daughters of the Empire, led by Mrs. Colin Campbell, was granted an interview with the Princess and they presented her with a life membership and a life member's badge.

Finally, on Tuesday, July 16, the last evening he spent in the city, the Duke hosted a garden party on the grounds of Robert Rogers's house,

Incherra, and those of Greenoch House, the home of John Galt, which was next to it on Roslyn Road. The party was delayed because of rain, a not unexpected problem in the stormy, wet summer of 1912. A large marquee was set up for the guests on the Galts' lawn and a smaller one was placed near the steps of Incherra, under which the Duke and the Princess received their guests. Later in the evening, the Camerons gave a dinner for the Duke and Princess at Government House.

All these events allowed people to make personal contact with the Governor General, to shake his hand and perhaps exchange a few words with him. Later, they reported that he seemed down to earth and gracious; their feelings of loyalty to the Crown, already strong, would be much stronger for having met him. As for the general public, *Dominion Magazine* reported that "There was no lack of enthusiasm, but it was shown in a controlled, good mannered way. Even in public the visitors were never mobbed."

On Wednesday evening the viceregal party left the city. The city's farewell was filled with warmth and demonstrated the real affection many Winnipeggers felt for the representative of the Crown in Canada. As they drove from Roslyn Road to the CPR station, turning the corner onto Osborne, Princess Patricia noticed an old lady with three white dogs. The Duke leaned forward and made a special bow to her, ever the charming Edwardian gent. They had a parade of cars behind them, one of them full of "Indian braves" in all the "splendour of paint and feathers." At each corner more cars spontaneously joined them and by the time they reached the station, there were over 1000 vehicles in the parade. At the station, the band of the 90th Winnipeg Rifles played "Auld Lang Syne" and then they were gone.

In its July 20 issue, *Town Topics* put into words the feelings of many Winnipeggers when the visit was over:

> With the departure of the GG and his charming daughter on Wednesday evening a great blank will be felt. They both have endeared themselves to all with whom they have come in contact and it was with real sadness on the part of those who have been intimately associated with them that farewells were said.

The carload of "Indian braves" in paint and feathers in the vicere-gal motorcade was how most Winnipeggers saw Aboriginal people. They were likely performers from the Wild West Show at the exhibition and may not have been been from Manitoba at all; they may have been Americans travelling with the Wild West Show, but they nevertheless represented the "typical Indian" to white Canadians in 1912. Dressed in buckskin clothing, doing trick riding in the Wild West Show, and living in a village of teepees on the grounds, the Aboriginal people at the exhibition were part of the show, an educational display about how things used to be before the March of Progress swept over western Canada.

Where, then, were the real First Nations of Manitoba? For the most part, they were not seen in the city because they were confined to reserves and schools, living under a sort of endless house arrest. There were, of course, still many Métis people living in the city and general area but probably they were not anxious to advertise their heritage. Some of the people living in shanties around the fringes of the city were likely also Aboriginal. Occasionally Aboriginal people came to Winnipeg to sell blueberries or saskatoons or handicrafts door to door, but, for the most part, First Nations people were invisible in the city in 1912.

In 1912, the Aboriginal population of the expanded Province of Manitoba was 10,500. The people were distributed over the territory of Manitoba much as they are today; that is, the larger communities were in the north, and the southern reserves, in areas of white settlement, had small populations. Only three communities, Norway House, Fort Alexander, and St. Peter's/Peguis Reserve, had populations over 500 people. The major difference is that the census records virtually no First Nations people in Winnipeg, whereas today the community in the city is quite large.

This situation is in sharp contrast with 1870, when Manitoba entered Confederation. Then, in the area that is now Winnipeg and in parishes stretching away from it along the Red and Assiniboine rivers, Métis and other Aboriginal people were very much in the majority.

A group of Aboriginal people camped on the Industrial Exhibition Grounds.

The almost complete disappearance of these people from the area is one of the more startling changes brought about after the transfer of the area to Canada. As early as 1882, Monseigneur Jean d'Artigue, a visiting Catholic priest, wrote of the changes that a Métis native of Red River would have seen upon returning to the city of Winnipeg:

> the virgin plains under the effort of the settlers, have partly converted into cultivated fields; ... his father's house is no more, and on its place is erected perhaps a magnificent building ... his old friends are dead or have emigrated to wild lands; the steamboats have replaced the canoes on the Red River ... and houses which would do honor to a great city the Indian wigwam and log cabin of the half-breeds.[5]

Along with the Métis, the Ojibway, Assiniboine, and Cree people who had once hunted over the Winnipeg district had also disappeared. Early travellers' accounts usually mentioned a "few lodges" of hunters camped at the forks of the Red and Assiniboine rivers, and nineteenth-century paintings of Upper Fort Garry normally depict groups of Aboriginal people camped near the walls.

The signing of the treaties and the establishment of the reserve system had resulted in the gradual removal of Native people from the area around the city; the pass system meant that people could not easily leave the reserves where they lived to visit Winnipeg.

The Aboriginal community closest to Winnipeg in 1912 was St. Peter's Reserve, north of Selkirk along the banks of the Red River. St. Peter's had actually been reclaimed by the federal government in 1907. In that year, government representatives had convinced most of the men of the reserve to surrender the land their community had lived on for almost a century and move to a new, larger reserve in the Interlake—the present-day Peguis Reserve.

Chief Peguis had been the leader of the St. Peter's people until his death in 1864. He was born in the Sault Ste. Marie region and moved with a group of followers to the Red River about 1800, part of a larger migration of Ojibway people. Peguis's policy toward the whites who soon began arriving in the Red River colony was always conciliatory and friendly. In fact, without his help, it is unlikely that the Selkirk Settlers would have survived in their new home. He continued his policy all through his life, converting to Christianity, rescuing the survivors of the Battle of Seven Oaks, and showing his friendship in many ways. By 1912, seventy-five per cent of the St. Peter's people were Anglicans who looked upon St. Peter's Church and graveyard, where Chief Peguis is buried, as their spiritual home.

The men of St. Peter's had provided labour to the Hudson's Bay Company through much of the nineteenth century, working on the York boats and later on lake steamers. They farmed and raised live-stock on the land along the river.

The removal of Chief Peguis's people from their reserve is one of the more shameful episodes in the history of Aboriginal-white relations in Canada. The land was needed for white settlers, much of the arable land in Manitoba having been already taken up, and, as a result, the St. Peter's people were moved. Their new home in the Interlake was rough country covered by dense bush and it was many years before it was made liveable.

By 1912 the move was far from complete. While 400 people had moved to Peguis Reserve, 800 still remained at St. Peter's. In his report for the year, Indian Agent John Watson was confident that "a great many more will follow this summer."

Watson had a low opinion of his charges and in his 1912 report to Ottawa he wrote,

> I cannot say that there is much improvement with these people.
> They have lived so long on the old reserve adjoining the Town of
> Selkirk, where they could get odd jobs and just worked when they
> had to in order to live, that they have become very indolent.

He believed that "now that they are moving onto their new reserve and away from the bad influences of the town, I expect they will do better." Watson implied that the people must be segregated because the Aboriginal person tends to "pick up the evils of the white man but I am sorry to say is not as quick at learning the virtues. The same applies to their morals, which have fallen to a very low level."

However, in seeming contradiction to this, he complained that the isolated community at Deer Lake was "still living in the old Indian style, and little if any progress is noticeable in the way of civilization."

A recurring theme in the Indian Agents' reports is the power of the school to "civilize the Indian." Graduates of boarding schools were seen as civilizing agents who would convert their relatives once they arrived back in their home communities. One agent reported that in his district, "The ex-pupils from the industrial and boarding schools are maintaining their good record, taking the lead and being good examples to others on the reserves."[6]

When the men became farmers or pursued some trade, such as shoemaking, which they had learned at the school, they were praised as good examples. Girls, it was hoped, would become domestics, working as servants in white homes. The agent at Norway House, William Calverley, proudly described the work of a young Aboriginal woman who worked in his home, and said that

> it has not been necessary to give any orders concerning meals and
> housework. When visitors are expected that information was all
> that was necessary. The house would be clean and neat, dinner
> well cooked and daintily presented on a table well set, all her own
> work and she would be neat and clean and well-mannered.[7]

Whether this young woman was paid for her work and what her living conditions were are not included in the report; nor are we told her name.

Calverley was not, however, a supporter of the official line on residential schools. He wrote with unusual candour that, in his experience, when a child was taken "from home people and surroundings which are natural to his childhood ... for a number of years ... and then returned to his people a stranger to customs, habits and pursuits, the result is as a rule, in this district a failure." On the other hand, when a child is kept in touch with "his people, customs and pursuits which will be his when he leaves school, the result is, as a rule, good."[8]

Disease hung over the Aboriginal population of Manitoba like a black cloud, as it had for many years. From twice to ten times as many Aboriginal people as whites died of tuberculosis at this time. The standard methods of dealing with this terrible killer, only developed in the previous decade—dispensaries for anti-tubercular drugs, hospitals, and sanatoria—were not available to Native people scattered in small communities and, in some cases, with no doctors to care for them. The much higher death rate was the result. Less serious diseases like measles or pneumonia often led, in Native communities, to the weakened patient's contracting tuberculosis.

There were a few bright spots on this bleak landscape. One was provided by the exploits of a young man called Joe Keeper. He had been born at Walker Lake and taken to the Brandon Residential School, where he spent the years from 1899 to 1909. In the latter year, he won a foot race in Brandon and so impressive was his skill as a runner that he was moved to Winnipeg to train at the North End Athletic Club. In 1910 he set the Canadian ten-mile record at a competition in Fort William and in 1912 he and two other members of the North End club qualified for the Canadian Olympic Team and travelled to Stockholm to compete in the Olympic Games. Mr. Keeper worked as a carpenter in the CPR shops and lived at 807 William Avenue. In 1916 he volunteered to fight in France and the next year he won the Military Medal for bravery at the Battle of Cambrai. Later in life he worked for the Hudson's Bay Company. Many members of his family, including the politician Lorne Keeper and the actor Tina Keeper, have subsequently made enormous contributions to Manitoba and Winnipeg.

For most Aboriginal Manitobans, however, 1912 fell in the middle of a dark time. Many people lived in the highly restrictive reserve system under the thumb of Indian Agents who watched and reported on the intimate details of their lives. They were expected to "improve" themselves by becoming in some way useful in the surrounding white society and yet they had very little power to make any changes to their situation. This was the fate of people who had peacefully and in good faith signed treaties with the Crown, turning over millions of hectares of territory. Although they had made a major contribution to the wealth and prosperity of the Canadian West, they did not, in 1912, enjoy many of its benefits.

∽⒮AUGUST⒮∽

Holidays, Real Estate

I n 1912, holidays were a luxury out of reach of most Winnipeggers. People worked long hours for six-day weeks and holidays meant only a quick excursion to the beach or an outing in one of the city's parks. Middle- and upper-middle-class people, however, enjoyed holidays of greater complexity and length. But, even for those fortunate enough to be able to take a longer vacation, the rest of the year consisted of hard work. On Saturday, September 21, *Town Topics* included the following ruminations on the summer holiday season that had just ended:

> The daily round is now pretty thoroughly established again, after the summer, and Winnipeg's army of vacationers is back again on the firing line. You find it hard to realize that the time since you returned from your outing is as short as the calendar shows it to be. You had the time of your life at Winnipeg Beach, Detroit Lakes, or the Lake of the Woods, where primeval beauties lured your restless spirit back to nature. They say there are more than ten thousand islands in the Lake of the Woods. That for every island there is a joy for the weary heart of the overwrought city man and woman. Likewise in those other places. And in every place where business and household cares are left behind. You just simply hated to come away from that care-free camp. Didn't you now? And this proves my contention that repose is a mighty uncommon thing. It proves that you took your vacation, just as

you take everything else, including your business, meals and medicine. In big gulps. You bolted it.... The truth is we live in an atmosphere of metaphorical headache, and don't relish anything, whereas if we were normal we would relish everything, even going back to work. ... we are not rested after vacation and ... next year our surcharged and outraged nerves will demand a far lovelier time.

The writer suggested that Winnipeggers try to find repose throughout the year by dropping everything once in a while and relaxing. However, taking time to relax in such an environment was looked on with a certain amount of suspicion. Winnipeggers took on the task of taking a holiday in the same way they did everything else, with energy and determination. Lying in a hammock would not do; instead, people, if they could afford it, mounted expeditions to faraway places. If they went to a cottage at a lake, they entertained and held regattas and race meets at a fevered pace.

The coming of May caused Winnipeggers to begin thinking of the lakes and beaches where they went to cool off. Now was the time to sell cottages and, for those with a lot of money to spend, J.H. Ashdown's cottage at Lake of the Woods was for sale. It had eight rooms with an outside kitchen, a boathouse with two bedrooms, and six hectares of the Canadian Shield. No price was quoted. On May 2, an advertisement appeared in the *Winnipeg Telegram* for cottage lots at Sandy Hook. Prospective buyers were reassured that "Your home in Sandy Hook is protected by restrictions that will permanently ensure its freedom from undesirable associations." The associations referred to were, no doubt, the noisy and happy Jewish and working-class vacationers just a few kilometres away at Winnipeg Beach.

Later in May, Robert Rogers took a party to Kenora in the private rail car that was one of the perks of being a federal cabinet minister. They spent the weekend in Nepahevin, Rogers's summer home. His guests were his son and daughter-in-law, his neighbours from Roslyn Road, Mr. and Mrs. Fred Heubach, and Raymond Carey, who, later in the year, married the Heubachs' daughter Clare.

On Friday, May 24, the Victoria Day holiday was celebrated with a wide variety of public events. At River Park there was a baseball game between the Winnipeg and Duluth teams; there were lawn tennis and football matches and the Spring Regatta at the Canoe Club. Horse race enthusiasts went to the exhibition grounds to watch a matinee of races. All the cricket teams in the city played; there were matches at Assiniboine Park, the university grounds on Broadway, the CPR field, and the River Heights field.

In Portage la Prairie, the official Manitoba trials for the Olympic games were held. Four athletes had already been nominated by the Manitoba branch of the Athletic Union of Canada, but they still had to make it through trials not only in Portage, but also in Hamilton and Montreal, before being named to the Canadian team. The trials at Portage were open to everyone who thought they might be good enough for the Olympics. The Manitoba team nominees were three Winnipeg men, Joe Keeper, John Kirkness, and Army Howard from the North End Athletic Club, and Jacob Wirth from the Brandon YMCA. Only the Winnipeggers appeared at Portage; Wirth was in Ontario competing in trials there. All four men eventually qualified to go to the Olympics in Stockholm.

The beginning of July and the end of the school year is the real start of summer on the prairie. Winnipeggers abandoned the city in huge numbers, heading for Lake of the Woods, Lake Manitoba, or Lake Winnipeg. The CPR special trains to Kenora began on July 1 and were taken off on Labour Day. The Camper's Flyer left Winnipeg every Saturday at 1:30 in the afternoon and got to Kenora at 4:30. The Camper's Special, which had a dining car attached, left at 5:00 p.m. and arrived in Kenora at 8:15. A train left to come back to Winnipeg at 8:15 and arrived in the city at 11:15 p.m. The round-trip fare was three dollars but regular visitors could buy a season ticket for only four dollars. Clearly, there was no wish to encourage casual visitors to this resort area.

Winnipeg Beach, a lakeside resort created by the CPR, was also only reachable by train. "The Beach" was packed with holidayers on the first of July. *Town Topics* described the scene.

> The antics of the weather man were largely responsible for the
> mad rush to the Beach this week-end and over the holiday; like
> the cave-dwellers of old the flat-dwellers of the city rose up

and went down to the sea, the only refuge from the heat laden
atmosphere of town homes and offices. On the morning of the
holiday train after train of heated but happy humanity arrived at
the Beach, and by noon the popular little summer resort presented
an animated scene ... cottagers entertained, hotel strove to please,
and even tent dwellers made merry with their guests beneath the
home canvas.

Many people felt that a beach patrolman, a good swimmer who
knew first aid, was needed at Winnipeg Beach, "to guard against
the casualties that have too often cast a gloom on Beach festivities."
The description of swimming in the waves of Lake Winnipeg, which
appeared later in *Town Topics* in July, will be familiar to anyone who
knows the lake and reinforces the need for a lifeguard.

> Nothing daunted by the unfavourable weather, a large crowd
> of city visitors spent the week-end at the Beach and braved the
> elements with true western spirit. The lake, wind-whipped and
> tumultuous was in an angry mood, and though presenting a fine
> spectacle with its huge rollers and white crests, kept the timorous
> majority on shore ... the 'intrepid spirits' spent the greater part of
> Sunday in bathing and seemed to enjoy the sport of jumping the
> rollers as they swelled up to the beach.

Just as the CPR had developed Winnipeg Beach, the Canadian
Northern Railway was creating beach resorts on Lake Manitoba.
The CNR ran special excursion trains to take people from the city to
Oak Point on Lake Manitoba on that August long weekend. A train
for civic employees left at 8:45 a.m. and another for Sparling United
Church pulled out at 9:35 a.m. The round-trip fare was one dollar.

After a day at Winnipeg Beach, the Moonlight Special train took
people back to the city. *Town Topics* reported that "a jolly campers
dance" was enjoyed after the Moonlight left on Saturday night, so
that cottage owners could enjoy themselves without being jostled by
the mobs of day-trippers from the city. The society columns in the
Winnipeg newspapers followed the activities of the middle classes at
the lake as carefully as when they were in town. They tracked the

A gaily decorated pier at Winnipeg Beach in 1912.

Lake of the Woods and Winnipeg Beach visitors and events with great precision, making it clear that the social structures and hierarchies of the city were largely transported to the lake in the summer months.

In Winnipeg on July 19, the International Regatta began, with participation by members of the Canoe Club and the Rowing Club, and music supplied by the band of the 79th Highlanders.

More regatta events took place the next day, followed in the evening by an informal dance at the Royal Alexandra Hotel, at which, *Town Topics* reported,

> Lovely cool weather, a good programme, a splendid floor, and a room made festive with Union Jacks, and the colors of the clubs were all that was needed to make the dance a huge success. During the evening the president of the club, Mr. George Galt, in his genial manner, introduced the victors to Mrs. C.S. Riley, who presented the prizes.

George Galt had founded the Winnipeg Rowing Club in 1883, soon after arriving in the city from Toronto, where he had already achieved a reputation as an oarsman. The club had been active from the beginning, because there were many men in the city who were interested in rowing sculls, A.M. Nanton and Justice H.N. Howell being only two.

Lord Strathcona made the Rowing Club a gift of the land on which their clubhouse sat and contributed money each year, practically the only donation he made to a Winnipeg organization. Winnipeg crews had a good deal of success at international competitions, winning events at the US National Regatta in Saratoga in 1895 and many other American events in the years after, and participating several times at Henley Regatta in England. In 1910 the Winnipeg crew, led by champion rower Conrad Riley, won the Henley Stewards Challenge Cup, the only year the cup had left England up to that time.

A very different kind of water sport took centre stage on Friday, August 2, when preparations began for the first series of international yacht races ever held on the inland waters of western Canada. The Lake of the Woods International Challenge Cup had been donated by Lieutenant-Governor Cameron and the Lake of the Woods Yacht Club defended it against a team from White Bear Yacht Club of White Bear Lake, Minnesota. F.L. Patton of Winnipeg was skipper of the defender. On Friday, August 2, the *Daphne*, a Canadian yacht owned and skippered by L.W. Caldwell, won the first race of the series. The next day, the American yacht *Quaker Girl*, owned by L.P. Ordway and skippered by his son, won the second race. On Monday the Americans won the final race in the series and they took home the cup. Mr. Ordway was very complimentary about the Canadian performance in the races and Fred Heubach bought *Quaker Girl*, the winning boat, doing what he could to ensure that the result would be different next year.

The following weekend, the residents of Sandy Hook on Lake Winnipeg held their first annual regatta, an altogether less pretentious affair than the Lake of the Woods yacht races. The regatta featured water polo, greasy pole climbing, a boys' boat race, a girls' boat race, foot races, and swimming races.

For the many families who could not afford a cabin at the lake, the city provided other things to do in the summer. At the end of August each year, the city-wide Playfest took place at the Horse Show Amphitheatre on Colony Street. The Playfest was the culmination of the free summer playground program operated in the city. The program was in its fifth year by 1912 and was administered by a commission that included representatives of the School Board, the Parks Board,

Sunday in Assiniboine Park, summer 1912. A trip to the park was a dress-up occasion.

the YMCA and City Council. The supervisor of the program was H.R. Hadcock, who was in charge of physical training at the YMCA

Public playgrounds, where city children could get outside and enjoy the benefits of fresh air and exercise, were an important part of the program of progressive city planning reformers at the time, promoted in publications like the magazine *The Playground*. Winnipeg playgrounds were operated in thirteen schoolyards around the city, from 3:00 in the afternoon until dark. Each one had a director, almost all of whom were school principals, and a lady assistant, who were all schoolteachers. About half the playground directors had attended the YMCA school in Springfield, Massachusetts. The programs placed a heavy emphasis on games, and leagues were formed for competitions. But there was also dance instruction and educational events such as Tooth Brush Day, when dentists visited all the playgrounds to talk about oral hygiene and sell toothbrushes for the token price of five cents.

On the August long weekend, children and their parents went to City Park in special streetcars to participate in a field day. There were demonstrations of dances like the tarantella for girls and the oxen dance for boys, and there were games of volleyball and dodge ball.

During the first three weeks of August, outdoor movies were shown in the schoolyards after dark. A sheet was hung out the second-storey windows of the school and a projector, donated by the Motion Picture Exchange, was set up on the back of a truck about 100 metres away. Crowds of 500 to 1000 children and their parents gathered around to watch educational films about the spread of tuberculosis and the germs carried by flies, as well as more entertaining comedies and dramas.

F.J. Billiarde, the hard-working provincial Superintendent for Neglected Children, in his annual report to the city for 1912, reported that "sometimes when a pathetic scene would be on, there was not a sound to be heard, and when Tom and Jack got into trouble, a perfect storm of cheers and laughter swept the crowd."[1]

Between films, slides with improving messages, such as "Don't be a Growser, Play the Game" and "Remember Flies Breed Filth; No Filth, No Flies," were projected on the screen.

The beginning of September brought the Labour Day holiday, which, in 1912, was celebrated as the holiday of working people. There was a huge Labour Day parade and a sports day at the exhibition grounds. After the parade, which consisted of elaborate floats constructed by the various unions, had passed through the streets, the largest crowd ever poured into the grounds to see union and company teams compete in track and field, baseball and soccer games. The YMCA also sent teams to compete.

The star of the day was undoubtedly Joe Keeper, one of three Winnipeg athletes who had competed in the Stockholm Olympics. Keeper, the child of a Scottish Hudson's Bay Company officer and his Cree wife, was an exceptional athlete: he had placed fourth in the world in the 10,000-metre run at Stockholm. The crowd went wild when, wearing his Olympic sweater, he easily won the eight-kilometre race that September afternoon.

The baseball tournament included company teams from Stovel Printing and the Hudson's Bay Company. Lathers Union won the cup in an exciting game played against the Sheet Metal Workers. The soccer champions were the Celtic Soccer Club, who defeated the Foresters team in the final game. The City Light and Power Team won the tug-of-war, beating the Manitoba Government Telephones crew.

That same Labour Day, a crowd of 10,000 people made their way to Kirkfield Park, a racetrack on the edge of Sturgeon Creek directly north of St. Charles Country Club, to watch the ninth annual Winnipeg Auto Club races. The enormous crowd reflected the growing enthusiasm Winnipeggers felt for cars. The Auto Club meet featured a one-mile "Race Against Time" for the prestigious Gas Power Age Trophy, won by the famous Barney Oldfield, driving a Christie racing car. He made the circuit in 54.5 seconds, breaking his previous record. Oldfield, who had started his career as a bicycle racer, was in his tenth year of auto racing and was able to command fees in the range of $10,000 for appearances like the one in Winnipeg.

Billy Rogers won the twenty-five-mile Dunlop Trophy Race, driving a Ford. The other front-runners were Ben Davies, driving an Underslung American, W. Masters, driving an EMF, and George Connor at the wheel of a Cadillac. There were ten other races, including some stock car events.

After Labour Day, most people in the city went back to work and holidays were forgotten, at least until winter vacation season began again in January. In December, a travelling lecturer brought a new holiday place to the attention of Winnipeggers, one that became a favourite destination. On December 3 there was a free public lecture by the Honourable Walter Gifford Smith of Honolulu on the "Hawaiian Wonderland," complete with motion pictures of Kilauea Volcano erupting. Mr. Smith, formerly a city editor of the *San Diego Sun*, hoped to promote interest in Hawaii as a winter playground for Canadians. The volcano was probably not much incentive to make the trip, but the palm trees and warm temperatures would have been.

≈≈≈

While many Winnipegers spent the last days of August 1912 enjoying the end of summer, one part of the city's business élite was busy preparing for an important group of overseas visitors. On September 1, a special train rolled into the CPR station, carrying forty investors from Britian. This group, which included members of the British aristocracy, had pooled their money into a syndicate called the Canadian Agency, and they had come to inspect their growing real estate investments in Winnipeg. For the rest of the day, they were given a lavish, whirlwind tour of the city that was growing at a dramatic pace, thanks largely to the enthusiasm of outside investors like themselves.

In 1912, Winnipeg and western Canada were nearing the end of a real estate boom that had been driving prices upward for almost five years. Fortunes had been made, at least on paper, by speculation in land, and both local investors and those from other parts of Canada and from Great Britain were still eager to buy. However, news of war in Libya and later in the Balkans between Turkey and her many enemies began to put a chill on the London money markets and it became more difficult for Canadians to raise capital there. Some prudent individuals began to warn that the end of the wild ride was in sight, although during 1912 they were largely ignored.

Western Canada had been growing steadily for over a decade. In the golden years before 1912, people demonstrated their faith in the future of the West by moving there in huge numbers. Their arrival set in motion an explosion of development on every front: new railroads were laid down; new towns sprang up with all their requirements for lumber, hardware, roads, bridges, electricity, coal, and food supplies; every new settler family needed an outfit of equipment in order to begin their new life. Winnipeg, the gateway to the West, grew wealthy feeding all this burgeoning growth.

Everyone wanted land, a space on which to farm or do business. Some people still took up homesteads—160 acres of land was theirs for free as long as they made certain improvements in the first three years. Much of the best homestead land had been taken earlier, and many people bought land from the CPR, the Hudson's Bay Company, or some other corporation or individual. In Manitoba in 1910–1911, only 3082 homesteads were "entered" or claimed by settlers who then had to make improvements, such as building a house and breaking the land, to actually receive title. This small number compared unfavourably with 25,227 in Saskatchewan and 15,964 in Alberta, where enormous amounts of rangeland had been brought under the plough in the previous two years.[2] The largest single group of new arrivals in these areas were the 750,000 Americans who crossed the line between 1900 and 1912. Many of these immigrants came with cash in their pockets, having sold established farms in Minnesota or the Dakotas, and a lifetime of experience farming the prairie. Stories are still told of how they arrived with boxcar-loads of furniture and farm implements and how they did not have to pass through the difficult adjustment period suffered by homesteaders from Britain and elsewhere. In Manitoba some older farms in the best districts, close to a rail line, had been worked for a generation and, as the original homesteaders in the areas

The old and the new Winnipeg in 1912: the new Grain Exchange Building on Lombard
Avenue across from a crumbling stable from the 1870s. During the boom, much of the
old brick and wooden downtown was replaced with concrete and stone buildings.

around Brandon, Portage la Prairie, or Neepawa sold up and moved
to British Columbia or back to Ontario to retire, they were getting
twenty-five to thirty dollars an acre, and some very good farms were
selling for forty to fifty dollars an acre.[3]

The CPR still had about ten per cent of its enormous original land
grant for sale, much of it going for ten dollars an acre. The railroad
preferred to sell to real farmers who would produce crops that the
railroad could carry to the Lakehead, rather than to speculators who
would hold the land, waiting for the price to rise.

The land fever was fed by stories like the case of the town of
Coronation, Alberta, about 150 kilometres east of Red Deer. Before
September 1911, Coronation did not exist. Then it was announced that
the town would be a division point on the CPR rail line—a guarantee of jobs
and investment. On the morning of September 27th, the first lots went
up for sale. People had come the previous day on the train and slept in
tents, so they could be first in line to buy town lots. One man purchased
a lot and immediately hauled a store onto it, moving the building with ten
teams of horses. Minutes later, he was open for business, selling building
materials to his new neighbours. The first issue of the *Coronation News*
went on sale that afternoon. By October 27th, 600 people lived in the
town and 175 buildings had been erected. Real estate prices rose daily. It
is little wonder that so many were bitten by the speculating bug.

The Great West Life Building on
Lombard Avenue, completed in 1911.

Winnipeg was certainly in the grip
of the fever; the editor of *Dominion
Magazine*, the Winnipeg monthly that
made boosting the city its main theme,
assured his readers in May 1912 that
Winnipeg real estate was like stocks
and bonds: a solid investment. It was
"without risk"—music to the ears of
the thousands of people who were
gambling their savings and borrowing
heavily to buy Winnipeg properties.
While the editor did admit that some
land sharks had been selling remote
outside lots in suburbs that did not
really exist, small investors had been
warned; there was nothing to worry
about.

The same month, on May 25,
the finance columnist of *Town Topics* observed that the profits that
promoters had made selling lots in various western towns were now
being invested in Winnipeg. He echoed the supreme confidence of the
Dominion editor when he wrote: "Real Estate is now an investment in
Winnipeg and not a speculation. That cannot be said of most of the
western cities, not excepting Vancouver."

Agents trying to sell lots in Winnipeg usually pointed to the
tremendous growth in the value of land. In February, *Town Topics*
reported that the Chevrier family's old Blue Store property on Main
Street north of McDermot sold for $5000 a front foot—probably the
highest price ever paid for Main Street property. The owner of another
downtown lot had just completed a multi-year lease agreement that
would net him $7000 a year more than the original purchase price.
The land on which the new Albert Hotel would be built, on Albert
Street, had brought a price of $64,000. Two lots on the corner of River
and Osborne sold for $55,000, earning a profit of about $30,000 for
the owners, who had held the lots for only two years. Lots purchased
in 1905 doubled, trebled, or quadrupled in value by 1910; why should
not similarly placed lots increase in value by the same ratio by 1915?

In January, *Town Topics* made the basic argument that all speculators must have been repeating like a mantra in those heady months. Winnipeg was

> a growing city, and will continue to grow, and with this growth property values in all sections are bound to keep pace. It needs only the announcement of some railway operations or industrial development to send prices away up in any section, and then we witness a new standard of values set. For this reason, in a city like Winnipeg, no property can ever be described as permanently stagnant, as development proceeds too rapidly.

In early February, for example, H.A.D. Chalmers Real Estate was selling residential lots in Transcona, far beyond Winnipeg's city limits, where the Grand Trunk's new shops were under construction. The price was $200, and, said the Chalmers ad in the *Free Press* on February 3, "This is a splendid chance to get in on a money making proposition. Get in while you can get in at these low prices. The chance won't last long."

Much of the money invested in western Canadian and Winnipeg real estate poured in from Great Britain. By 1910 Canada surpassed the United States and Australia as a place for Britons to invest. In 1911 British investment in Canada was twenty times what it had been in 1902, most of the money going into municipal and railroad bonds and real estate.

The *Canadian Annual Review* for 1912 included a long analysis of western real estate speculation. It quoted Sir William Wiseman, a British MP, who believed that "a great deal more money is bound to be made in real estate because the [Canadian] cities are all growing." The same analysis noted that British investors such as Lord Northcliffe, A.J. Balfour, and Sir Thomas Lipton—three Winnipeg streets, Lipton, Ruby, and Lenore, still bear his name and those of his two daughters— all owned properties in Winnipeg.

The tour of the Canadian Agency investors on September 1 featured many of the most attractive real estate developments in 1912 Winnipeg. This syndicate had invested heavily in Tuxedo Park, the suburb southwest of the city being developed by Frederick Heubach and his firm, and also owned about 360 hectares south of Tuxedo. This latter area was to be an industrial suburb that would include working men's housing and a variety of factories. The brand-new, $3,000,000 Canada Cement Plant was already in operation, the first, they hoped, of many industrial enterprises. Their holdings elsewhere in the West included a huge tract of 100,000 hectares near Edmonton.

The group of investors was accompanied by A.M. Grenfell, the chair of the Canadian Agency, and R.M. Grenfell, Captain Newton, and W.E. Stavert, all of Montreal, who were the Canadian representatives of the investors. Stavert was a high-ranking officer of the Bank of Montreal who seems to have specialized in bankruptcies and had acquired the assets of several smaller banks for his employers. His presence suggests that the Bank of Montreal was also involved in the syndicate's investments. During his visit, he established himself as a Winnipeg old timer by marvelling at how much Winnipeg had progressed since he had lived in the city in 1885, a youthful clerk in the Bank of Nova Scotia. He told the *Free Press* how, in those far off days, he had slept with a pistol cocked at his elbow.

The party also included some young members of the British aristocracy: Earl Stanhope, Earl Winterton, and Lord Hyde, all under thirty, were on the train. After a brief stop at the Royal Alexandra Hotel, the group set out in a cavalcade of cars to see their holdings in the city. They toured the newly opened Bank of Commerce western headquarters on Main, drove down Portage Avenue, crossed the St. James Bridge, and visited the Tuxedo site, the area set aside for the University of Manitoba, and the Canada Cement plant. After a drive around Assiniboine Park, they went back downtown by way of Crescentwood, with its impressive large, new houses. After lunch at the Royal Alexandra, some of the visitors went to a baseball game to see the Winnipeg Brownies finish in last place in the Central International League playoffs; others went to Kildonan Park. They were given tea at Government House and returned to the hotel for a banquet in their honour. The banquet was attended by 100 people and was hosted by Fred Heubach in his role as president of the Industrial Bureau. The after-dinner speaker was Sir Arthur Lawley, who talked about British Empire issues. The special CPR train was held for half an hour so the guests could finish eating before setting out for Saskatoon, the next stop on their trip. The attention lavished on these visitors demonstrates the importance of British capital in the development of the West.

Although much of the money that fuelled Winnipeg's real estate boom came from outside investors, most members of Winnipeg's élite and many less prosperous citizens also speculated and invested in western land. Speculating in real estate was a long-established feature of the British/Ontario culture shared by so many of Winnipeg's business élite. In his book about Hamilton in the 1860s, Michael Katz writes:

> Given the limited investment opportunities of the time, land occupied the place that the stock market some day would assume. As one historian has written recently, the buying and selling of land for possible profit, whether on a very small or a very large scale, was almost a universal pre-occupation, almost, it might be said, the Upper Canadian national game.[4]

According to Katz, speculating was not seen as a disreputable activity; quite the contrary, "it meant the man was enterprising, promising and worthy." These are words that many people in Winnipeg would have used to describe John Machray in 1912. The nephew of the late Robert Machray, Anglican Archbishop of Rupertsland, and a respected local lawyer who was in charge of the considerable investments of both the Anglican Church and the university, Machray and his partners in various deals were riding the crest of the real estate boom. A great deal is known about his business because of its eventual and spectacular failure. When Machray finally went bankrupt in 1932, revealing that he had lost close to $2,000,000 of University of Manitoba and Anglican Church funds in bad investments, a Royal Commission inquired into his activities. During the inquiry, many former partners described the deals he had entered into in the boom years leading up to 1913.

In 1912 Machray was at the "top of his wave," as his partner, Robert Dennistoun, later wrote. Machray himself remembered the "palmy days" of 1912, when "we all thought we were millionaires."[5] Caught in the speculative fever, he counselled Dennistoun and, no doubt, many others, to give him money to invest for them and not to miss the chance of a lifetime.

Machray had very little money of his own, other than the right to run a bank overdraft, but, in addition to the church and university investments,

John A. Machray.

he controlled the funds of small investors who entrusted him with their savings. He was well connected, not only through his uncle and his duties as Chancellor of the Anglican Archdiocese and Bursar of the university, but also through his wife Emily, the daughter of E.L. Drewery, owner of Redwood Brewery and an important community leader in Winnipeg. Machray's connections were impressive; his law partner, Fred Sharpe, said at the Royal Commission hearings: "He always had unlimited confidence in his ability to raise money and he did raise money."[6] Unfortunately, Machray's business skills and honesty were not all that his partners and clients might have hoped.

Machray signed covenants or partnership agreements with other lawyers and businessmen such as John and George Galt, the prosperous owners of G.F. and J. Galt, wholesale grocers, and of Blue Ribbon Limited, in order to invest in property. In the so-called Strathcona Point Syndicate, Machray had the Galts as partners, along with federal cabinet minister Robert Rogers, and local people such as C.W. Rowley and Lee McCarthy. They bought a tract of land adjacent to the new site of the Manitoba Agricultural College, south of the city. It was purchased in 1911 from R.A.C. Manning, a local Tory organizer, and Colin Campbell, a provincial cabinet minister, before it was generally known that the college would be moving to the site.

Machray didn't do business only with the British-born élite of the city. He became an associate of the three Diamond brothers, Jewish businessmen, with whom he bought land just north of the Salter Bridge. Harold Trenholme, the manager of the Bank of Commerce on north Main Street, who became, in 1912, the son-in-law of Archbishop Matheson, was also a partner in this syndicate and may have been the person who connected the Diamonds with Machray.

Machray built various apartments and houses in the city, a speculation that, given the terrible housing shortage, did not seem to involve much risk. The Wellington Apartments, which still stand on Wellington Crescent, and the two duplex houses immediately to the west of them on the same street, were all built by Machray and various associates in the years around 1912.

Machray also, like many others, promoted a subdivision in 1912. He had purchased a large tract of land west of Winnipeg in St. James near the Deer Lodge Hotel and had it surveyed into lots to form the Deer Lodge Subdivision. During 1912 he offered, through his agents, the Stewart and Walker Real Estate Company, building lots on Sharp Boulevard, and along Duffield, Moorgate, and Conway streets. Distinctive concrete pillars were erected at the junction of these streets with Portage Avenue to mark out this middle-class neighbourhood, so conveniently located on the streetcar line.[7] Newspaper ads for this subdivision claimed it was sixteen minutes by streetcar from City Hall, which might have been true if the car did not pick up any passengers along the way. Sewer lines were to be put in at the earliest possible date and a new bridge across the Assiniboine to City Park was planned. It was promised that Sharpe Boulevard would soon be Winnipeg's most "artistic" and popular thoroughfare; only houses costing more than $3500 would be allowed in the area and no unsightly buildings or undesirable businesses would be tolerated.

Frederick Heubach was another well-connected real estate developer in the city. Early in March the papers carried an announcement that Heubach, Finkelstein and Heubach had just floated a $1.5 million loan in London ($25 million in today's dollars). David Finkelstein said there was no precedent in Canada for a private loan of that size. They planned to use the money to start on the Tuxedo suburb, putting in streets and sewers.

The *Town Topics* real estate reporter was full of confidence about the suburb. On March 2, he wrote:

> Mr. Heubach, Fred Heubach, that's the name that fits him best—
> stepped over to London and there the force of his proposals
> struck home. These world investors realized the situation and
> its possibilities. The money is now put up. In a year or two the

result will be a suburb more permanent as the ideal home centre
of Winnipeg than any district yet touched by the combined skill
of the beautiful home builder and the landscape architect.

Frederick Heubach was, like Machray, an old timer in Winnipeg:
his first job in the city, in 1879, was in the real estate department of the
Hudson's Bay Company as the private secretary of Land Commissioner
C.J. Brydges. He was later involved in various real estate firms and
in 1905 formed the Tuxedo Park Company, selling shares to raise the
capital to buy a large tract of farmland southwest of the city.

Tuxedo was to be an exclusive and expensive suburb and Heubach
engaged the firm of Frederic Olmsted, the designers of Central Park, to
lay out the plan. The area was enhanced by the opening of City Park in
1909, a large and elegantly arranged area designed by Frederick Todd,
a student of Olmsted, whose portfolio included, among other things,
part of Mount Royal Park in Montreal.

In February 1912, both Machray and Heubach were still ambitious
men on the rise, men whose neighbours and friends would have said
had very good prospects; the difficulties and failures that overtook both
their firms were still in the future, and there was every reason to believe
that they would prosper as Winnipeggers only slightly earlier had done.
There were plenty of encouraging examples all around them.

Augustus Nanton had made at least part of his fortune this way.
Arriving in Winnipeg after the first great real estate boom, in 1883,
Nanton had just been made the junior partner in the Toronto firm of
Osler, Hammond and Nanton. His benefactor, E.B. Osler, had married
a wealthy Scottish woman and proceeded to make a fortune acting as
an agent for Scottish investors. Nanton's assignment was to discover
new areas for large investments by their Scottish clients. Over the years
Nanton's canny and conservative management of the investments of
many clients, such as the North of Scotland Canadian Mortgage
Company, made money for them and for himself. He never granted a
mortgage where the risk was too great and, in the first fourteen years of
his career, he never had to foreclose on a borrower. Nanton had made
many trips out on the prairie during the 1880s, travelling on the CPR
as far as the rails would take him and then continuing by buckboard,
sleeping under the stars. He was, therefore, able to give sound advice as

to where the good land was located and invest in some of it on his own account. By 1912 he was one of Winnipeg's millionaires, and a board member of several companies, including the Hudson's Bay Company and the CPR.

George Allan was another Winnipegger who began his career as an agent for outside investors. Allan, a lawyer and member of the prominent Toronto family who donated the Allan Cup, who eventually became governor of the Hudson's Bay Company, also

Fred Heubach, the developer of the Tuxedo garden suburb.

made scouting trips in the 1880s and 1890s, looking for places to invest. R.T. Riley had likewise come to the west in the 1880s to look after the investments of someone else: Senator W.E. Sanford of Hamilton. Unlike Nanton, Riley was in Winnipeg at the time of the boom in the early 1880s. He describes selling off town lots belonging to his clients in the fantastic auction sales run by Big Jim Collican.

> I was very skeptical of these town sites ever amounting to anything and I was careful to advertise them as the property of the Honourable C.P. Brown, Colonel Kennedy and W.E. Sanford and others. I never signed my name to anything except as agent. I paid Collican between $4000 and $5000 a night in Commissions on sales....[8]

Riley built his own fortune and his own businesses, eventually breaking away from Sanford to work independently. He was conservative with his own money, as he says in his memoirs—"I bought tax sale and cheap lands, half breed claims, etc."—and always resold as soon as he had made a small profit.

"Half breed claims" were the land grants given as compensation by the federal government to the children of the Red River Métis under one of the provisions of the Manitoba Act. The Métis were given "scrip," or documents that entitled them to 240 acres for each eligible person. The equivalent of over two million hectares in prairie lands was issued as scrip in a complex process that worked itself out between 1870 and 1925. The disposal of Métis scrip and how many Métis actually benefitted from it has been and continues today to be a matter of great controversy. Many people in Winnipeg in 1912 had profited from buying and selling scrip. Arthur Wellington Ross, for example, is described by Thomas Flanagan as "one of the biggest buyers of Metis lands in Manitoba."[9] Ross employed "claim runners" to buy up scrip as it was issued to the Métis so that he could resell at a profit. Ross had made and lost a fortune and was dead by 1912, but his sons Hugo, who died in the *Titanic* disaster, and Donald were successful young men with an important place in the community.

Augustus Nanton, a man of comparatively high principles, revealed that he, at least, saw the ethical problems in speculating in scrip when told his partners: "I do not want to buy scrip from dealers and scalpers who rob the half breeds, but I will buy direct from the owners at a good price."[10]

W.F. Alloway and his partner H.T. Champion had also invested in scrip and in much other land besides in the early days. As old timers, they were in the enviable position during the boom of having land to sell and, between 1906 and 1912, they liquidated all their holdings, doubling the capital of their banking firm. Around 1900 Alloway had purchased a large number of lots, along the south side of Portage Avenue between Main and Smith streets, for $90,000. This property was all later resold for a total of around $500,000. One of Alloway's most famous deals involved taking, in payment for a carriage and two fine horses, the strip of land between Portage Avenue and the River and Walnut and Maryland streets. He later sold the land for $30,000.[11]

Operating at a less exalted level, dozens of other promoters and developers offered the general public a chance to get in on the boom. John Haffner, the general agent for Hanover Place, a suburb to be built northwest of the exhibition grounds in the neighbourhood around the present Sisler High School, was typical of many people trying to sell subdivision land in Winnipeg at this time. The new underpass on McPhillips, carrying traffic under the busy CPR main line, was a selling point for this subdivision. Haffner invited prospective investors to send for a folder and a copy of Chataway's Map of Winnipeg. This annual city map was a fascinating mixture of reality and fantasy—all the subdivisions actual and future were laid out, with streets and avenues fanning out across the prairie. That many of the streets on Chataway's map didn't exist, or were just tracks across the prairie or through the scrub oak with surveyor's stakes marking the way, was not important because it was not intended to help travellers find their way but to guide investors who traded in lots, hoping to get rich. Although John Haffner did offer customers a ride in his Ford car—"make an appointment to visit Hanover Place. Our autos are at your service"— he also invited eager small investors to buy a lot by simply clipping the coupon in his newspaper ad. We will never know how many trustingly sent their cheques accompanied by the coupon, which said: "I enclose $15.00 for which kindly reserve the best 175 foot lot in Hanover Place. I agree to pay the remaining instalments of the purchase price in 9 monthly payments of $15.00 each."

The most colourful real estate agent in town was Fred Hilson, an auctioneer who called himself "The Man with the Hammer" in his flamboyant newspaper ads.

> Say friend, go to Hilson's to buy
> You can't do better, don't try.

Hilson sold literally everything from his auction rooms at 127 Princess, where the St. Charles Hotel was later built. Every week, up to 700 people crowded in to bid on furniture, furs, food stuffs, and real estate lots. Hilson announced in January that he had sold 17,000 lots all over western Canada and not one of his buyers had lost money. "I am continually hammering at you to get in on these money making opportunities," he shouted from the pages of the *Free Press* and *Telegram*.

Town Topics ran a piece in April, satirizing the seedier side of the business. Entitled "Real Estate Investments: Able Unbiased Honest Information for the Asking," it featured imaginary letters from potential real estate buyers and answers from the "expert" at the paper. The gist of the expert's answers is that if the paper is getting ad revenue from the real estate company, then it's a good place to put your money. If the firm refuses to advertise with them, they pan the project. Some of the fictional developments are funny, though: advertising Winnipeg-style projects in remote parts of Manitoba's north, such as boulevard lots in Norway House and the Brummagem addition in South Port Churchill. They recommend the latter lots—Port Churchill is destined to be one of the world's greatest seaports, and the Brummagem addition, which is only six and half miles from what will be the main downtown corner, is put on by the reliable firm of Skinnem and Guller, who never make any trouble about coming across with the paper's top rates. Like all good satire, the piece is close to the truth. On January 10, the *Free Press* ran a story about William Beech, who owned forty lots in Port Churchill and who argued that the Hudson Bay Railway should have its terminus there because, unlike Port Nelson, it had a deep, natural harbour. There was, at this time, very real and greatly overheated speculation in real estate around The Pas, the starting point of the long-planned Hudson Bay Railway, which was finally beginning construction.

We can get a glimpse into the workings of a busy real estate office of this time in the files of M.R. Grant, who, with his partner, operated out of 401 in the McArthur Building. People living in Britain and other parts of Canada used Grant's services. Grant had written to a Mr. Broderick, in Midland, Ontario, advising him that there were many people moving to Riverview and there was a heavy demand for lots. In March, Mr. Broderick wrote back that he did not want to sell his lots in Riverview, a new middle-class neighbourhood in the south end of Winnipeg: "I think I ought to be able to get a better price after spring has opened up and building operations are under way."[12]

Grant wrote to other clients as well. To W.H. Atkins, in Roxborough, England, he said: "We are glad to know that you had a pleasant journey across the pond and hope that ... you will return in the spring prepared to buy some more property. We may in the way of encouragement tell you that your Riverview property is increasing in value very rapidly." Another of Grant's customers, James Archibald of Watrous, Saskatchewan, received a note from Grant informing him that the Selkirk Avenue streetcar line was to be extended to McPhillips that spring. This, said Grant, would have the effect of increasing the value of Archibald's property on Pritchard Avenue, because it would bring it within easy commuting distance of the CPR shops. He noted, therefore, that "you should be able to sell your property this spring at a good profit."[13]

Notre Dame Avenue construction in 1912. On the left, the steel work of the Lindsay Building is almost complete; on the right, construction of the Street Railway Chambers is just beginning and a construction shed is visible on the site.

The current boom was linked with that other, more famous, Winnipeg boom of the 1880s by a letter Grant received from S.A. Bailey of Victoria. Bailey asked Grant to sell seven lots in Point Douglas for him. He had paid $1550 for them in 1881 and needed to get at least $13,000 in order to cover the taxes and interest and still make a profit. Bailey's letter might have served as a useful reminder to speculators that it can sometimes take a long time to realize a profit on an investment.

A. Lawrie of Forest, Manitoba, wrote asking Grant to sell his lots in Elmwood because "I hear there is a boom on there now and the present may be an opportune time for disposing of them." Joseph Finkelstein, who lived in Winnipeg on Henry Street, also asked Grant to sell some property for him: lots on the corner of Ellice and Edmonton. Dozens of similar letters came in that spring, all asking for lots to be sold so the owners could cash in on the boom.

The actual construction of houses and apartments was often done by the lot owners as part of the speculation. John C. Wilson is an example of a builder who made and lost a great deal of money in Winnipeg in the years before 1912. He was a carpenter by trade and used his savings to buy some lots at the corner of Alfred and Charles streets in 1902. He built two houses on the lots and sold them, but lost money because of inexperience. He tried again with some property on Langside between Sargent and Ellice, and this time he made a profit of $15,000 on the houses he built. He continued expanding his business until the slump of 1907, when he was forced into bankruptcy. With the resumption of the building boom, he was very proud to have managed to pay off his debts and was the contractor who built, among others, the Preston Apartments on Broadway and the Almonte and Rosetta apartments on Wolseley Avenue, all of which are still standing.

During 1912 the feeling grew that the boom might be nearing its end, although many were reluctant to believe it. Warnings about an inevitable crash were given by reputable people, such as the presidents of both the Bank of Commerce and the Bank of Toronto, who warned against speculation in subdivision lots in January 1912. In *Town Topics* on January 20, the real estate columnist agreed with this advice and noted that reputable firms in Winnipeg did not deal in worthless subdivision lots. For example, he reported that the firm of Mark Fortune and Company had lately made several sales of property on Wellington Crescent and in River Heights, and plans were underway to construct several expensive residences. The message was clear: there were speculators in Winnipeg but there were also respectable firms dealing in properties that were of solid value.

In response to another bank president's speech, warning of the coming crash, the *Town Topics* real estate writer agreed that everyone knew this.

> This elevation of prices and taking off layers of profit cannot continue ad lib. But while the layers can be taken off what sane man is going to desist from doing so. There is always the chance that the next layer of profit will never come, but there is no westerner that will not take a chance on that. Then there are so many now that can so well afford to take a chance. Mr. Wilkie can also make up his mind that the westerners who have accounts in his bank are going to use their credit to its limit in order to deal in real estate....

Some of the blame, said *Town Topics*, belonged to the policies of the banks themselves: "If the banks were more stringent with their credits, especially to the big men, there would be less real estate speculation. The little fellows strain too much; they see the big fellows without brains but with the banker's ear, flounder through the mire to success."

British writers had begun to predict an end to the boom, as well. A letter published in the *Economist* in November expressed concern that western prosperity was so heavily dependent upon wheat. The money earned from selling wheat, mostly to Great Britain, constituted fifty-seven per cent of the total earnings from agricultural exports and ninety-one per cent of the value of all grain exports. The all-wheat economy of western Canada left the country dangerously exposed to any fluctuation in wheat prices, and the writer, like many other people, said that farmers should be diversifying in order to protect themselves. Although the Balkan war had cut off the flow of Russian wheat to world markets, driving up the price for the Canadian crop, a fall in prices could happen just as easily. Such a drop in the 1890s had precipitated a major depression in the West.

The *Canadian Annual Review* for 1912, in a long feature article on real estate in the West, reminded investors that there were unscrupulous speculators at work in Winnipeg and that employment of a good agent or a personal investigation of the city are the best means of protecting oneself.

> The truth seems to be that the real values of subdivisions in or
> around a city such as Winnipeg have depended and must always
> depend upon 1) their proximity to the expanding portions of the
> town, 2) their ability to attract residents or industries, 3) the class
> of construction in the former case and the proximity to railroads
> in the latter.

"Let the buyer beware," warned the *Review*. "If the purchaser of a lot is taking his chance as the American cowboy would in a game of cards he has chiefly himself to blame should the result be disastrous...."

Everyone seemed to have conveniently forgotten the terrible aftermath of the boom of 1881 and 1882 in which so many speculators had been ruined and the young city's economy all but ground to a halt. In the later 1880s and 1890s, a local business paper, the *Commercial*, had often editorialized about the contrast between respectable businessmen, who worked steadily to create wealth, and the speculators, who were vultures, parasites, and sharks who fed upon the industry of others, producing nothing, adding nothing to the wealth of the country, but taking profits that others had earned.[14] In 1912 speculation was respectable once again.

In a speech reported in the June 22 *Town Topics*, R.T. Riley worried that some of the subdivisions being sold out on the horizon were relatively worthless and yet wage earners were pouring money into them. He gave the example of one subdivision that had been placed on the market some time ago by a prominent real estate firm. He had predicted then that the development was five years ahead of its time, but fifteen years would have been closer to the mark. At present, there were only three houses in an area with room for 80,000 people. The owners of the lots in this area would eventually get tired of holding them and would find it impossible to sell for what they had paid. He did not feel the same about "inside" real estate in the centre of the city—he did not think that the value of Portage Avenue or Main Street lots would drop in the future.

Like R.T. Riley, most of the doomsayers made a distinction between subdivision lots and inside property, on the main streets of the city, which, although it was considerably more expensive, was said to be likely to hold its value after the end of the boom. In November 1912, the *Victoria Colonist* quoted Robert Mason, a British capitalist, who said, "I know of no such investments in the whole world as inside property in the big western cities of Canada ... every one of my holdings in Edmonton, Winnipeg and Vancouver is worth today 50% more than when I bought it and continuing to increase in value."

The inevitable end of the boom did finally come during 1913. English and European investors began to turn their backs on Canada, preparing for the great bloodletting that would soon begin. Investment in Canadian securities fell off and economic activity slowed across the Dominion. As early as January 1913, Sir Edmund Walker, president of the Bank of Commerce, lamented the difficulty of selling Canadian securities in London and New York, because of the fear of war in Europe. People were beginning to realize that "real estate speculation was proceeding at too rapid a pace," which caused them to be more careful about where they invested, he said. Transactions in inside city properties had probably been larger than ever but the subdivision promoter had not prospered. Speaking at the same Bank of Commerce Annual Meeting, Vere Brown, the bank's inspector of western branches, tried to play down the general effect of the coming fall in real estate values:

> The existence of an extensive speculation in real estate cannot be denied, but an exaggerated impression prevails, particularly abroad, as to its bearing on the commercial prosperity of the country ... speculation ... has been confined to such channels that a serious shrinkage in values could not have but an inconsiderable effect on the prosperity of the country as a whole.[15]

Speaking to his shareholders a year later at their January 1914 Annual Meeting, E.B. Osler, president of the Dominion Bank, described the damage done during 1913:

> I look forward with some anxiety to 1914.... We have a stoppage in the expenditure for railroad building; there has been a cessation in the enormous outlays that have been made in the past few years in building up western towns. We have had a set back and in some measure we have deserved it.[16]

At the 1914 Bank of Commerce Annual Meeting in the same month, Vere Brown confirmed that speculators had been ruined by the crash, and that "the losses on inflated outside properties—which will doubtless be severe before the readjustment of values is complete— will fall almost wholly on the professional real estate operators and innumerable small speculators."[17]

In June 1912, *Town Topics* had predicted this fate for the small speculator, whereas larger investors were protected by the banks.

> The pinch falls heavy on the little fellow, but the banks have to go easy on the big fellow with a big line. If he gets away the loss

will tell. He is humoured and his affairs are nursed until ill times pass by. But the little fellow will be turned over to the assistant manager to be summarily closed out whenever his account shows signs of danger.

Even many of the "big fellows" eventually succumbed to the effects of the collapse of 1913. For John Machray and Fred Heubach, the slowdown in the economy and the resultant decline in the demand for new housing meant that they, like many other people, were left with large holdings that could not be sold. During the Royal Commission that investigated his business dealings after his bankruptcy in 1932, a witness testified that Machray had decided, in late 1912 and 1913, to hold onto his real estate holdings and pay the taxes and charges in the hope that land values would recover. In November 1912 alone he paid $14,000 in taxes to the city, and by 1921 Machray and his partners owed $58,000 in taxes on the Deer Lodge subdivision where very few lots had actually been sold. They managed to have the section of the tract north of Ness Avenue returned to farmland and it was sold to the Assiniboine Golf Course, netting enough money to pay the tax bill. As project after project in Machray's portfolio suffered the same fate, he moved closer and closer to the inevitable bankruptcy of 1932 and the scandalous collapse that accompanied it. Machray's ruin was complete when he was actually charged with the theft of the money entrusted to him by the university. He pleaded guilty and died in Stony Mountain Penitentiary a few months later.

Frederick Heubach was likewise left holding a large amount of land in Tuxedo that would not see house construction until the 1920s. He passed away in 1913 and his son gave up his interests in the garden suburb they had dreamed of building and moved to England. Development of the Town of Tuxedo was left to their partner, David Finkelstein, who became mayor of Tuxedo until the 1950s and did see the suburb become a reality.

∽September∽

Mitzraim

Sunset on September 12, 1912, marked the start of two days of Rosh Hashanah, the beginning of the year 5673 in the Jewish calendar. Although Winnipeg was the most cosmopolitan of Canadian cities in 1912, it was still very much an Anglo-Saxon and Protestant city in outlook, and it is unlikely that many Winnipeggers were aware of the Rosh Hashanah observations taking place in synagogues and Jewish homes in the city.

The Jewish presence in Winnipeg dated back only forty years, but there were Jewish families in the city when it was incorporated in 1873. Most, like Edmonde and Adolphe Coblentz and Reuben Goldstein, were businessmen, making their living as merchants. By the time of the 1881 census, there were about twenty-one Jewish families in the city. Then, in June 1882, everything changed dramatically: over 300 Russian-Jewish refugees arrived at the CPR station, fleeing persecution in Russia.

In the Russia they had left behind, Jews were confined to the "Pale of Settlement" and excluded from trades and professions; they were subject to quotas at educational institutions; military service for their men was long and brutal and involved forced conversion to Christianity. Many Jewish conscripts died during their terms of military service. With the assassination of Czar Alexander II in 1881, the situation of the Jews worsened considerably. One of the radical students who killed the Czar was Jewish and this was reason enough to trigger a series of 200 bloody pogroms in which forty Jews were killed and hundreds more badly injured. Rioting peasants invaded Jewish villages, destroyed houses and belongings, raped women, and looted shops. In 1882 the so-called May Laws were passed, further restricting where Jews could live, own property, and work.

As the years passed, there were other outbreaks of anti-Semitic violence in Russia, the worst being in the years from 1903 to 1906. The pogroms were officially sponsored by the government of Nicholas II, seeking to find a scapegoat for the growing chaos in Russia. In 1903–04 alone, forty-five Jews died and over five million rubles in property was destroyed.

In many of Winnipeg's Jewish homes, families carried memories of this persecution and violence. Many years later Mrs. Polly Fireman recalled the horror of watching her father die: "I went upstairs by way of a ladder to get some money because the Cossacks asked my father for money. I gave all the money to the Cossacks but they hung him with a string. I had typhoid then and they figured I would die anyway, so they didn't kill me."[1]

With the threat of violence hanging over them, Jews were obliged to pay for protection. Hyman Gunn, a Winnipeg tailor, related how his father, a miller, had to give the local police chief in his Russian town a bag of flour every week, and "the graft he was paying made it so we couldn't live."[2]

Persecution drove over half the Jewish population of the Russian Empire to emigrate during the thirty years before World War I. Most went to the United States, but many, like the 300 refugees who arrived in Winnipeg in June 1882, came to Canada. The famous author Sholem Aleichem had an uncle, Nissel Rabinowitsch, among the group for whom, in June 1882, Winnipeg was the end of a long and brutal journey. In spite of the efforts of the local Jewish community and non-Jewish Winnipeggers to provide food and such essentials as bedding for the new arrivals, the first days in Winnipeg were grim. On his first night in the city, Rabinowitsch slept on the floor of the immigrant sheds on Higgins Avenue, hungry and tortured by lice. Some of the men went to work unloading a lumber barge, earning enough to buy food; life in the new world had begun.

But it was difficult to adjust to the rough conditions on the Canadian frontier. Rabinowitsch, who was remembered by his famous nephew

Rabbi Israel Kahanovitch shortly after his arrival in Winnipeg in 1907.

as a man who loved books and who might have been a great Yiddish poet in different circumstances, lamented that all his time and energy was spent in exhausting labour: "It is natural under such circumstances that we cannot think of anything of a higher order, such as we were accustomed to do at home. Nor have we enough time to recite our daily prayers. We come home at night wearied and exhausted and sleep overcomes us before we have even eaten."[3]

Nissel Rabinowitsch's life in Canada was similar to that of many of his fellow refugees. He worked as a labourer for the CPR until he had saved enough money to begin selling household items to rural families as a travelling peddler. Eventually, he opened a general store, where he made a modest living until his death in 1897. He did finally have time for his prayers and was among the founders of both the Shaarey Zedek and Rosh Pina synagogues.

By 1911, with natural increase and successive waves of immigration, the census reported that the Winnipeg Jewish community had grown to 8934 souls. The community had become more cosmopolitan, with the arrival of people from parts of the Austro-Hungarian Empire and the influx of a large number of Roumanian Jews between 1900 and

1903. After the failure of the 1905 revolution, Winnipeg became home to political refugees representing all shades of opinion on the left.

Most religious Jews in Winnipeg at the time were Orthodox, but this is not to say the community did not contain all the various shadings of Jewish religious feeling. As early as 1884, there had been a Reform synagogue called Beth El where sermons and some of the prayers were in English. In 1912 a Reform congregation, Shaarey Shomayin, owned the synagogue on the corner of Dagmar and William, across from the Public Library. The rabbi, Solomon Philo, proved to be a little too liberal for his congregation, who dismissed him after he performed a marriage between a Jew and a Gentile. The following year this congregation amalgamated with Shaarey Zedek in the Dagmar Street building.

The original Shaarey Zedek Synagogue at Henry Avenue and King Street (315 King) was built in 1890, the first of many synagogue buildings erected in Winnipeg. Three years later it was followed by Rosh Pina, also on Henry Avenue. These and several other synagogues, such as Beth Abraham, the Roumanian synagogue on Charles Street, were all thriving in 1912.

But the largest congregation was undoubtedly that of Rabbi Kahanovitch at Beth Jacob in the heart of the Jewish district on Schultz. He served the largest Orthodox congregation in western Canada: Beth Jacob Synagogue could seat 700 people and had cost $7000 to build, an enormous sum for its largely working-class members. If the rabbi whom people choose reflects their own values, then Rabbi Kahanovitch reflected well on the members of Beth Jacob. He was a scholar who had distinguished himself during his studies in Poland and Lithuania, as well as a happily married man with a family of lively children. He was tolerant of the views of others, including the agnostic and left-wing secular Jews. He quickly assumed the role of community leader after his arrival in 1907 and eventually was recognized by many as the chief rabbi of the whole Canadian prairie region.

He was called upon by his congregation and others to perform a wide range of functions: settling disputes, drawing up employment contracts, organizing the provision of kosher meat in the city, and raising funds for causes such as the Talmud Torah school, Zionist groups, the United Hebrew Charities, which supported a number of social services, the Jewish Old Folks Home, the Jewish orphanages,

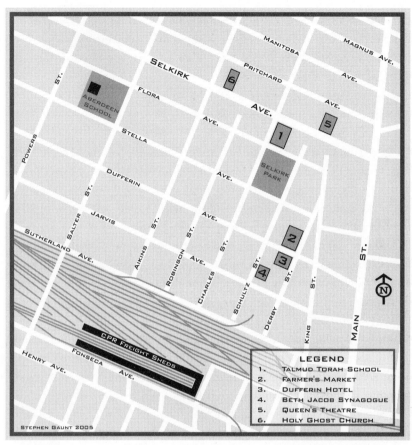

The streets north of the CPR yards were the centre of a vibrant Jewish community.

and many, many others. For the rabbi, fundraising often meant going from door to door with his collection box, reminding people of their obligation as Jews to give to charity.

The main alternative to Orthodox Judaism in Winnipeg was the secular Jewish organizations founded by left-wingers. This was in contrast to Eastern cities, where congregations of Reform and Conservative synagogues were the main non-Orthodox Jewish groups. Secular Jews organized various cultural groups and educational facilities, such as the I.L. Peretz School and the Arbeiter Ring School.

The Jewish community—and by 1912 it could be said to be a community, with its own institutions and identity—was the largest of what we might call the non-British ethnic groups in the city. This is not an entirely accurate description because, based on figures collected for the 1916 census of the prairie provinces, almost twenty-five per cent of Winnipeg's Jewish population in that year was born in Canada. But this group is, nevertheless, a good one to look at to discover how the British-born majority reacted to people different from themselves, what means they used to integrate such people, and how the Jews reacted to these efforts.

As a general rule, people who were not one of the 425,000,000 inhabitants of Britain's vast, worldwide empire were not exactly welcomed with open arms by their British-born neighbours in Winnipeg, nor were non-white British-born folk made to feel welcome. In 1912 the Manitoba Trades and Labour Council petitioned the government to make it illegal for Chinese men to employ white women. This was already against the law in other provinces such as Saskatchewan, and in September three Chinese restaurant owners in that province were convicted of this offence and fined ten dollars. The legislature of British Columbia sent a delegation to Ottawa in March to ask that a new treaty being concluded with Japan ensure that Asiatic immigration was controlled. They argued that "the immigration from Oriental countries still continues in a degree constituting a menace to white labour and the desire to preserve B.C. as a white man's domain."[4]

There was no clear consensus in Canada about how or even whether non-British newcomers were to be integrated into Canadian life. Some people believed that there was nothing to impede any newcomer from becoming a citizen and, indeed, people could become legally naturalized after three years in Canada. They were required to swear an oath that put a heavy emphasis on loyalty to the person of the sovereign, a symbolic shift from being the subject of one king to being a subject of the British Crown. They promised to defend King George V "to the utmost of my powers against all traitorous conspiracies, or attempts whatsoever which shall be made against his person, crown and dignity." The new Canadian also promised to inform the King about any "traitorous conspiracies" of which he was aware. There was also a point of view that held that the foreign-born could never become full citizens with the same relationship to the Crown enjoyed by the British-born. This idea gained in popularity during the war that soon broke upon the country and led to the internment of thousands from eastern and central Europe, including many who

The Queen's Theatre on Selkirk Avenue was a centre of Yiddish culture in Winnipeg.

had become Canadian citizens. It was many decades before non-British people were able to feel they truly belonged in their new country.

As for the Jews, they were generally further along in the process of integrating into the dominant "British" society in Winnipeg than others who arrived later. At the same time, they were building a distinct community of their own. It was in the years around 1912 that the Winnipeg Jewish community could be said to finally emerge from its formative years of struggle for survival, and begin to establish the wide range of institutions that would give it real permanence and provide its members with the services and supports they needed.

The substantial brick Talmud Torah (Hebrew Free School), the cornerstone of which was laid in July 1912, is an example of one of these institutions, and its opening was a moving symbolic moment for many eastern European Jews. Sheppy Hershfield later remembered marching with his classmates from their old Hebrew School to the new building. He looked at the crowd and saw his parents, their eyes full of tears: "Only as an adult I realized they were tears of joy at the thought that their children were walking freely down the street on their way to a great Jewish undertaking."[5]

The Winnipeg B'nai B'rith, established by Max Steinkopf, dates from this period, as does the Montefiore social club with its library and sports teams, founded by several young businessmen in 1911.

The Hebrew Sick Benefit Society, which offered health insurance and a range of other services, was set up in 1906. Specifically left-wing groups like the Yiddisher Ygend Farein, which opened a school in 1914, also appeared around 1912. The Jewish Folk Choir was founded in 1910, the same year city's Yiddish paper, the *Canadian Israelite*, began publishing. The United Hebrew Charities was organized between 1910 and 1912, and in 1911 the North End Relief Society was set up; in 1912 the Jewish Old Folks Home of Western Canada opened its doors, and the next year two Jewish orphanages were operating. Zionist groups also began to appear at this time.

St. Giles Presbyterian Church on Selkirk Avenue had been sold in 1907 to the Hebrew Sick Benefit Society and members of the Yiddish Dramatic Club and had been transformed into the Queen's Theatre. Culturally one of the most important institutions in the area, the Queen's was, by 1912, home to a thriving Yiddish theatre presenting plays starring local actors and international stars such as Molly Picon, on tour from the United States. That the theatre was a comfortable refuge for the people of the neighbourhood is clear from this cranky November 17, 1911, editorial from the *Canadian Israelite*:

> In the Queen's it is common to hear soda-water bottles uncorked throughout the performance, usually at the most melodramatic points in the play. It is not unusual to hear peanut shells being cracked, apples being crunched. It just isn't nice! After all, not too long before curtain time people have had their full evening meal at home. Is it therefore necessary to pack large family baskets and trundle them into the theatre?

In politics, the community was quite active by 1912. Hart Green was the Liberal MLA for North Winnipeg, and, in the municipal elections of 1912, Alter Skelatar, a Conservative, was elected to City Council for Ward 5 and Moses Abraham was elected to the school board. Charles Salzman, a Social Democrat, ran for election to the school board in 1911.

Jewish women, like their counterparts in other parts of the city, played a major role in establishing social agencies. In 1912 Mrs. Chaia Rosenblat and Mrs. A. Aronovitch raised the funds to make a down payment on a house for the Jewish Old Folks Home. Together with a group of other women, including Slava Shragge, Rachel Woldinger, and Rebecca Abramovitch, they succeeded in getting the home established.

In the 1880s and 1890s, there was no specific Jewish neighbourhood, but Jewish Winnipeggers had lived in the area south of the CPR station on streets such as Henry and Lily. By 1912 Main Street between Rupert and Higgins avenues was home to many Jewish businesses. Between Pacific and Alexander, there were three clothing shops, belonging to Sam Schachter, Victor Zitsow, and Louis Katz. In the block north of Alexander, Ralph Udow and Robert Mindell also operated clothing stores and Leon Abramovitch sold hardware and furniture. Between Logan and Henry stood the Bon Accord Block, with the offices of professionals such as Dr. Oskar Margolis, who lived nearby at 39 Lily Street, the law firm of Finkelstein and Levinson, and Aronovitch and Leipsic Real Estate. Further along the same block was Nathan Rosenblatt's Hardware and Clothing store and Steinkopf and Lawrence, Barristers.

In 1912 the centre of the Jewish community was moving north, but some families still lived in this older area in the streets east of the blocks on Main where Jewish businesses were located. By simply counting Jewish-sounding names in the Henderson Directory, admittedly not a foolproof method, we can estimate that about a quarter of the homes on Henry Avenue and Lily Street were occupied by Jews. Some of the more successful families who had been in Winnipeg for decades lived in this area south of the CPR. Max J. Finkelstein, a partner in the law firm of Finkelstein and Levinson, lived at 114 Henry Avenue. He was well known in the city as one of the lawyers who saved the Russian radical, Savaa Federenko, charged with murder in Russia, from being extradited and sent home to certain death. Max's father, Charles, who was the owner of a successful cartage business, lived two streets away at 71 George Street.

Other Jewish professionals and businessmen had begun to move further south. David Finkelstein, a lawyer who was a partner with the Heubachs in developing Tuxedo and who became mayor of Tuxedo for over thirty years, lived in the Cornwall Apartments on River Avenue. Moses Finkelstein, the owner of Northwest Hides and Furs, who had been the first Jewish alderman in Winnipeg, lived on Broadway in the Preston

Apartments. Max Steinkopf, the first Jewish lawyer called to the bar in western Canada, had moved further south to 422 Wardlaw Avenue.

Middle-class Jewish families were also beginning to move north of Selkirk Avenue and to the more desirable streets east of Main. For example, lawyer and MLA Solomon Hart Green lived at 143 Polson Avenue. In the 1916 census of the prairie provinces, the first time the Jewish population in different districts of the city was counted, the ma-jority—about eighty-seven per cent—lived in Winnipeg North, but nine per cent lived in Winnipeg Centre and five per cent in Winnipeg South. The proportions were probably similar four years earlier in 1912.

In 1912 the densest concentration of Jewish residents was just north of the CPR yards in the district bounded by Jarvis and Selkirk avenues and Main and Robinson streets. Here, almost every second house was home to a Jewish family, with the concentration of Jewish homes being greater on the south side of the neighbourhood, along Jarvis and Dufferin avenues. The area was known to some non-Jews as Jerusalem and to others it was "Jew Town." Among Jews it was often called *Mitzraim*, which is the Hebrew word for the Egypt of the captivity: a place from which to escape. In 1912 this district was the centre of a thriving and energetic Jewish community with its own synagogues, schools, social agencies, newspapers, a complex political landscape, and a Yiddish the-atre. There were also Polish and Ukrainian and German immigrants in the district, as well as Anglo-Canadians who had lived on streets such as Selkirk prior to the big influx of new immigration after 1900. Like im-migrants everywhere, the people in the area were focussed on the future, filled with hope and dreaming about what their children would accom-plish. This spirit was captured by their twenty-six-year-old MLA, S. Hart Green, during his maiden speech in 1910 in the Manitoba legislature:

> As the representative of the most cosmopolitan constituency in
> the province, I can assure the house that in after-years some of the
> best men Canada will produce will spring from the melting pot in
> which these different races are being blended into Canadians.[6]

Green's choice of the image of the melting pot is interesting because this is an idea that modern Canadians associate with our neighbours to the south, while we have taken the very different road of "multi-

The south side of Jarvis Avenue between Main and King streets. Many Jewish businesses operated out of shops built onto the front of dwellings.

culturalism." In 1912, however, it was clearly the policy of the various levels of government that the new immigrants would be transformed as quickly as possible into Anglo-Canadians, with the schools acting as the transforming agency. Many leaders among the immigrant groups supported this policy and the new arrivals certainly recognized the need to assimilate enough and learn enough English so that they and their children could get better jobs and earn a decent living. But there were also plenty of institutions designed to keep native languages and cultures alive in the midst of the Anglo-Canadian majority.

The neighbourhood had grown very rapidly over the preceding ten or fifteen years. From an area with only scattered houses, many occupied by Anglo-Canadian employees of the CPR, the area was transformed to one of the most densely populated in western Canada. Laura Rockow later recalled her family's simple tarpaper shack on Jarvis Avenue in the 1890s, when the Rockows were one of a very few Jewish families in the area. The little house often became buried in snow in the winter because nothing stood between the Rockows and the open prairie. Laura's father, who started out as a peddler in the rural districts around Winnipeg, was, slowly but surely, able to improve his family's situation until in 1910 he built a new house at 104 Aikins with such luxuries as an indoor bathroom and a basement.[7]

By 1912, all over the North End, a building boom was underway: small wood-frame houses on twenty-five-foot or thirty-three-foot lots, fifty per cent of them not even connected to the city sewer and water system, were quickly thrown up to meet the demand for housing. Often, several families were crowded into a single small dwelling. Lots frequently had a house on the street and one, two, or three more small shacks in the backyard. In the long triangle between Derby, King, and Jarvis, an area that would have fit easily into many of the large lots along Roslyn Road, were crowded forty-two households and numerous businesses. Rented accommodations for new arrivals were often dark, airless, and dirty. People put up with these conditions because they had no choice and because their misery was tempered by their high hopes for the future. As Jacob Freedman, who arrived in Winnipeg in 1904, recalled, "They [his family] lived at that time on Stella Avenue. All the houses were small. Sometimes the walls were black with the cockroaches and bedbugs but at that time we didn't mind very much. We were all young. It was a new country."[8]

But living conditions were so bad that the government had to take action. As far back as 1904, spurred on by an outbreak of typhus that killed 138 people, the city had conducted a study of the causes of the disease and found that a major factor was the deplorable sanitation in this particular part of the city, where most houses had "box closets" or outdoor privies with a box instead of a pit to hold the sewage. A Board of Health and a strengthened Health Department were set up and various strategies, including the abolition of box closets and the connection of all houses to sewer and water, were pursued. The incidence of typhus fell off as a result. In 1909 the province had amended the City of Winnipeg Act, giving the city the power to regulate apartments and tenements. A tenement inspector began to levy fines and force landlords to improve the conditions under which their tenants had to live. But conditions changed only slowly as long as there was a shortage of cheap housing and landlords were reluctant to comply.

Dominating the entire area and contributing to the general unpleasantness were the enormous yards of the Canadian Pacific Railway—the largest privately owned rail yards in the Empire. With room for 12,000 rail cars on 190 kilometres of track, the yards roared and crashed day and night, spewing smoke, cinders, and dust out over the nearby streets as dozens of trains a day rolled through in both directions and yard engines continuously shunted cars. The yards were also a vast industrial site with a foundry, locomotive and car repair shops, one of the largest chimneys in the city, storehouses, a scrap yard, and enormous coal bunkers. Along the streets bounding the yards, both north and south, were businesses associated with the railroad: scrap yards, factories like the Vulcan Iron Works, and cartage companies with large stables, all adding to the smell and noise and general ugliness.

The population of the North End in 1912 was, as Hart Green had said, cosmopolitan. Selkirk Avenue, which in the 1920s and 1930s was known as the Jewish Main Street, was in transition in 1912, with a large number of Anglo-Canadian families interspersed among their eastern European neighbours. These working-class people of English origin, many employed by the CPR, had been living on the streets of the North End for two decades. St. Peter's Anglican Church still stood on the northwest corner of Selkirk and Aikins at this time and the rector, Samuel Fea, lived next door.

Richard Heap and his three sons, at 334 Selkirk, were typical of the Anglo-Canadian residents of the street. Heap was a man of eighty-one in 1912, a genuine Winnipeg old timer. Born in Lancashire, he had served as a sergeant-major in the British army and in 1885 had helped to train the Winnipeg militiamen who went to fight in Saskatchewan. He had worked for thirty-five years for another English immigrant, E.L. Drewery, as supervisor of the Redwood Brewery's aerated water plant. His son Robert, still living at home with his father, was now a foreman at the Redwood Brewery. Another son, Thomas, who worked as a conductor for the Street Railway, lived a few doors away at 330 Selkirk.[9] Further east, at number 234, lived Frederick Dowling, who was also a Street Railway conductor. Number 258 was the home of A. McMartin, a conductor on the CPR. Jobs like these made men like McMartin and Dowling the élite of this working-class neighbourhood.

Some Anglo-Canadian residents of Selkirk Avenue had businesses. Patrick O'Connell owned the Market Hotel on Princess Street behind the City Hall; Richard Beattie, who lived at 358 Selkirk, was a plumber with a shop at 965½ Main. Percy Linklater, of 222 Selkirk, had been operating a hardware store at the corner of Stella and Main for many years. He came to Winnipeg in 1872 and worked for James Ashdown for a few years before opening his own store. His son, William Linklater, continued in the business for many years.

Many lots in the crowded North End held two or even three houses.

Another hardware merchant and tinsmith was Edward Wasdell, a neighbour of the Linklaters. Edward's father, Joseph, came to Winnipeg in 1881 and had owned a hardware business at 889 Main. The hardware and tinsmith business, now operated by Edward, had been moved to 140 Princess Street, facing Market Square.

Other residents of Selkirk with non-Jewish names were engaged in a variety of working-class occupations: William Low was a teamster, James Melvin a concrete finisher, William Gilchrist and John Waite were listed as stonemasons, William Williams was an electrician, and Peter Ghidoni worked as a waiter at the Royal Alexandra Hotel. William Capstick of 370 Selkirk worked as a trucker for the CPR. Five children lived at home with him and they all worked: William and Edward were both employed in the warehouse of Tudhope Anderson, a farm equipment company; Millicent was a cigar maker; John was an electrician; and Annie worked as a clerk for the Street Railway.

There were a number of widows on Selkirk; one of them was Agania Frank, whose late husband, Alexander Frank, had been drowned just three years before. A deeply troubled man, who had been in what the papers called a state of high mental and nervous tension, he ran out of the house one evening, shouting that he felt like he was on fire. His body was discovered the next day, floating in the Red River.

Frank was a member of an aristocratic Austrian family—his father had been Minister of Agriculture in the Imperial government. In

Winnipeg he had found work as a notary in the law firm of McNeill, Elliot and Deacon, and he had also been acting unofficially as the Austrian consul: he was awaiting official appointment at the time of his death. Overwork was named as a cause for his breakdown, and, given the number of Austro-Hungarian subjects flooding into the Canadian West, it is easy to imagine that he was indeed overworked. Frank left his widow with three boys and a girl. By 1912 his oldest son, William, was working as a clerk at the farm equipment firm of Tudhope Anderson, perhaps introduced to the boss by his neighbours William and Edward Capstick.

Stretching east from the corner of Aikins and Selkirk, on the north side of the street, was the imposing property of Holy Ghost Roman Catholic Church, with its gothic church, rectory, school, and residence for the Benedictine teaching sisters. Holy Ghost was established in 1898 to serve the growing Polish community in Winnipeg. There was friction between Polish Catholics and the largely French and Irish hierarchy of the church in Canada, and this had led to the formation of the breakaway Polish National Catholic Church. Archbishop Langevin had difficulty finding Polish priests for the West, but in 1898 he had found a Polish Oblate, Father Albert Kerlawy, to travel to Winnipeg to set up the Holy Ghost parish. Max Major, editor of the Polish language *Gazeta Katolicka*, lived nearby at 305 Selkirk, where his wife ran a Catholic bookshop. Another bookstore, listed as a "foreign bookstore" in the city directory, was operated by Frank Dojacek at 333 Flora Avenue, about a block away. Dojacek, who eventually had a long and successful career as a publisher and merchant, had immigrated from Bohemia in 1903 and had been selling Ukrainian and other foreign-language books, music, and musical instruments in his shop and by mail order since 1906.[10]

The Ukrainian community in Winnipeg at the time was small— about 3500 people compared to perhaps ten times that number living on farms in rural Manitoba. It was nevertheless an active community, publishing several newspapers and supporting institutions such as the Ukrainian National Home and the Taras Shevchenko Educational Association, located at Manitoba and Powers. A Ukrainian man, Theodore Stefanyk, was elected to City Council in 1911, and in 1913 Orest Zerebko, a teacher, became the first Ukrainian to graduate with a BA from the university. Under the Education Act, schools with enough native Ukrainian speakers could have bilingual education and a Ruthenian teacher training school had been operating since 1907. Young teachers, like Zerebko, passed through this school and went out to work in rural communities, providing the children of the Ukrainian farm families with an education they would not otherwise have had.

Like their neighbours, the Jews were mostly working-class people or small merchants and tradesmen, often with stores along Main Street. Jews, Ukrainians, and Poles, barred by prejudice and poor English-language skills, were not yet well represented among the better paid workers in large organizations like the CPR or the Street Railway; when they were hired, it was to do labouring jobs. The city reported that it employed 55 "Hebrews," 102 "Galicians," 165 Germans, 66 Austrians, and 67 Russians in a workforce of about 1000 in 1908, mostly in un-skilled labouring jobs.[11]

Jewish tradesmen, such as tinsmiths or blacksmiths, who were un-able to get employment elsewhere, operated their own small enterprises, often out of the same buildings in which they lived. Nathan Fogel lived behind his grocery store at 264 Selkirk, as did Moses Duboski, who had a produce store at 303 Selkirk. Louis Gronbach had a butcher shop at 354 Selkirk and lived next door at 386. Further west, at number 493, H.I. Oretski had just opened a general store in the front rooms of a house. Over the years he expanded the business until Oretski's Department Store was known as the Eaton's of the North End. Ninety years later, there are still businesses like this along Selkirk Avenue.

In many houses, young people left school at fourteen and began working; Jewish boys were often expected to begin contributing to their family's income after their bar mitzvah. Boys could make money at an even younger age selling papers after school and many Jewish boys did this. Newsboys were licensed and, of 215 in Winnipeg, 108 were listed as being "Hebrew"; the others were a mixture of Polish, English Canadian, Ruthenian, and German lads, and, rounding out the cosmopolitan nature of the newsie community, one Syrian and one Turkish boy.[12]

Dr. S. Hershfield wrote that "Selling papers suited us well: first it could be done after school and during summer holidays; secondly we were our own bosses and it did not interfere with our playing baseball or football; and lastly it was a most exciting and adventurous occupation."[13]

Sam Fogel later remembered his days as a newsie:

> I used to board the streetcar after school and go downtown to
> pick up the papers. My brother and I had this corner Donald
> and Portage on the northwest corner. When the *Titanic* was sunk,
> we sold papers there till eight in the evening and we made sixty
> dollars that day. I used to bring the money home and give it to my
> mom; it used to be a pleasure to come home and give money.[14]

Samuel Freedman, later chief Justice of Manitoba, recalled how,
when he was a student at Strathcona School, his job was to collect the
books and homework of his two older brothers, who both rushed off
after classes to start selling papers.[15]

Girls worked too, and Laura Rockow, after she had finished school
and studied at a business college, went to work for the Canadian
Northern Railroad in the freight office. She started there at age sixteen
in 1907 and by the time she left to get married in 1915, she supervised
six other typists.

The streets south of Selkirk Avenue were inhabited by working-
class and lower-middle-class families. On Flora Avenue between King
and Salter, among other people, there lived three labourers, several
caretakers, two clerks, a warehouseman, and a peddler. There were
also tradesmen, some with shops on Main: a blacksmith, a printer, a
tinsmith, a plumber, and a harness maker. There were three tailors, one
of whom, Hyman Gunn, was a manufacturer employing other tailors
in his factory on Logan. Living next to Gunn, at number 309 Flora, in
the other half of a duplex, which Gunn may have owned, was Rabbi
Kahanovitch of Beth Jacob Synagogue. The rabbi always lived on
Flora, first at 309 and later at 281, until his death in 1945.

On Stella Avenue, the street south of Flora, lived people with a similar mixture of occupations: six labourers, eight clerks, and a number of
tradesmen such as Kolman Bass and Israel Baronowsky, partners in a
blacksmith shop a couple of blocks away on Dufferin. John Bernack, who
lived at 292 Stella, was a partner with M. Chess in the Manitoba Fruit
and Produce Company, located on Jarvis between King and Derby.

William Genser, president of the Genser Real Estate company with
an office in the McIntyre Block on Main Street, lived at 367 Stella.
He had come to Canada from Austria, settling first in Montreal and
moving to Winnipeg in 1900. One of his sons, Morris, was a talented vio-

William Genser, successful real estate agent.

linist who led the pit orchestra at the Walker Theatre. Moshe Genser had a long career as a musician, and as a music store and furniture store owner. Among many other accomplishments, he was one of the founders of the Winnipeg Symphony Orchestra and of the local musicians' union.

Further east, at 232 Stella, lived Hyman Katz, who was a partner in the Manitoba Hat and Knitting factory at 56 Princess Street. Katz was just one of several clothing manufacturers in the Jewish community, the first having been Moses Haid, who opened the Winnipeg Shirt and Overall company in one room in 1899.

The real heart of the Jewish district in 1912 was at the corner of Dufferin Avenue and Derby Street, where David Morosnik's open-air produce market drew housewives from all over the North End. Morosnik had been one of the earliest Jewish immigrants in the 1880s. Over the years he had made his living buying and selling horses. He still lived with his two sons at 263 Dufferin, in a house next to the open yard used for the farmer's market. One son, Louis, was a law student at the firm of Andrews, Andrews, Burbidge and Bastedo. Louis, only twenty at this time, had already had a career as a newspaperman, covering the courthouse for the *Manitoba Free Press*. It was there that he met the local lawyer, A.J. Andrews, who convinced him to take up the law. By the time of his death in the 1950s, Louis Morosnik was a leading member of the Winnipeg bar, well known for his colourful and dramatic courtroom style.

The market was in the open yard between the buildings at the northwest corner of Dufferin and Derby. Farmers from north of the city brought vegetables, chickens, and dairy products to sell to local housewives, in a setting not very different from the ones in eastern Europe, where many of the women would have shopped before coming to Canada.

James Gray, whose family lived in the North End for a time, describes the scene in the market in his book *The Boy from Winnipeg.*

> There seemed to be horses everywhere at the Jewish market on
> Derby Street, where my mother did her weekly shopping for
> vegetables and butter and eggs. My mother was a slow shopper,
> which suited us fine for we would walk around and pet the horses
> that were tied behind the farm wagons, or were being shod in a
> near-by blacksmith shop. Some had stripped leather arrangements
> over their noses to keep off the flies. Some even had a sort of shawl
> covering from which long strings dropped, again to keep off the
> flies.[16]

Dr. Hershfield describes going to the market with his mother to get a chicken for the Shabbat meal, and how she "would walk from stall to stall looking for a chicken for the shabbos ... she would haggle with the farmer in Ukrainian about the price, finally buy it and take it over to the little shed where a shochet would kill the chicken."[17]

Across from the market was the Dufferin Hotel, where the farmers would go for a quick drink to warm them on the way home. Next to the Dufferin stood the Minuk Block, the property of Peter Minuk, known as the "King of Dufferin," who operated a real estate office around the corner on Derby Street. The block had a dance hall upstairs and several businesses at street level, including Joseph Charach's barbershop. He lived behind the shop with Isaac Charach, also a barber, two of five Charachs who were barbers in the area. D. Charach, who lived a few doors away, took a different road and opened the New York Photography Studio at 576 Main Street.

One block south of Dufferin is Jarvis Avenue, the southern limit of the Jewish district. Sutherland Avenue, one block further south, is mostly given over to industrial uses and storage yards. Jarvis has the same mixture of residences and businesses as further north, but also facilities linked to the railroad, such as a huge cordwood storage yard, a scrap iron business, and John Gunn and Sons Lime Storage yard.

On the northwest corner of Derby and Jarvis stood the Gould Hotel and, just west of it, the Hay and Feed business operated by Moses Berg. Across the street was the Gunn Block with eighteen

David Morosnik's farmer's market at the corner of Dufferin and Derby.

apartments. West along Jarvis, at the corner of Jarvis and Schultz, lived Sam Hollander, who is listed as a Hebrew teacher in the city directory. Across the street from Hollander was the establishment of May Mararo, dressmaker. David Rusen lived on the next block to the west and was a partner in a wholesale fruit business further east on Jarvis. Two of his neighbours were Henry Jones and Natisch Zbysko, labourers, and S. Shapira, who operated a dance school. In the next block, between Charles and Robinson, stood a multi-unit row house, 303 to 317 Jarvis. The tenants here included Harry Libowich, a jeweller, Moses Perlman, a peddler, an electrician named Kion Nichichowitch, and David Zimmerman, a merchant.

In this very mixed neighbourhood, how did everyone get along? Certainly, the larger Anglo-Canadian population, in other parts of the city and the country as a whole, expressed anti-foreign sentiment, some of it quite shockingly racist in nature. George Fisher Chipman, the editor of the *Grain Growers Guide*, published two articles in the *Canadian Magazine* that contained attacks on the intelligence and character of Winnipeg's "Galicians" and other "foreigners" living in the North End. There were many similar articles in magazines and newspapers at the time. In his 1912 novel *A Manitoba Chore Boy*, E. Wharton Gill, an Anglican clergyman and novelist, gives us a sense of the kind of prejudice that greeted eastern Europeans before they ever reached Winnipeg. His main character, a young Englishman, had been travelling steerage but on the CPR train to Winnipeg from Montreal, the English-speaking steerage passengers joined the second-class passengers and, the young man says, "The Galicians, or whatever they were, were put in the carriages by themselves, fortunately for us."[18]

Galicians and Ruthenians, designations that tended to be used for people we would now call Ukrainians, had a few defenders. J.S. Woodsworth, who operated the All People's Mission west of Salter on Stella Avenue, did plead for understanding and help in supporting the new arrivals so that they could successfully establish themselves in their new home. William Sisler, the principal of Strathcona School, while focussed on integrating the children of the new immigrants, also spoke with compassion about the difficulties Ukrainian families faced in making enough money to live. Michael Sherbinin, a Ukrainian intellectual who lived in Winnipeg for about ten years before leaving in 1911, likewise made pleas for understanding and tolerance.

Jewish Winnipeggers faced prejudice, as well. In the schoolyards of the North End, Jewish children sometimes had to fight prejudice with their fists. Maurice Bregman remembered that at Argyle School, the public school attended by most children in the Mitzraim district, "There were a number of anti-Semitic children there, older bullies that made our lives miserable. They used to bait us and they would gather the other kids around them and they would throw stones at us and call us Jews and Christ-killers," and Dr. S. Hershfield recalled that at Strathcona School, "We formed a gang and no goyische boys ever dared to attack us for we had already fought and beaten all the goyische gangs in our neighborhood, and Jewish children could now walk to and from school without fear of being beaten up."[19]

In the classrooms at schools like Argyle and Strathcona, the children struggled to learn English and many of them idolized their teachers. One former student later recalled that "We must have been hard to put up with because we admired them [their teachers] so much that we wanted to be close to them. We walked around at recess hanging

Students from many different backgrounds attended Strathcona School in 1912.

on their skirts and sleeves.... We wanted to be like them and were ashamed of our parents and grandparents."[20] Dr. Hershfield paints a somewhat different picture of his reactions to assimilation attempts. He and his friends enjoyed visiting Woodsworth's mission and the Robertson Church Mission of Robert Mutchmore on Burrows, and admired the two men in charge, but converting to Christianity never crossed their minds. They were mostly attracted by the games and the children's parties put on for them; they were happy and comfortable in their Jewish culture. One mission they did not visit was operated on Pritchard Avenue by a convert from Judaism. "We despised his efforts at proselytization," wrote Hershfield.

One of the most persistent anti-Semitic ideas was and is the so-called "blood libel": the charge that Jews use the blood of Christian children to bake Passover mozza. In the years from 1911 to 1913, a blood libel case was making its way through the Russian courts. Mendel Beilis, a Jewish worker in Kiev, was accused of murdering a twelve-year-old Russian boy, Andrei Yushchinsky, and using his blood to bake bread. The police had discovered the true killers, but the Imperial government, for which anti-Semitism was an established policy, pushed the local authorities to manufacture the case and Beilis spent two years in jail before he was finally acquitted.

The case was followed all over the world and in May 1912, a group of Winnipeg Jewish leaders sent a letter to City Council, saying, in part:

We desire to associate ourselves with the protests being made all
over the world against the attempt made in the city of Kieff to
revive the ludicrous charge of ritual murder—known as the blood
accusation—against Judaism and Jewish people among the ignorant
and inflammable populace of eastern Europe the blood accusation
has often given rise to terrible outbreaks of mob violence.[21]

The effect the "blood libel" had on ordinary people's lives is illustrated in a 1914 letter sent to Joseph Wolodarsky, then living in
Winnipeg, by his sister Pesel, who was still in Russia. She tells him
that one of their neighbours, Shloime Pletzel, hired a non-Jewish boy,
fifteen years old, to help him with his work. When Pletzel fired him
because his work was not satisfactory, the boy, afraid to go home with
this news, ran away to Kiev to find work there. When the boy's mother
heard he was no longer at the Pletzel's house, she demanded to see him
and called in the police. Finally, a letter came from the boy, proving he
was still alive and working in Kiev. Pesel wrote: "If that letter had not
arrived, who knows where Shloime and Cholya might be right now;
probably in jail somewhere. Can you imagine brother, how lucky you
are that you are so far from here. Though it may not be so great for
you either, one always has a home where there is freedom."[22]

The Winnipeg Jewish community spoke out against racism when it
occurred. In 1912, in addition to the Mendel Beilis trial, one of the most
important issues for Jewish Canadians was a private member's bill
making its way through Parliament in March. The stated intent of the
bill was to secularize the historically Presbyterian Queen's University.
To accomplish this, the legislation stated that no religious test would
be required of faculty other than a profession of Christianity. This
clause, intended to open up faculty positions to non-Presbyterians,
clearly excluded Jewish professors—a group admittedly quite small in
1912. There were protests across the country and in Winnipeg a huge
public meeting was held in the Queen's Theatre, addressed by Jewish
leaders such as Rabbi Kahanovitch, Baruch Goldstein, editor of the
Canadian Israelite newspaper, as well as R.L. Richardson, publisher of
the *Winnipeg Tribune*. A resolution deploring the clause and "affirming
the principles of equality and liberty that form part of the basis of the
constitution of the Dominion" was sent to the Committee on Private Bills.

The offensive section was eventually removed from the bill, although faculty were still required to have "a good Christian character."[23]

Anti-Semitism in Canada, although a very real part of everyday life, was of a different sort from the state-sponsored persecution many Winnipeggers had known in Russia. This became clear to Jews in Manitoba as early as the summer of 1882, a few months after the arrival of the first large group of Jewish refugees, when one of the newcomers, Kieva Barsky, was attacked with an iron crowbar by Charles Wickes, a fellow labourer on a CPR construction crew. Barsky charged Wickes with assault and Wickes was jailed for one month. The judge in the case, Chief Justice Woods, spoke eloquently from the bench, condemning the sort of blind prejudice that had caused the assault.

For those who wished to, bridging the gap between the two cultures was not always easy. Laura Rackow recalls that, when she was a small girl on Jarvis Avenue, although "most of our gentile neighbours seemed to resent our presence," the Scottish woman living next door did try to be friendly. One day the woman called her over to her yard and offered her a cookie: "I still remember the feeling of horror that came over me as I gazed on that innocent little cookie. It was 'traif' (not kosher) and I ran out of the yard and home as fast as I could before the sight of it could contaminate me."[24]

Many of the children brought up in the little wooden houses of the Mitzraim district entered a wide variety of careers, and made contributions to the life of the city and the country that were truly remarkable, given the poverty into which many of them were born. Few traces of the neighbourhood remain now, but here and there, a clapboard cottage survives on its narrow lot. If we listen closely, the echoes of Yiddish or Polish or Ukrainian voices seem to drift in the air. We might even catch sight of a skinny boy bounding up the steps and through the kitchen door, his pockets full of change from the papers he has just sold downtown.

OCTOBER

Grain

On October 8, 1912, the *Winnipeg Telegram* carried the news that Vere Brown, the superintendent of western branches for the Bank of Commerce, had returned to the city after his annual fall tour of the wheat country. He estimated that the crop would be good, although not a bumper crop, and that the grades would be high. The actual size of the 1912 crop was not finally calculated by the Dominion Bureau of Statistics until after all the 100-bushel wagonloads of grain had been delivered and passed through the system, but Brown's impression proved, as was usually the case, to be accurate: 1912 wheat production was 224,000,000 bushels, a slightly smaller crop than the preceding year, and the quality was good.

To Winnipeggers, the next best thing to the official figures was the estimate made each year, before the harvest was even complete, by E. Cora Hind, the agriculture editor of the *Manitoba Free Press*. Every fall since 1904, Miss Hind had travelled all over the west by train and buggy, climbing through fences and estimating yield, farm by farm, district by district. She was always very close: in 1904 she had established her reputation when she estimated 55,000,000 bushels and the crop came in at 54,000,000.

In a city where so much depended upon the size and quality of the wheat crop, the estimates of people such as Brown and Hind were eagerly awaited. A good crop meant mortgage payments would come in on time, money would continue to be made at the Winnipeg Grain Exchange, and the orders would flow in for all the things the city had to sell.

Out across the prairie, an extraordinary phenomenon had been unfolding since early August, when the harvest began: a torrent of wheat was flowing east to market. Farmers, elevator operators, railroad officials, grain inspectors, grain traders, and shippers were now running a frantic race against the clock as they laboured to move as much of the western crop as possible to the head of the Great Lakes before Lake Superior froze in December, greatly slowing the flow until spring.

In a thousand farmyards, in the early dawn, farmers murmured gently to their giant Clydesdale horses as they harnessed them to grain wagons full of wheat. The same teams had worked with the farmer all through the short, fierce, growing season, ploughing and seeding, harvesting and thrashing. Now they hauled the grain to the local elevator, where it would begin its long journey to a mill, perhaps in Winnipeg or Kenora or in Britain.

The elevator operator, the local face of the grain industry, weighed the grain, assigned a grade, and took a sample to establish the "dockage"—the percentage of the load that consisted of weed seeds, dirt, and broken kernels. He then dumped the grain into the pit below the floor of the drive shed and "elevated" it up inside the elevator with the bucket conveyor, directing it into the bin that held other grain with the same grade.

Each country elevator was a small tributary to the enormous river of grain that flowed east to Winnipeg and thence to the head of the Great Lakes. The river had grown larger year by year for many years, but in the past decade it had turned into a massive flood. Since 1902 there had been a fifty-six per cent increase in wheat production in Canada, from 97 million bushels in 1902 to 224 million bushels in 1912. In the same period exports had grown from 32 million bushels to a total of 95 million bushels. Another 20 million bushels left the country in the form of flour.

Most of this increase came from new wheat lands broken in the three prairie provinces. Manitoba, the oldest and most densely settled province, increased her wheat-growing area by only twenty-eight per cent. The big change was in Saskatchewan, where the wheat acreage in 1900 had been just 487,000 acres; in 1910 it was 4,228,000, an increase of eighty-eight per cent. In Alberta the growth was from 43,000 acres to 880,000 acres, an increase of ninety-five per cent.[1]

As long ago as 1885, wheat had surpassed furs in importance as an export from Manitoba; its value grew until by 1912 it was the major

The Ogilvie Mill in Point Douglas as it appeared in 1903.

export of Canada. This dramatic change resulted from the favourable combination of several factors.

First, a large market existed for Canadian wheat in Great Britain. Since the repeal of the Corn Laws, Britain had become the world's largest importer of wheat. In 1912 over eighty-five per cent of Canadian exports went to Great Britain, where Canadian grain joined wheat from all over the world flowing into the concrete silos of the gigantic Cobourg and Alexandra granaries in Liverpool or the Millennium Mills on the Victoria Docks in London.

Then, there was the short growing season of the prairies, which were ideal for hard red spring wheats much in demand with millers because they "add strength to a blend." This means that when blended with cheaper, softer white wheats that are grown in warmer climates, red spring wheats can produce dough that will hold more water and rise higher, resulting in loaves with greater volume.

Before the 1870s, red spring wheat had a small market because the stone-grinding technique used in flour mills caused the exceptionally hard outer bran to be mixed into the flour, giving it an unacceptably dark colour. This problem was solved with the introduction in the 1870s of steel rollers, first developed in Hungary by András Mechwart. The rollers scrape open the wheat kernels instead of crushing them and then complex sifters remove the bran and produce high quality white flour. The value of red spring wheat and of the lands where it could be grown skyrocketed.

Red Fyfe was the first great red spring wheat variety grown in Manitoba. It was brought by early settlers from the United States and probably originated in Poland. It did very well in Manitoba soils, produced good quality flour, and fetched a good price. Red Fyfe gave Manitoba and the northwest an export crop to finance the construction of the railroads and other infrastructure needed to support an export wheat industry. In 1882 Ogilvie Mills, operators of a large, new, steel roller mill in Winnipeg, distributed a poster in Manitoba, explaining to farmers why they should be growing Red Fyfe:

> Important to Farmers: The standing of Manitoba wheat abroad has been seriously injured by the large proportion of Canada Club and other soft mixed varieties produced last year. Pure Red Fyfe is the most valuable wheat that can be produced here, and it is the variety upon which the reputation of the "New North-West" as a wheat producing region will mainly depend. No soft or mixed wheat is worth as much by 15 cents per bushel, and this difference in price will hereafter be made by the undersigned millers and wheat buyers. ... soft wheat can be raised anywhere, while pure Red Fyfe is always sought by millers ... sow only Red Fyfe.

However, in 1888 an early frost caused widespread damage to the wheat crop; a replacement was needed for Red Fyfe that would mature more quickly and avoid frost damage. Department of Agriculture scientists began using the relatively new technique of plant breeding in an attempt to produce such a wheat. The process, begun in 1892 at the Brandon Experimental Farm, ended when Charles Saunders, the Dominion Cerealist, introduced Marquis wheat, a purely Canadian variety that matured ten days earlier than Red Fyfe and was perfect for the export trade, because of its superior milling and baking qualities. In 1911 Manitoba farmer Seager Wheeler helped to establish Marquis's reputation by winning a prize for the best bushel of wheat grown in North America at a New York agricultural show. First widely planted in 1913, Marquis fed the booming western economy with a reliable and valuable export for over twenty years.

The elaborate and costly system required to move millions of bushels of grain from individual farms all over western Canada was largely headquartered in Winnipeg. Winnipeg had fought hard to gain control of the western grain trade. In the early 1880s inspection and grading of western grain had been controlled by the Toronto Board of Trade, Toronto being the headquarters of the Ontario grain trade. Inspectors were examined and appointed by the Toronto board and standards of quality for the various grades of grain were decided in Toronto. As the size and importance of the western crop began to grow, the Winnipeg Board of Trade wrested control of western inspection and grading away from Toronto. In 1883 the Winnipeg Board of Trade took over the examination and licensing of inspectors in the west; in 1888 a Western Standards Board was established to set the grade standards for western grains; and after 1890 all appeals against grades were taken to a Board of Arbitration in Winnipeg. By gaining control of the inspection and grading of the western crop, Winnipeg had the means to develop western varieties as unique and valuable commodities. The famous Number One Northern grade, for example, became synonymous with high quality wheat.

Grades are assigned to lots of grain on the basis of factors such as weight per bushel, plumpness of kernels, and the presence of proven varieties. Standards like these, applied by impartial government grain inspectors, were the best guarantee possible for both buyers and sellers that they would receive fair value. Foreign customers liked the Canadian system. So great was and is the trust placed in the Canadian system that Canadian shipments were and are accepted and traded on the basis of the inspector's certificate. Visual inspections of the grain itself were usually required before a shipment was accepted from other countries, such as Russia and even the US. The reason for this lack of confidence is suggested by a Russian police report of the time, which stated that officers had discovered, in a grain warehouse, "quite

The trading floor of the Winnipeg Grain Exchange in about 1920. To the left are the large chalkboards where prices from other grain markets were constantly updated.

a little mountain, as they put it ... of sand and grit of all kinds evidently intended for mixing with the oats before shipment."[2]

The Winnipeg Grain and Produce Exchange was founded in 1887 as a market in which western grain could be purchased for use in the mills of Britain and Europe. The Exchange did not trade grain on its own account, but was an association to which a wide variety of buyers and sellers belonged. The buyers were the representatives of Canadian and foreign, mostly British, millers, and the sellers were the elevator companies and commission agents who handled the sale of other people's grain. By 1912 the Exchange had developed into one of the great wheat markets of the world, the volume of wheat traded there exceeding at times that at Chicago and Minneapolis. Its vast new building on the corner of Rorie and Lombard was finished in 1908. In addition to the Exchange's trading room, the building contained the offices of most of the grain traders, the elevator companies, shipping companies, and the Winnipeg offices of the Board of Grain Commissioners, as well as most of the other companies and associations connected with the trade. It was expanded a number of times and was for a while the largest office building in western Canada. It loomed above Portage and Main and could be seen for a great distance down Portage Avenue, a symbol of the dominance of the grain industry in Winnipeg.

Since 1904 Winnipeg had also had a futures market and the brokers who traded in this market were members of the Exchange. The futures market allowed traders to "hedge" to prevent risk. Clarence Piper, manager of the Empire Elevator Company, attempted to explain this complex procedure, which excited the suspicions of so many farmers, in his 1915 book *Principles of the Grain Trade in Western Canada:*

> As fast as purchases are made in the country, the amounts thereof are reported to the head offices in Winnipeg. The companies then sell immediately the same amounts for different deliveries according to the position of the grain when purchased ... this is hedging by which they have done two things ... they have bought some grain which they have in their possession and they have sold a contract to deliver a like amount of the same grain at a future time. If the price advances their cash grain becomes that much more valuable but at the same time they lose an equal amount on their sale for future delivery since they have already sold at a price that much below its new value. On the other hand, if the price declines, their cash grain becomes less valuable but at the same time they gain an equal amount on their sale for future delivery since they have already sold at a price that is much above its new value.[3]

This system made the business of buying and selling grain more stable. Hedging benefitted farmers, Piper argued, because without this kind of protection, people buying grain in the country would have to offer lower prices to provide a cushion against possible price fluctuations. Unfortunately, hedging also provided speculators with an opportunity to gamble, purchasing grain and banking on a price rise in the future. Most farmers associated the futures market with this sort of speculation, calling it a "gambling hell," and it added to their suspicion and hostility.

The trading floor of the Exchange was a large, rectangular room two storeys high on the sixth floor of the Grain Exchange building.

Entering the room from the south, one would see, on the right, a set of chalkboards mounted about three metres above the floor with a walkway in front of them, on which the Exchange staff recorded prices paid for various grains in Minneapolis, Chicago, Duluth, and other grain market centres, continuously updated as the prices came in by telegraph. Three times a day, the Liverpool prices were received via the transatlantic cable and posted. Since so much of the western crop was sold to British mills through Liverpool, in 1912 the Liverpool price minus the cost of shipping the grain to that port formed the basis of the Winnipeg price for the day. A large, electrically operated, "wheat clock" was also mounted on the east wall to register price changes on the trading floor.

Up-to-the-minute information was essential in the sometimes highly volatile grain market, so the Exchange was wired to the outside world. Along the wall were telephone booths so the traders could keep in touch with the firms and individuals they represented. At the far end of the room was an area for telegraph operators, who sent the prices on the Winnipeg market to the outside world and received information about prices on other markets.

The actual trading floor had a pit, an octagonal area surrounded by a raised barrier with steps leading up from the outside and down to the central area. These steps allowed the traders to see each other and the bids and offers they were making. Beside the pit, in a high "pulpit," stood the Chief Recorder, in 1912 a diminutive Scot called Bill Little. With the help of two assistants, he recorded all the transactions taking place between buyers and sellers of wheat, oats, barley, and rye. From the opening at 9:30 until the close at 1:15, 12:15 in summer, he had to interpret "the seemingly incoherent shoutings and signalings of the brokers and traders in the pit below...."[4] He also manipulated the electrically controlled wheat clock.

Little later recalled the days before 1914 as "hectic and sometimes frenzied times. The pit would be jammed daily with a crowd of active traders. The noise would be indescribable, the excitement intense." One morning Little, who had asked the board of the Exchange on more than one occasion to add another trading pit, finally cracked under the incessant strain and collapsed in the pulpit. He was off work for nearly a year after suffering a complete mental and physical breakdown. He returned to find that the Exchange had finally installed the second pit. Wheat was traded in one and the remaining grains—barley, oats, rye, and flaxseed—in the other.

Agreements to buy and sell were made verbally on the floor and reconciled at the end of the trading day by the Clearing House, operated by Exchange members. In 1912 the Clearing House dealt with 400,000,000 transactions. Three kinds of trades took place on the floor: the sale of farmers' grain, usually handled by commission agents acting on the farmer's behalf; the so-called "cash" grain market involving the sale of grain already owned by various middlemen, such as the line elevator companies or other grain buyers; and the trade in futures. The buyers were brokers representing Canadian millers, or exporters making up shipments of grain for overseas buyers. Agents handling farmers' grain charged a commission of one cent per bushel, for which they provided various services, such as acting as the owner's agent in disputes over grade, managing the paperwork involved in keeping track of the grain as it moved from the country to Fort William, and trying, as the seller, to get the best price possible for the grain.

Winnipeg also dominated the elevator business. Of the 1997 elevators scattered over the prairies, a few were farmer- or government-owned, but in the fall of 1912, most prairie farmers would likely sell their grain at an elevator owned by one of the large private grain companies with headquarters in Winnipeg.

Some companies and individuals who were significant later in the Winnipeg grain trade were still relatively small in 1912. James Richardson and Sons had only twenty-six elevators, mostly in Saskatchewan, and James Richardson himself—the man who, in the 1920s, laid the foundations for the massive enterprise that still survives today—had just arrived in the city to work as the company's local vice-president. Henry Sellers, whose father and grandfather had managed terminal elevators at the Lakehead, and who became one of the leaders of the grain trade by the end of his career, had also only recently moved to the city from Port Arthur and was working with the Hargraft and Gooderham Grain Company.

Among the larger players were the milling companies, Ogilvie Mills and Lake of the Woods Milling. They had been the first to build lines of country elevators to feed their flour mills in Winnipeg and at Keewatin.

George Carruthers, one of the most important members of the Exchange in 1912. He was the local representative of the Carruthers Grain Company of Montreal. In the background, Bill Little presides over the noisy chaos of the trading pit.

The Canadian Elevator Company, owned by William McWilliams and Alvin Godfrey, two Winnipeggers of American origin, operated over 100 elevators in Manitoba and Saskatchewan communities.

Nicholas Bawlf, one of the founders of the Winnipeg Grain Exchange and of the grain business in the city, had sold his interests in his original enterprise, the Northern Elevator Company, in 1909 to F.H. Peavey and Company of Minneapolis. Then Bawlf had set out with his son, William, to build a new company, N. Bawlf Grain Company, which was in the process of constructing a new line of country elevators. Bawlf also had interests in the Alberta Pacific Grain Company, the firm that helped to make future Prime Minister Richard Bennett a millionaire.

John Charles Gage was an American who had moved to Winnipeg in 1903 and built the International Elevator Company, which, by 1912, had forty elevators in Manitoba and Saskatchewan. Gage had also taken the next step in the elevator business and purchased, with Alex Reid, the Western Elevator Company, which operated a terminal elevator at Port Arthur, giving them an integrated operation from the country point to the Lakehead.

Until 1904, all the terminal elevators at the Lakehead were owned by the CPR. In the years since, line elevator companies had begun to acquire terminals so that grain from their country points would pass into their own terminals and they would receive income from storage and handling charges in both places. In 1912 the farmer-owned Grain Growers Grain Company leased two of the CPR terminals at the Lakehead to work with the line of country elevators they were leasing from the Manitoba government. New terminals were being built to accommodate the growing shipments of grain. N.M. Patterson built his first terminal elevator in 1912 and a new government-owned terminal was planned.

Because they made their money on per bushel charges, grain traders' and elevator companies' incomes grew as the size of the western crop grew. The same was true for the bankers who financed the grain industry and for the railroads and shipping firms that hauled the grain. The city was riding high on the booming wheat economy of the West: many of Winnipeg's largest fortunes had been made in the grain trade and several of the city's largest businesses were elevator companies. Until wheat, oats, and barley trading were taken over by the Canadian Wheat Board, starting in the late 1930s, the Grain Exchange was probably Winnipeg's most important engine of growth and it created enormous wealth for the city.

Individual farmers, on the other hand, were probably not making much more than a living wage, their income being dependent upon the price fluctuations on the grain markets. Most were also carrying debts from buying land and starting up their farms. The contrast between the prosperity the grain trade was producing in Winnipeg and the farmers' income fed the suspicion and animosity farmers felt toward the Winnipeg-based companies that handled and bought and sold their grain. These suspicions were an important force in Canadian politics in the decade before 1912.

Farmers suspected that elevator operators were cheating them on weights and grades, and it was a fact that some grain buyers in country elevators tampered with their scales. This problem was, to a great extent, solved by having government inspectors check and license the scales in all elevators.

Farmers also brought the charge of price fixing against the companies that owned the country elevators and purchased grain through them. The *Winnipeg Tribune*, under its independent Liberal publisher, R.L. Richardson, wrote in 1899 of a "gigantic combination" and a "syndicate of syndicates" working to cheat western grain growers. It was true that five large companies owned most of the country elevators in western Canada, but that they colluded in fixing prices was never really proven by any of the royal commissions and investigations conducted. Prices tended to be the result of outside factors, such as conditions in other grain-growing areas, rather than price fixing.

The Grain Exchange Building was the largest office building in the city and symbolized the importance of the grain business in Winnipeg.

The farmers' solution was to ensure they had the right to bypass the elevator by loading their own boxcars at sidings and shipping their grain east, independent of the line elevator companies, in the hope of getting a better price. This right to a car had been enshrined in the Manitoba Grain Act in 1900 and was successfully tested in the courts in 1902 in the famous Sintaluta case. W.R. Motherwell and Peter Drayman, two members of the Territorial Grain Growers' executive, successfully argued that the CPR was not following the new regulations.

The Grain Growers moved beyond the country elevator to take on the Winnipeg Grain Exchange, as well, and they made some headway, succeeding, with the help of Rodmond Roblin's Conservative government, in getting their own Grain Growers Grain Company a seat on the Exchange.[5] The struggle between the private companies that dominated the Grain Exchange and the farmer-owned cooperatives, such as the Grain Growers Grain Company, and later the prairie Pools, was far from over and the two sides hurled charges and counter-charges at each other for many years.

Terminal elevators at the head of the lakes were also a source of irritation for the organized farmers. They knew, because it had been proven in a 1908 audit, that at least some of the terminal elevator operators mixed grain of different grades to create more Number 1 wheat than had been taken into the elevator. Farmers considered this to be theft. In response to their demands, government inspectors and weighmen were stationed in the terminals to supervise the binning of grain and audits, or weighovers, began to be done regularly. Many farmers wanted all terminals nationalized. The government was not willing to do this, but construction had begun on a government-owned terminal at Fort William, the first of a series of such large elevators the government later built and operated.

All these concessions and safeguards, as well as a sophisticated system for grading grain and regulating the industry, were finally consolidated in the Canada Grain Act, which came into effect in July 1912. This new Act was administered by the Board of Grain Commissioners and their staff, and it provided Canadian farmers with a level of protection against abuses unknown in any other grain-growing country.

The impressive success of the Grain Growers movement in securing remedies for the grievances of their members was founded on the fact that they constituted a sizeable voting block at the time. Also, the Liberal government and Interior Minister Clifford Sifton, in particular, were pursuing a policy of filling up the West with new homesteaders and were anxious that nothing should happen to make the West seem like an undesirable place in which to settle. In the same way, in Manitoba, the government of Rodmond Roblin, in spite of the fact that Roblin himself was one of the founders of the Grain Exchange and a partner in a private grain company, always made sure to accede to farmer demands.

Credit must also be given to the quality of the Grain Growers leadership in this important decade. Men like W.R. Motherwell, who later served as agriculture minister in both Regina and Ottawa, lobbied more skilfully and expressed themselves more clearly than the farm leaders who had preceded them. Agricultural historian H.S. Patton said of the Grain Growers 1902 pronouncements on the issue of the farmer's right to load his own boxcar:

These resolutions, whose explicit businesslike character contrasted
significantly with the vague and spacious declarations of the old
Patron's Lodges, were carried to Ottawa. The government was
impressed and the Grain Growers' resolutions were incorporated,
in almost the very language of the petitioners, in the amendments
to the Manitoba Grain Act.[6]

The general political atmosphere created by the progressive movement in the US and Canada also favoured the Grain Growers. Progressive
politicians such as Teddy Roosevelt focussed public attention on trusts
and monopolies in business and promised to curb their power. The grain
trade was the target of progressive rhetoric in both countries, and the
general suspicion people felt about the industry was strengthened by
books like *The Octopus* and *The Pit*, two popular novels published by
Frank Norris around the turn of the century. Both portrayed the grain
trade and institutions such as the Chicago Commodity Exchange as mon-
strous conspiracies designed to cheat the American farmer.

The Canadian industry, like that of the United States, had developed
as a bulk-handling system, moving grain in carloads and shiploads instead of the inefficient and labour-intensive bags used in other wheat-
growing areas. Bulk handling necessitated a sophisticated grading and
tracking system so that each owner's share of the whole was followed
through the system with paper records. The system depended upon
the immense network of elevators through which all this grain flowed,
from the small, wooden, country elevator to the vast, concrete silos of
the terminal elevators in Fort William, Port Arthur, and farther east
in other lake ports and in Montreal, where the largest elevator in the
world had been opened on October 1, and on to the huge storage
elevators in ports like Liverpool and London.

The bulk-handling system made inspection and grading extremely
important. The initial grade was assigned by the country elevator operator, but the new Grain Act established that inspectors paid by the
Board of Grain Commissioners, who were thus seen to be impartial,
would sample and grade all grain produced on the western prairies.
All grain cars, whether they were being used by individuals or elevator companies, were sealed by the station agent in the place of the
grain's origin. That official also filled out the bill of lading that would

travel with the grain to the Lakehead. When the long trains of boxcars rumbled and shrieked into the CPR and Canadian Northern yards in Winnipeg, the seals were broken by an employee of the board and each car was sampled. All these samples were taken to the board's offices in the Grain Exchange Building and a grade was assigned. This sort of comprehensive sampling and grading by inspectors paid by the government had begun in 1899 and it continued until the 1950s. It provided a check on the grades assigned by country elevator operators and thus benefitted farmers. It also guaranteed those purchasing grain that they would get what they were paying for.

The work of gathering samples from boxcars was back-breaking. The board's sampling crews worked in shifts twenty-four hours a day, seven days a week, during the heavy autumn season. The twelve- to fourteen-man crews could sample a whole train in the time it took to change the engine and crew. It was difficult to get men to do this work. In 1918 Chief Grain Inspector George Serls wrote:

> When help is wanted for sampling we have always to go around the city and pick them up as best we can. The sampling of cars is such hard work that it is almost impossible to get men to stay at it. During the months of September and October, we are engaging men every day on account of so many quitting after they have tried the work.[7]

For each of the thousands of cars, the method was the same. The car doors were opened by removing a few boards at the top of the doorway. A grain sampler climbed in and drove a hollow brass grain sampling pole, perforated with holes every few centimetres down its length, down into the load of grain in the car. He twisted the pole to trap the grain sample and turned the brass knob at the top to close the holes. Then he withdrew it and dumped the sample onto a square of canvas, which was then tied shut and labelled. This process was repeated a prescribed number of times in the car until a representative sample of the grain was collected. Once the sampling was complete, the car was sealed again and the next car was tackled. The canvas bags of grain samples were taken to the board's office in the railyard, where a clerk completed the appropriate paperwork. The bags were then taken to be graded in the board's inspection department on the eighth floor of the Grain Exchange Building.

If the samplers were at the bottom of the board's hierarchy, the grain inspectors were near the top. It took years to learn the craft of grain grading and the inspectors had to pass examinations set by a group appointed by the Winnipeg Board of Trade: the Board of Grain Examiners. The job of the inspectors, working in the board's inspection room on the top floor of the Grain Exchange Building, was to visually grade the samples. They worked on benches set under the north-facing windows, to secure the best light. Each sample was dumped onto a square of brown paper. About half the sample, about half a kilogram, was cleaned by shaking it through a standardized screen. The resulting "screenings," any material that was not the kind of grain being graded, was weighed and the "dockage," the percentage of foreign material in the grain, was set. The dockage was an important factor in setting the final price of the grain shipment and having it set by a disinterested government inspector was seen by farmers as an important safeguard.

The inspector then examined the grain sample and, sometimes with the help of standard samples kept in the inspection room, assigned a grade. He recorded the grade and dockage and passed the sample on to a clerk, who prepared a certificate for the owner of the grain and updated his daily report that would go on ahead of the grain. The sample and its paperwork were kept in a metal box in the department in case the grade was later appealed. The owner of the grain could request a reinspection and, when the car reached Port Arthur, it would be put aside and the Chief Inspector at the Lakehead would look at a sample and assign a grade. If they were still not satisfied, the owner could apply to the Grain Survey Board for one last appeal, but the word of this board was final.

The trains left Winnipeg and chugged eastward through the Shield to the Lakehead, where the grain was shovelled out of the boxcars and elevated into the vast concrete silos of the terminal elevators. In Winnipeg it had been transformed into a graded commodity that could be bought and sold on the Winnipeg Grain Exchange, the market where western grain was purchased by the hungry world. In 1912 Canada operated the most highly regulated grain industry in the world, and Winnipeg, with its various institutions for accommodating the trade, was at the very heart of the system.

⌒♥NOVEMBER♥⌒

Heating, Militia, Hunt Club

A lthough the fall of 1912 was mild, Winnipeg knew that winter was coming. As people turned to the problem of restocking their coal bins for the coming cold weather, they found that prices had remained very high, largely because of the labour strife in coal mines in Alberta, Britain, and Pennsylvania, which had cut off production for long periods since January. Coal dealers reported "difficulty in getting supplies since the suspension of mining in the spring, impossibility or delay in getting orders filled and delay in transportation," because there was a car shortage in the west.[1] High prices meant that people turned to cheaper soft coal and wood to heat their houses.

The city's health officer, Dr. A.J. Douglas, was not pleased with this development. He had been trying to convince people that it was false economy to burn soft coal because of its tendency to damage equipment and, more important, because it produced so much more smoke than harder coal. To control the "smoke nuisance," city health officials encouraged the use of hard coal or coke or smokeless soft coal like the Pocahontos brand. Even wood produced less smoke than soft coal. If persuasion failed, fines were levied against people producing excessive amounts of smoke.

Another method for controlling smoke was to instal a smoke consumer, which returned coal gases to the firebox to consume the impurities before they went up the chimney. Several of the big boilers in the city, like those at Eaton's store, the Royal Crown Soap factory, the CPR yards and the street railway powerhouse had smoke consumers.

A 1912 ad for coal.

Private homes could instal the Schaller System, advertised as being in use in the newly constructed St. Regis and St. Charles hotels, which could be installed in two hours and would "re-consume the waste coal gases and utilize them into heat."[2]

For poor people, the rise in prices was a terrible disaster; for the rich of the city, the problem was not so much the price as the availability of the coal. Augustus Nanton's house burned a ton of coal a day in really cold weather,[3] but he could afford it. He may have got a special price on coal; since 1905 he had been the managing director of the Alberta Railroad and Irrigation Company, the Galt family enterprise that operated the coal mines at Lethbridge. Nanton had bought up shares in the Galt family business in 1904 and 1905, and in 1912 he, in turn, sold the mine to the CPR. He was made a director of Canadian Pacific two years later.[4]

Most people had to pay the going price for coal, however, and since heating the home occupied such a central position of importance in Winnipeg, there was a great deal of discussion over the merits of different types of coal. The technology of heating homes with coal remained the same for many decades into the future, and H.G.G. Herklots, who arrived from England in the 1930s, commented even then on the phenomenon of Winnipeg's obsession with heating fuel:

> When talk of snow has abated, men begin to talk of fuel. And they continue to talk of it right through the winter, referring to it casually even, in moments of anticipation and recollection, on summer evenings by the lake side. What do you burn, what do you burn? It is the great, all engrossing question.... As each man has his own tobacco and hesitates to smoke another, so has each man his

own coal.... Men savour the names of coal as some men savour the names of wine. Drumheller there is from Alberta, Galt and McLeod ... Cannel coal and Pocahontos from the States ... inexpensive Souris, the poor man's coal, that looks like solid mud....[5]

People could even tell what sort of coal a given house was burning:

> At night sometimes, when the temperature is really below zero, the chimney smoke pours thickly from the houses on the street. The fuel fancier stands back to watch it (pulling his fur collar around him as he does so). 'That house is burning hard coal and that one coke,' he says. 'I fancy they've got Souris over there.' All this and more can be deduced from the ash piles staining the snow behind each house. In this land there is very little privacy.[6]

Anthracite coal was the hardest coal available and the most expensive. Bituminous coal was the softest coal and the cheapest. Other factors had to be taken into account in deciding on the quality of coal; for example, the amount of slate running through the coal. The veins of slate were the same colour as the coal, but they could be easily seen by a canny buyer. Emily Holt, in her useful book *The Complete Housekeeper*, cautioned homeowners, therefore, never to buy coal sight unseen, unless the coal dealer was known and trusted.

Coal came in a number of sizes—pea, nut, egg, range, grate, and furnace. The size one ordered depended upon the kind of grate in one's furnace. Holt pointed out that "Obviously it would be a great waste to buy coal so small it would stream out between the grate bars or the bottom of the fire-box, and almost as much so to buy it so big one lump could not lie close enough to another to admit of proper burning."[7]

Emily Holt advised that September would be a good time to have the year's coal delivered, but that it should not be brought until the household was ready for it. Steps, windows, and walls nearest the coal chute should be covered with paper or an old carpet to prevent the dust from getting into the house. She suggested that someone be stationed in the coal bin to wet down the coal with a watering can as it was dumped into the house, so the dust wouldn't spread. For the same reason, she warned that all the registers and the door to the basement should be kept shut.

The work of making the fire was a task that involved complex skills, the mastery of which gave rise to a good deal of pride. In 1935 Herklots, who had never stoked a furnace before in his life, bragged, "I have learnt so to fling the coal through the little furnace door that it makes no mess upon the basement floor, and spreads as it falls within. I am a master of checks and draughts; I know the purpose of the slicer door."[8]

Emily Holt described the process in detail. After cleaning the fire-pot and ashpan of ashes, the fire-pot was half filled with kindling. Then a roll of paper was lit and held up the chimney to start the up-draught. Now the kindling was set afire and, with the dampers at the bottom of the furnace door open, allowed to burn for a while. Then heavier kindling and a layer of coal were shovelled onto the fire. When this was burning well, the fire-pot could be filled with coal that would burn slowly for many hours. One last duty was necessary to prevent coal gas from getting into the house: to close the dampers and let the coal burn for about fifteen minutes to drive the coal gas up the chimney before opening the registers to let hot air into the house.

Holt also described the lighting and care of cooking stove fires and fireplace fires. She advised burning quick lime or oyster shells in the stove to loosen the "clinkers" from the grates. Clinkers were mineral deposits left behind when a fire that was too intense burned up mineral deposits in the coal.

Wood was burned too, in furnaces and fireplaces. Once the only fuel available in Winnipeg, wood had slowly been supplanted as affordable supplies of coal and the railroads to transport it became available. But wood continued to be used: Herklots, describing the city in the 1930s, might have been speaking of the Winnipeg of 1912: "Many acres of Winnipeg's great sprawling area are filled all year with high stacks of wood; many square miles of bush and forest must be burnt in our houses each winter."[9]

~ ~ ~

Winnipeg newspapers in November 1912 were full of ominous news from Europe. On Monday, November 4, they reported that the uprisings against the Turkish Empire were over. In the Balkans, the

Turkish army had been defeated by the Bulgarian army, the Turks had begun to retreat to Constantinople, and the Ottoman Empire had sued for peace. The fighting ended with the humiliating defeat of the Sultan and his armies, but not before terrible atrocities had been committed and the first aerial bombardment in history had taken place—an Italian pilot dropped bombs on the Turkish army in Libya from his plane. Although the fighting was over, hardly anyone believed there would now be peace. After all, German armaments makers were working at top speed to produce battleships and submarines to challenge Britain's hegemony at sea, and the First Lord of the Admiralty, Winston Churchill, was responding by laying down the largest warships the world had ever seen.

The weakness of the Ottoman Empire created tremendous instability in the area and the great powers moved to take advantage of this. As news of the defeat in the Balkans reached Canada, British and German warships were steaming to the Golden Horn to "protect Christians" living in Constantinople. A prophetic editorial in *Dominion Magazine* for November said that the war in the Balkans threatened Canada's prosperity because European capital would now have to go to build weapons, not railroads and municipal improvements in western Canada.

Was Canada ready for the war that was beginning to seem inevitable? Certainly, the military was held in high esteem by most of the country's middle and upper classes for a number of reasons. Canadian successes in South Africa, general romanticized notions about the army and the Empire, the influence of activities such as scouting and military drilling on schoolchildren, and the widespread belief that a war was on the horizon all contributed to support of the armed forces. The budget of the militia department was one of the largest in the Canadian government, surpassed only by Public Works, Railways and Canals, and the Post Office.

Many Canadian schoolchildren were involved in cadet units—40,000 cadets attended summer training camps in 1912—and there was regular military drill for school students. In Winnipeg, this consisted of learning to march and drilling with broom handles, not rifles. There were city-wide competitions and the winning teams might receive a set of rifles or a ceremonial sword. There were officers' training

Enlisted men of the Lord Strathcona's check harness at the Fort Osborne Barracks, located on what is now the west lawn of the Legislative Building.

courses at the universities and a start had been made in organizing a university regiment in the western provinces. The Boy Scouts, a relatively new organization, intended by its founder, Lord Baden Powell, to produce "a far superior soldier than if he received merely the usual cadet training,"[10] had good support in Winnipeg: the North Winnipeg Troop was the largest in Canada. The connection between the Scouts and the military was reinforced by their participation in the annual Decoration Day Parade.

The militia, Canada's part-time fighting force, theoretically consisted of every man between the ages of eighteen and sixty, but in reality there was a permanent force of about 3000 and a part-time militia of about 57,000 men who might be ordered out for up to thirty days of training a year. The military was well supported by community leaders in cities like Winnipeg, as it had been for many years. Many of Winnipeg's élite had actually seen active service with the militia at some time in their lives, during the Fenian raids or fighting Riel, and some continued to serve as officers in the city's regiments.

In the decade between the end of the Boer War and 1912, the federal government carried out a reform of the militia, "Canadianizing" it by replacing the British General Officer Commanding with a Canadian Militia Council and creating a new command structure to make the force more efficient.

In Winnipeg, there were 110 permanent force troops with headquarters at Fort Osborne Barracks. Lord Strathcona's Horse numbered eighty-three, and the rest were officers and men from support units such as the Army Service Corps. The commanding officer at Winnipeg was Colonel Sam Steele, a genuine war hero with a somewhat salty reputation. Steele had turned sixty-three in January. He was a barrel-chested veteran with a Victorian moustache, showing signs of the hard drinking and years of tough service with the Mounted Police all over eastern Canada and in the Yukon during the gold rush, and with Lord Strathcona's Horse in South Africa. "He has not been a carpet soldier," said the *Free Press*, "but has seen plenty of action in the service of his country. Presiding now at Fort Osborne Barracks as the Commanding Officer of Military District 10, he is held in high esteem by his men." This was not entirely true: Steele, with all his rough edges, was not always popular with the polished professional officers he sometimes commanded. No one dreamed in 1912 that he would continue to serve his country through four years of war before his death in 1919.

The refurbishment of the country's barracks, begun after the Boer War, was part of national reforms to Canada's military. Buildings were in poor condition and not large enough to accommodate all the men in the permanent forces. Since 1903, officers and non-commissioned officers had had the option of living out in the community and received an allowance to do so, but the other men lived in poor conditions like those at Fort Osborne. The buildings were not new: the Drill Hall on the corner of Osborne and Broadway dated from 1886. During 1911 and 1912, over $11,000 was spent on repairs to the barracks—putting in washrooms, fixing roofs, installing a new boiler, and doing extensive new construction. With the well-known efficiency of armies everywhere, no sooner were the repairs completed than the demolition of the Fort Osborne Barracks began: the land on which the barracks stood was sold to the province in February 1912 to allow space for the construction of the planned new Legislative Building.

Over the next few years, Fort Osborne moved west to its new location in Tuxedo in the former buildings of the Manitoba Agricultural College

General Sam Steele, fourth from the right, arrives to inspect the troops on summer training at Camp Sewell. To his left is Captain Homer-Dixon, son-in-law of Lieutenant-Governor Cameron.

and the old barracks were slowly demolished. The final curtain fell in 1919 when the old, wooden Drill Hall was lost in a spectacular fire.

Beginning in 1912, the annual summer training camps for militia were lengthened and more training took place through the year. The training camps had been declared officially dry, ending the drunkenness that had reached scandalous proportions in the past. The militia was required to train, under Permanent Force instructors, for twelve to sixteen days a year, but not everyone attended the training camps. Only about 40,000 of the 57,000 men in the authorized establishment went to training camps, and one critic estimated that of these, only about 25,000 who could be considered "well trained."[11] Although the turnout was improving by 1912, it was hard to get men to spend time training when the acute labour shortage meant they could earn much higher wages in the summer working at other jobs.

The Winnipeg militia units had their summer training at Camp Sewell, twenty kilometres east of Brandon, from June 30 to July 5. Over 600 members of the 79th Cameron Highlanders, the 90th Winnipeg Rifles, and the 100th Winnipeg Grenadiers climbed aboard

The Winnipeg Grenadiers in their expensive busbies. Behind them is the Hudson's Bay store and the Empire Hotel is visible on the east side of Main Street.

a special twenty-car CPR train on the evening of Saturday, June 29th. The *Free Press* described the scene at the station: "In spite of the sultry, sizzling evening, their departure was marked with a spirit of gaiety and anticipation of five days of excellent training."

When the Winnipeggers arrived at Camp Sewell, they joined militia units from all other parts of the 10th Military District—from Regina to the Lakehead—already in camp. The total number of men under canvas was about 4000. On July 1st the national holiday was celebrated with a huge sports day, complete with music provided by several regimental bands. Civilians from the surrounding country came to enjoy the contests and military music. The camps were important to the local economy because Brandon and Carberry merchants supplied the troops. There is no mistaking the festive, holiday mood that comes through in the newspaper accounts, but presumably some useful training was done during the five days in camp.

Two new militia regiments in Winnipeg had recently been founded: the 79th Cameron Highlanders in 1910 and the 100th Winnipeg Grenadiers in 1908. Both these units reflected the growing population of the city, which enabled Winnipeg to support more than the 90th Winnipeg Rifles, for many years the city's only militia regiment. Colonel Steele was a moving force behind the development of these new units.

At first, money was a problem for the Grenadiers; the elegant officer's uniforms with their fur busbies cost $150 and the bill for outfitting 300 troops was $11,000. But the dress uniforms, the bands and the pomp and ceremony, were key elements in attracting young men to join up and so the money was found and the regiment was established with H.N. Ruttan as colonel. Ruttan, the Winnipeg city engineer, was a veteran of 1885 and a former colonel of the 90th Winnipeg Rifles. In 1912 he was promoted and his replacement was J.B. Mitchell, a former North West Mounted Policeman and an official of the Winnipeg School Division. The Grenadiers' chaplain was Bertal Heeney, the rector of fashionable St. Luke's Church.

The Camerons had begun as a project of the Winnipeg Scottish Society and, when established as a regiment, they were first commanded by R.M. Thomson, another 1885 veteran and a successful Winnipeg lawyer. Thomson had put up the money in 1911 for a company of the Winnipeg Camerons to go to London for George V's coronation. They were the guests of the British Army Cameron regiment and made up part of the Canadian contingent in the Coronation Day parade. Thomson was replaced in 1912 by James Cantlie. The regimental chaplain was C.W. Gordon, the minister of St. Stephen's Church and, under the pen name Ralph Connor, a successful novelist.

In April 1912 a third infantry regiment, the 107th Winnipeg Light Infantry, was established, completing the 20th Infantry Brigade. This was actually a revival of the 92nd Light Infantry Regiment, which had been formed in 1885 to fight in Saskatchewan but which had been disbanded in 1888 because the city could not support two militia units. The first colonel was D. McLean, a former mayor and MLA from north Winnipeg.

The regiment was headquartered at the McGregor Street Armoury and counted many North Enders with non-British backgrounds among its members—Lieutenant E.R. Levinson, a young lawyer, Captain Theodore Stefanik, and Lieutenant Skelatar, one of the city's first Jewish aldermen, turned out next to the English and Scots members of the regiment. Training had commenced in April at Fort Osborne under instructors from the Royal School of Infantry and the regiment was putting together a thirty-two-piece band, an important weapon in attracting new recruits.

The longest established and best known of the Winnipeg militia regiments was the 90th Winnipeg Rifles, a mounted rifles regiment formed in 1883. By 1912 the 90th had an impressive history, having fought in Sudan in 1884, in Saskatchewan in 1885, and in South Africa. The 90th numbered among its officers many powerful and influential businessmen and lawyers. Its honorary colonel was J.A.M. Aikins, a Conservative MP, a wealthy lawyer, the son of a Lieutenant-Governor, and a future Lieutenant-Governor himself.

The regiment played a central role in the ceremonial and symbolic life of the city. The members of the 90th who had been killed fighting Riel in 1885 were memorialized both in St. John's Cathedral churchyard, where they are buried, and with Charles Wheeler's magnificent column on Main Street, located in a place of honour before City Hall. The graves were the focal point of the Decoration Day parade, which, every May 12th, honoured the veterans of all wars and kept alive the memory of the 90th's victory over Riel. Ella Sykes described the 1911 parade.

> On May 12 there was a procession in Winnipeg to commemorate the Fish Creek and Batoche engagements, in which the Red River Rising was put down. A column opposite the Town Hall marks these victories, and from here the bands with detachments of different corps marched by. And then came the veterans. All the men who had fought against Riel strode by in their Sunday best, but wore slouch hats with red bands and a couple of small brown ostrich tips ... the whole procession, on its way to St. John's cemetery to lay flowers on the graves of the dead heroes.[12]

In fact, the Decoration Day Parade commemorated much more than the 1885 campaign against Riel; over 600 active militia, veterans of numerous wars, and Boy Scouts marched in this parade, to the music of various regimental bands. They started at Fort Osborne Barracks with a memorial service and then marched for three and a half hours through the streets all the way to St. John's Cemetery and back. Thousands watched the parade, which included survivors of

Veterans of many British wars, mustered and ready for the Decoration Day Parade.
The man with the side brim of his hat pinned up is a veteran of 1885.

the Wolseley Expedition and the Northwest Rebellion, as well as the
Fenian raids, a naval contingent, and a large group of veterans of the
South African War. Marching with the rest were Sergeant Matthew
Ormoston, who had fought in the Indian Mutiny in the 1850s, and
Captain Bruce, who fought in the Zulu Wars.

The veterans of the Wolseley Expedition and the Northwest
Rebellion were represented in the parade in large numbers. It had only
been twenty-seven years since 1885 and so most of the men who went
to fight Riel were still in their prime and perfectly able to stride along
and take part in the ceremony to honour their fallen comrades. There
were also a number of men who, having come west to fight in 1870,
had stayed in Winnipeg and now formed part of its political and commercial élite. Marching in the parade were Hugh John Macdonald, Sir
John A.'s son, a Conservative politician and magistrate who had been
in uniform during both 1870 and 1885; the banker W.F. Alloway, who
first came west with Wolseley; Charles Bell, the secretary of the Grain
Exchange who, through his work with the Historical Society, was one
of those responsible for creating the historical underpinnings of the
British Ontarioan group that dominated Winnipeg; and Sir Daniel
H. McMillan, former Lieutenant-Governor, Liberal politician, and
wealthy grain merchant, who also served in both 1870 and 1885. It is

likely that these men shared a common view of their military service: that they had helped to secure the West for civilization and progress by crushing two revolts by the wild and savage Métis. For them, the commemoration of the 1885 fighting would have deep political and cultural as well as personal meaning.

The veterans—the soldiers of the past, the militia—the soldiers of the present, and the young Boy Scouts—the soldiers of the future, of Flanders, were cheered by Winnipeggers, who saw war in a romantic, nineteenth-century light. The horrors of World War I, in which 3000 Winnipeggers lost their lives, soon dampened their enthusiasm, but on that sunny May Sunday in 1912, the crowds were happy to cheer the men and feel proud of their victories.

The extent to which the military was involved in the social life of the city seems remarkable to us today and is a measure of the acceptance both the permanent force and the militia enjoyed among the city's élite. Parties like the one given on the evening of May 8 by Colonel Macdonnell and the officers of Lord Strathcona's Horse were attended by young women belonging to the Tupper, Galt, Nanton, McMeans, and many other such families. Flirting with the young officers was an attractive prospect for the young women, and, clearly, their parents thought it was an acceptable way to spend an evening. One of the officers, Captain Thomas Homer-Dixon, was married to the daughter of the Lieutenant-Governor, Donald Cameron. Homer-Dixon came from a wealthy Toronto family. He had defied his father's wishes and joined the British army instead of staying home to make money. He was wounded in the Ashanti War in West Africa, losing his hearing in one ear during a fight with the locals.

Another officer present at the party of May 8 was Count de Bury, a lieutenant, who held out the irresistible allure of European aristocracy. *Town Topics* reported the scene:

> The lower rooms of the officer's mess were all thrown open for dancing, supper being served about midnight in the billiard room. The girls looked particularly fascinating in their powder patches and quaint costumes. Masks were doffed at suppertime, when many surprises ensued.

In December the Cameron Highlanders gave a much more elaborate
ball. Colonel R.M. Thompson and his officers played host at the Royal
Alexandra, as they had for the past two years. It was a much more lavish
affair than the Strathcona's Ball, the Cameron's officers having deeper
pockets. The same kind of upper-middle-class families attended, demonstrating once again the elevated social status enjoyed by the military
in Winnipeg. The regiment took over the second floor of the hotel and
their band provided background music as the guests passed a guard of
honour of about "fifty stalwart kilties" to get to the ballroom.

Winnipeg's Scottish élite—Colonel Thompson and Mrs. Cameron,
the Lieutenant-Governor and Miss Thompson, Major Cantlie and Mrs.
Colin Campbell, Major Osler and Mrs. Waugh, Sir Daniel McMillan
and Lady Schultz, Colin Campbell and Mrs. Cantlie—joined in dancing "two Highland schottisches, strathspey and reel and lightsom and
Reel of Tulloch."

Having a Scottish background did not guarantee that you would
know how to do these old dances: *Town Topics* reported that fifty or
sixty people had been practising "for the event for several weeks."

The dining room of the Royal Alex was decorated with flags and
tartans, and the colours, which had been presented to the regiment
the previous May when the Winnipeg Camerons travelled to London
for the coronation of George V, were displayed near the fireplace. The
description of the Cameron's Ball seems bittersweet when we remember that within four years, many of the men of the 79th Cameron
Highlanders died fighting in France: at Regina Trench alone, 500 of the
Camerons, including Colonel Thomson and many other Winnipeggers,
perished in one of the war's most tragic frontal attacks.

≈ ≈ ≈

On Friday, November 22, a Charity Ball to raise money for the
General Hospital was given by the Women's Hospital Aid Society.
Both the dining room and the ballroom of the Royal Alexandra were
used and a buffet supper was served in the cafe from 10:30 until 1:00
a.m. An official set of Lancers was danced by the Lieutenant-Governor
and Mrs. G. Galt, Mrs. Cameron and F.W. Drewery, A.M. Nanton

Fox hunting near Winnipeg, 1912.

and Mrs. Homer-Dixon, Colin Campbell and Mrs. W. Alloway, and other couples.

In 1912 government grants made up a very small, although growing, proportion of the funding for agencies like the hospital, and the fundraising work of women like Mrs. Galt was extremely important. She and other ladies of her circle provided a great deal of the funding for the social agencies that were struggling to improve conditions in the poorer districts of the city.

The Margaret Scott Mission is one example of such an agency. The mission had operated out of 99 George Street, a building that still exists, since 1905. The mortgage had been paid off in 1912, thanks to a bequest from Hugo Ross, who died on the *Titanic* and whose mother and sister-in-law were both board members. By 1912 the mission employed eight trained nurses who visited new mothers and poor, sick people in their homes. The nurses were credited with reducing infant deaths in Winnipeg, which had the highest number of such deaths in Canada. The mission also started a program, later taken over by the school division, which taught schoolgirls about the principles of good health and nutrition. Board members such as Mrs. Augustus Nanton, Mrs. D.C. Cameron, Mrs. Stewart Tupper, Mrs. E.L. Drewery, and Mrs. Matheson, the Anglican Archbishop's wife, donated funds and raised funds from local firms and individuals.

The fundraising efforts of these and many other women continued year-round. Easter Saturday was Violet Day. To raise funds for the newly constructed Children's Hospital, ladies and girls went out selling artificial flowers. In 1912 the one-day event netted the enormous sum of $6750, mostly for the maintenance fund. In May, Mrs. Gordon Bell, the wife of the deputy minister of education, organized the annual tag day for the Ninette Sanatorium for tuberculosis patients.

Tuberculosis was a major disease in 1912, although the previous decade had seen the development of many innovations—new drugs, the use of sanatoria where patients were treated with good food and lots of time in the open air—which were slowly bringing it under control. *Town Topics* reported that since June 1910, when the facility opened, 274 tuberculosis patients had been admitted. Sitting on a wooded slope above the beautiful Pelican Lake in southwestern Manitoba, the sanatorium was successfully battling the terrible disease. The board included a number of Winnipeg people—Augustus Nanton, the Reverend C.W. Gordon, who had donated a cottage that could accommodate five patients, and E.L. Drewry were all board members. The IODE had made tuberculosis one of its main causes and the Brandon chapter had played a large role in building the facility. The Fort Garry IODE, under the leadership of Mrs. Colin Campbell, paid for one of the cottages at Ninette.

These are a tiny sampling of the widespread and comprehensive network of committees and boards representing all areas of the city and all classes and ethnic groups, which worked constantly to raise funds for good causes. Women played a major role in these activities and it was one of the areas in which they had an important impact on the life of the city.

~~ ~

A social event of a very different nature took place in November, when the Winnipeg Hunt Club held its annual meeting at the end of hunting season. The club, founded in 1908 and located in Charleswood, moved in the fall of 1912 to new quarters by the Red River, next to the new Manitoba Agricultural College, south of the city. The new clubhouse, which became the largest and most luxurious in western Canada, was almost complete in November. *Town Topics* expressed enthusiasm for the new building and the social life that would go on there.

Once opened, however, it is certain to attain immediate prominence as one of Winnipeg's favorite out-of-town resorts, which are not too numerous yet. Everything connected with the interior service will, of course, be upon the highest plane of club management, and the privilege of living in the country amid ideal sylvan surroundings, while within easy access of the city, is something that will undoubtedly be appreciated and taken advantage of by many. During the winter the members can run out to the club in a very few minutes by automobile, as the road is paved to the club-house gates. It is just a nice distance to ride or drive, to give a keen appetite for dinner, then in summer, the river affords another pleasant avenue of transportation.

There were plans to buy a launch that could take Winnipeg's busy entrepreneurs up the Red River to downtown after early-morning hunting, so they could be at their desks making money by 9:00 a.m. Only in Winnipeg would the aristocratic sport of fox hunting have to accommodate itself to the need to be at the office for the opening of business.

The club also had a huntsman's cottage, stables, and kennels for the hounds, and they were all occupied by November. A very successful hunting season had just come to an end and the future looked bright. *Town Topics* foresaw real benefits in the improvement of riding in general:

One thing the formation of a hunt club in Winnipeg has already done is to increase the number and improve the standard of hunters and saddle horses. This promises well for our forthcoming horse shows, and will mean keen competition and large entries in hunter and saddle classes. One very interesting feature of future horse shows should be the large entries of ladies hunters and saddle horses, judging by the numbers who have ridden to hounds this season.

At the club's annual meeting, the membership was fixed at 200 men and 100 women. It was said that this was the number the club can accommodate, and, *Town Topics* said, "it looks as though there will be a waiting list started at once with a long period of suspense attached to it, as is the case with other clubs of a social nature, whose attractions appeal to a greater number of people than their facilities can accommodate." Restricting membership to a certain number was also the best way to give the Hunt Club a highly desirable exclusivity.

The people involved with the club were the same society leaders who supported the Horse Show. The honorary president of the club was Douglas Cameron; the president, Augustus Nanton. The Master of the Fox Hounds was J.S. Hough, the Nantons' neighbour on Roslyn Road. Directors and committee members included W.H. Gardner, Captain Homer-Dixon, Major J.A. Cantlie, John Galt, W.J. Tupper, H.F. Osler, R.W. Paterson, and Walter Moss, all wealthy members of the Winnipeg élite.

The Hunt Club operated for a very short time; its activities came to an end with the outbreak of the war. After World War I, hunting was replaced by golf and the Southwood Golf Club took over the clubhouse and other facilities.

DECEMBER

Christmas, Old Timer's Ball

Winnipeg's stores had a wonderful Christmas season in 1912. The weather was warm and there was money in the city; most people had had work all year and some had made huge profits from the boom. Extra help had been hired and the papers were full of Christmas ads for Ashdown's, Birk's, Eaton's, the Hudson's Bay Company, and many other stores. Eaton's and the Hudson's Bay store spent enormous amounts on publicity, employing full-time staff to produce full-page ads for all the Winnipeg papers. The ads emphasized prices, suggesting that people in the city were out to find a bargain and decided on the basis of price where to shop. The ads also constituted a sophisticated "campaign," which started with reminders to shop early and avoid the crowds, and ended a few days before Christmas with lists of one-dollar items suitable for last-minute shoppers.

Ruth Harvey, the daughter of C.P. and Harriet Anderson Walker, owners of the Walker Theatre, recalled a girlhood shopping trip with her mother to the old Hudson's Bay store on Main. They entered the store near the grocery department, which was at the back.

> To step inside there on a December day, half blinded by the dazzle of sun on snow, was to be Ali Baba entering the vast gloom of the treasure cave. For a moment I could see only dimly the laden shelves and counters. But even before my eyes had adjusted to the light my nostrils were aware of many odors— coffee, apples, warm bread, spices, tea and oranges, mingled

with others pleasant but unidentifiable, in a symphonic smell of good food.[1]

Shopping was a dignified process, as Harvey remembers it. "Mama and I moved with leisure from section to section.... In due time our purchases would be sent to the house in a sleigh drawn by a horse with jingling bells on its harness. At each department we sat down on the chairs there and mamma took out her list. The clerk displayed, measured, weighed, and suggested." She lingers over the biscuits, describing them in loving detail:

> Here were the everyday biscuits and the special-treat biscuits. The bins behind the counter held the ordinary ones: social teas, fig newtons, oval arrowroots for the nursery, raisin biscuits and ginger snaps. But on the shelves above were tins of plumcake and shortbread from Edinburgh, and boxes and boxes of the very finest biscuits from England. They were packed for the colonies: boxed in tin and soldered tight against heat and cold and damp. From England they went by ship over the globe, to all the big red splashes on the map and all the tiny red pinpricks dotting the blue expanses of the oceans.... Every moment of my day and night, it was tea time someplace or other in the Empire. People were warming the pot, measuring the tea leaves, pouring on the boiling water, and perhaps while the tea steeped opening a box of biscuits like these.

The last stop in the store was to buy wines and liquors, where,

> as mamma ordered, the names took on an aura of festivity. First, claret for the holiday dinners. Even the children would have a few drops of claret in their glasses—enough to make the water a faint pink and to make us feel regal. Then brandy, to put around the pudding and set alight. And sherry, to serve to callers and put in the grownups pudding sauce.... And now mamma asked for rum. That was for past Christmas, for New Year's Day. It would go into the punch bowl with brandy and lemons and sugar and spices and hot water.

Winnipeg stores used every means to advertise, even an elephant from a visiting circus.

The Bay's ads at Christmas 1912 offered a bewildering mass of possible gifts. Just like today, everything was on sale and prices appeared to bear no relation to the actual value of the goods. Leather mitts with wool lining were selling for $4.50; for $1.25 more you could buy a wooden writing desk. Morris chairs were $9.50.

The Hudson's Bay store that Ruth Harvey remembered stood on the southwest corner of Main and York, a Victorian brick building of the 1880s, far from the retail district that was developing between Eaton's new store and Portage and Main. By 1912 the Bay was preparing to move their business to Portage Avenue as well, but it had been difficult convincing the London Committee to do that. When it had become known, in 1904, that Eaton's was going to build a department store in the city, the local Hudson's Bay Company commissioner, Clarence Chipman, had counselled the London board to expand the Main Street store, so they could continue to do business "in the face of any competition that may arise." The board refused to panic and approved only a $43,000 facelift to modernize the store.

No doubt, the renovations helped to keep the store from going under in the face of the Eaton's onslaught: in 1905 the Hudson's Bay

The Hudson's Bay store at Main and York.

sales figures declined by eleven per cent, but they did escape the fate of two other local department stores, Nash, Carson and Naylor, and Imperial Dry Goods, which were forced to close the first year Eaton's was in operation.

The continued growth of the city finally convinced the London board to approve a new Portage Avenue store and in February 1911, they authorized the local real estate firm of Oldfield, Kirby and Gardner to spend up to $1,000,000 to acquire lots south of Portage Avenue between Vaughan and Colony streets. The site was large, but the local Sales Shop commissioner, H.E. Burbidge, who was the son of the manager of Harrods in London, wanted to be sure the company had enough room for future expansion. Eaton's had not acquired enough property in their first purchase and had paid astronomical prices for land when they expanded their store. Burbidge took great care to keep the acquisitions quiet, in order to keep the prices down. Messages were telegraphed to and from London in code and Burbidge received correspondence at his rooms in the Royal Alexandra, rather than at his office.

At first W.H. Gardner, who was handling the purchases, was able to get some lots at less than market value; by March 15, 1911, he had secured, for $850,000, more than three-quarters of the land now occupied by the store. But then the news leaked out: on March 17 the *Free Press* ran a story reporting that Gardner was buying up lots for a British client. A speculative frenzy ensued. One woman who owned a house in the area received seventeen phone calls in one day from people trying to buy her property. A certain Charles McCarrey, who had purchased a lot for $12,000 a few weeks before, was now offered $14,000 for it. He refused and said he would hold out for double his money.

By April 1, in spite of the speculators, Burbidge was able to report to London that all the land had been purchased, with the exception of a short crescent of houses near St. Mary's Street, for which the price was too high. The final bill: $950,000, just within the authorized million dollars. The real estate fever moved elsewhere, but there were hard feelings. Several landowners accused Gardner of misleading them and there were a number of court cases, including one brought in November 1912 by Michael and Martin Kelly, partners in the successful contracting firm of Thomas Kelly and Sons. They had sold property on Portage Avenue between Vaughan and Colony but were not told about the Hudson's Bay store, and claimed that the price they were paid was too low.

Gardner survived with his profits intact. Although the London board authorized money to begin excavations in July 1913, the work was delayed and the new store finally fell victim to the economic downturn that set in that year. The land remained vacant for fifteen years, hidden behind advertising billboards, an embarrassing symbol of Winnipeg's reduced circumstances. It was 1927 before the new Hudson's Bay store began to rise on the corner of Portage and Vaughan.

For the shopping public, the new Eaton's store on Portage Avenue had, by 1912, become the western anchor for retail business on Portage. In December the full-page *Eaton's Store News* appeared every day and sometimes twice on Saturdays. The *News* alerted children to the store's Santa Claus Parade on November 30. Santa started out on Pembina, inexplicably entering the city from the south, and made his way from the underpass north to Stradbrook, then turned west. He travelled along Wellington Crescent to the Maryland Bridge and down Maryland to Portage, where he turned east and headed for the store.

Santa's image was not standardized in 1912. Instead of the roly-poly Santa with red cheeks that we are used to, he was often quite thin,

this Western Country, and to all friends, this store extends its
heartiest Eaton Greeting and Good Wishes for

A Very Merry Christmas and

A Happy New Year

THE **T. EATON C**O LIMITED

Santa helps Eaton's wish their customers a Merry Christmas.

giving his smiles a slightly sinister appearance at times. He was shown
in one Eaton's ad wearing a holly wreath around the fur trim of his hat,
an older, Victorian ornamentation.

At the store, Santa was available during certain hours morning and
afternoon to shake hands with the children and show them the mound
of toys in his massive toy trunk. There they would see plush animals,
dolls, tin automobiles and trains, games, and sports equipment.

Anyone walking east of Eaton's along Portage Avenue toward
Main Street would find plenty of shops, especially on the north side
of the broad avenue. There were small clothing stores like Stiles and
Humphries Clothing, Cornell Clothing, and Decatur and Ferguson
Clothing. There were a number of restaurants on this stretch of
Portage: the Olympia Cafe, the Venice Cafe, the Alberta Café, and
a Bowes Dairy Lunch, one of a number of Bowes outlets in the city.
These cafes were busiest at lunch when the office buildings around
Portage and Main disgorged their many typists and clerks and bosses
for the noon meal. The offices around the busy corner were occupied
by lawyers, real estate agents, trust companies, loan companies, and

insurance agents, all of which employed managers, clerks, stenographers, and messengers. The owners and managers were likely to give the Bowes Lunch a miss and go down Main in the first block south of Portage to eat at the Carlton Club or the Conservative Adanac Club. Or they might walk or take a cab all the way to the Manitoba Club on Broadway for their lunch.

Rounding the corner and heading north on the west side of Main, pedestrians encountered a mixture of offices and retail businesses, although by 1912 office buildings were definitely predominant. The Canadian Northern building, with its ticket office and telegraph office, stood next to Gordon Mitchell's Drug Store and Jerry Robinson's Department Store. While not as big as Eaton's or the Bay, Robinson's store was a profitable local business. Robinson had just completed a new addition that year, which expanded the rear of the store all the way back to Albert Street. The Main Street show window had a large display of lady's purses, all different and all costing $6.68. Robinson's sold everything you would expect to find in a large dry goods store, plus groceries.

Further north stood the McIntyre Block, with its seven floors of every kind of office imaginable—lawyers, insurance agents, tailors, and so on. Holt Renfrew was still doing business on this block of Main Street in 1912.

Across McDermot, past the CPR telegraph office, stood the Blue Store, Chevrier and Sons Clothing, "Outfitters to Mankind." This business dated from the 1870s when Noe Chevrier, who became a senator, opened his clothing store. Many people in Winnipeg couldn't read then, so he painted the store blue and called it the Blue Store, so they could find it. Earlier in 1912 the building and land had been sold, along with much of the rest of the block, to Sir Herbert Holt, the Montreal billionaire, for close to a million dollars. It was expected that the old store and its neighbours would soon come down to make way for a new office building. The belief was that Main Street would soon be all office buildings and the shopping district would move to Portage Avenue, because of the draw of Eaton's. This change did take place slowly and surely, and by 1929, when Jerry Robinson's finally closed, Main Street had very few retail establishments.

In 1912, Ashdown's store on the north side of Bannatyne marked the northern limit of the principal retail area. Beyond Ashdown's, the

Main Street in 1912. On the left, flying several Union Jacks, is Robinson's Department Store. Looming beside it is the McIntyre Block. On the right are the classical façade of the new Bank of Commerce headquarters and the new Union Trust Building, both still under construction.

Union Bank Building, with the Confederation Life Building across the street, marked the gateway to downtown for people coming from the north. The east side of the street was mostly office buildings like the beautiful new Bank of Commerce Building, officially opened in October. Farther up, across from City Hall and north of Pacific all the way to the Royal Alexandra, were many shops and offices and other businesses owned by Jewish businessmen. One of these was a young and ambitious Sam Bronfman who, with his father and brothers, owned the Bell Hotel. Rising above all these small businesses like a beached luxury liner, the Royal Alexandra stood on the corner of Higgins Avenue and Main Street.

Isolated though it may have been, the Royal Alexandra was still the best hotel in the city in December 1912. The Fort Garry was taking shape on Broadway but it did not officially open until the end of 1913. The Royal Alex had the Christmas season all to itself for one last time.

The Old Timer's Ball was one of the main social events in the hotel every year in December. In 1912, the tenth annual Old Timer's Ball was on December 18. It was hosted and organized by a slightly different group from those who sponsored most of the notable events at the hotel. The current Lieutenant-Governor's wife and the previous one, Mrs. Cameron and Lady McMillan, were involved, as were the wife of the mayor and Lady Roblin, the premier's wife, giving the ball an official tone. But many of the other women organizers were not from the upper crust. Mrs. J.T. Huggard, for example, was married to a reasonably prosperous lawyer, but the fact that he had come to the city in 1872 was the real basis for her involvement. Mrs. George Black's husband was the Provincial Auditor. They lived in a solid middle-class house at 244 Balmoral, not a background that would normally put them into the company of Mrs. Cameron. But Black had come to Manitoba with Garnet Wolseley's expedition in 1870 and was, therefore, a member of a very select group, one which was honoured and respected not for how much money they had, but because they had made the epic journey through northern Ontario to crush the rebel Riel.

People like James Ashdown and his wife, who were not usually mentioned in the society columns, would nevertheless come to this event because of its broader significance. The Ashdowns were very wealthy but the reason they were present at the ball was that they were true "old timers," having come to Winnipeg in the early days. The young English immigrant Ashdown, like a sort of prairie Dick Whittington, walked from St. Paul to his adopted home in the 1860s. Like Whittington, he became a wealthy merchant, leading citizen, and mayor of his adopted home. The Ashdowns, strict Methodists, were said to have preferred a quiet evening at home, reading the bible. But for the Old Timer's Ball, they made an exception.

Edward Drewery, another Englishman, came to Winnipeg in 1877 and his brother Fred followed in 1881. Together, they built the phenomenally successful Red Wood Brewery. The Drewerys were devout Anglicans and devoted family people who seemed to prefer to entertain on a small scale, inviting only their own children and their spouses to their home beside the brewery. However, the Drewerys came to the ball.

The Old Timer's Ball united people from different social levels in the common activity of commemorating the city's history, as seen through the eyes of the English Ontarioans who had driven Riel out and assumed a dominant role in Manitoba. Everything about the event hearkened back to Red River days. Even the invitation always had an old Red River scene engraved on the back. In 1912 the picture showed the old Cathedral of St. Boniface and a verse from Whittier's "The Bells of St. Boniface" appeared beside the illustration. The band of the 100th Grenadiers supplied the music for the program of twenty dances that were of a strictly "old time" variety. The evening began with a set of Lancers, an elaborate quadrille, a little like modern square dancing. Then came a mixture of Scottish dancing and local dances—the Red River jig, Highland Schottische, and eight hand reels.

Events like the ball seemed to make the history of the Red River settlement part of the Ontario immigrants' own history. By adopting the Scottish Selkirk Settlers as "imaginary ancestors," as one modern historian has put it, they grafted the Selkirk Settlers to their own histories and created a cultural tradition, just as ambitious New Yorkers constructed pedigrees that linked them with the revolutionary or even older Dutch and English colonial worlds, "to justify their assumption of dominance in the region."[2]

Dr. George Bryce of Manitoba College, a prolific writer of histories of Manitoba and the West, had produced yet another history in 1912, to celebrate the centennial of the arrival of the Selkirk Settlers.[3] One of themes Bryce included in many of his works was the triumph of civilization, as represented by the Selkirk Settlers and the later settlers from Ontario, over the wild and savage original people of the prairies. The Old Timer's Ball, as well as events like the Decoration Day parade in May and the widespread participation in "first footing," or New Year's social calls, on New Year's Day, all tended to support Bryce's vision and connect the community's modern leaders with the Selkirk Settlers of Red River days.

There were many other dances and parties in the hotel that December. On Monday, December 23, Mrs. G.J. Bury, the wife of the new western vice-president of the CPR, entertained in the Vice Regal suite of the Royal Alex. Her guest list for what must have been an official CPR Christmas dinner, the first she would have hosted, consisted of most of

Skating on the Assiniboine River.

the upper crust of Winnipeg, including the Lieutenant-Governor and Mrs. Cameron, and the Honourable Robert and Mrs. Rogers.

Outside the warm glow of Winnipeg's grand hotel, social events crowded the calendar. Several brides who had been married in the fall months hosted their first social events as married women. On Wednesday, December 4, Mrs. Frank Girdlestone entertained in her mother's house at 207 Academy Road. As was the custom, the young woman wore her wedding gown. A few days later, Mrs. W.L. McIntosh, formerly Miss Louise Robertson, entertained for two consecutive days in her suite in Lilac Court, also wearing her wedding gown. Mrs. W.H. Gardner, her mother, helped her out. Mrs. Henry Sellers, née Irene Mouslon, held her post-nuptial reception at her new home at 943 McMillan, helped by her mother and a few friends.

On Monday, December 9, Mrs. R.M. Dennistoun entertained at dinner in her house on Roslyn Road in honour of Miss Fetherstonhaugh of Montreal. She invited several Winnipeg couples and one or two eligible bachelors. Was Mrs. Dennistoun trying to match the well-off Montrealer with a Winnipeg groom? It is possible; several well-off young women from other cities were mentioned in the society columns during the year, staying with acquaintances in Winnipeg and honoured at various lunches and teas. The guest lists usually included one or two bachelors who might have been having trouble finding a wife in a city where men outnumbered women.

The palatial rotunda of the Royal Alexandra Hotel. In December 1912, the larger Fort
Garry Hotel was under construction and the Royal Alexandra was still the centre of
holiday entertaining.

A few days later, the first meeting of the afternoon skating club
proved to be a great success. The club met at the Horse Show
Amphitheatre, which was flooded in the winter for hockey and skating. The ice was judged to be good and the music excellent reported
Town Topics on December 28th: "The enthusiasm is very strong this
year and the members are keenly interested in waltzing and figure
skating." If a competent instructor was secured, Mrs. Robert Rogers
and Mrs. Morton Morse had promised to donate prizes for waltzing
and simpler figures.

There was public skating every day at the Amphitheatre, from two
to four in the afternoon and eight to ten in the evening. Ladies' tickets
were slightly less expensive than men's—six for a dollar versus five
for a dollar—to encourage the fairer sex. There was outdoor skating
nearby on the Assiniboine River just east of the Osborne Bridge, but
on cold days the Amphitheatre was much more comfortable.

On Christmas Day, Mrs. Jerry Robinson, whose husband owned the
department store, entertained her grandchildren at a "Christmas tree"
in her home on Wellington Crescent. The children were lucky to have

as grandparents the owners of one of the largest department stores in the city, a treasure trove of presents. Two days later Mrs. Nanton had a Christmas tree for her youngest son Augustus and his friends from 4:00 to 6:00, where "A mammoth Christmas tree was laden with gifts for each lad and lassie present, Mr. C.M. Taylor in a Santa Claus disguise presenting the gifts. A number of proud mothers joined the party at the tea hour."

On Christmas night, many people entertained with dinners and dances. Mrs. George Galt, whose house was often full of people, "entertained a group of 18. A large number of dinner parties ended up there and a jolly dance was enjoyed." Her neighbour, Mrs. Vere Brown, Mrs. Arthur Rogers, and Mrs. Hugh Sutherland also presided over large Christmas dinners in their beautiful homes. All over the city, families, from the very rich to the very poor, did the same. Winnipeggers in 1912 displayed the same charitableness that they do today at Christmas.

There were a number of different drives to raise money for poor families. The *Telegram* newspaper had its own Santa Claus, who collected money and then bought presents for children who would not otherwise receive one. The paper printed pictures of poor children in the city to loosen their readers' purse strings and dispatched a fleet of volunteer drivers in their cars to deliver the gifts. The campaign raised a lot of money. The workers in the CPR shops alone sent in the substantial sum of $249.

The 1913 New Year's reception at Government House attracted more visitors than it had for some years. Perhaps people wanted to greet the new Lieutenant-Governor, hosting the levy for the first time. The military were much in evidence, and very smart they looked in their handsome uniforms, a reassuring presence, given the news from Europe. The beginning of the new year was accompanied by the murmur of voices in Government House, an occasional burst of laughter, the steady movement of traffic in the streets as people went about "first footing," the warm welcomes at front doors as friends came to make their New Year's call, and the hiss of the wind in the bare branches of the trees. The city was beginning another year, full of confidence and hope, expecting, no doubt, that 1913 would be the year that Winnipeg would come fully into its own and surpass Toronto and Montreal in even more ways than in 1912.

But that was not to be. Rumours of war slowly cut off the flow of British capital during 1913. Winnipeg and the rest of western Canada did their best to keep the investment coming, but Britain became increasingly focussed on building ships and making guns for the great bloodletting ahead. In May 1913, Premier Roblin wrote an article for *Dominion Magazine* in the usual boosterish tone of that publication. He said that although some Canadian bond issues were not selling in London, a recent Manitoba loan was successfully floated and was actually oversubscribed. He was not surprised at this because, "If a concern of any kind is sound financially and its securities are desired and sought after, I do not think there is much wrong with it. This applies as much to a province as it does to a business concern."

But Sir Rodmond's reassuring words could not prevent the inevitable, and Winnipeg and Manitoba soon suffered for lack of investment capital along with the rest of western Canada. Bankruptcies and reduced standards of living for everyone followed.

It is often said that the building of the Panama Canal was a major factor in ending Winnipeg's dominant position in western Canada. Certainly, the canal was recognized at the time as an important development. In November, *Town Topics* reprinted an article from *Saturday Night*, by Agnes Laut, a nationally known journalist and a Winnipegger, in which she wrote about the effect of the Panama Canal. It was to be finished in 1913 and open in 1915. Vancouver would suddenly become the front door to Canada, not the back door. Some steamship companies were going to add only another five to ten dollars to the cost of a steerage ticket to take people to the west coast ports. Laut expressed concern that all up and down the east and west coasts of the US, ports were expanding their facilities in order to accommodate new trade, but Canada was doing nothing to get ready.

In reality, given the interruption of the war and the fact that the Port of Vancouver did not have facilities, including large grain elevators, to handle increased volumes until the 1920s, the canal did not have as much impact on Winnipeg as is sometimes claimed. It was not until 1919, when the Board of Grain Commissioners sent a test cargo through the canal, that it was established that grain could be safely shipped, without spoiling, by that route.

Of much greater significance was the abrupt end of foreign investment in the West in 1913, and the drop-off in immigration brought on by the war. This, coupled with the growth of Winnipeg's rivals, Calgary, Edmonton, Vancouver, and Regina, stalled the city's growth and greatly weakened its position of dominance over the prairie region.

Like all Canadian cities, Winnipeg suffered the loss of some of its best young men during the war and Winnipeggers poured vast sums into the war effort, surpassing other cities in their purchase of war bonds and their donations to war charities. The city never really recovered after the war; the conditions that had produced the great boom that ended in 1912 never reappeared and Winnipeg's influence suffered a long, slow decline.

In early 1913, however, Winnipeggers still dreamed of a glorious future. Let's give the last word to Sir Rodmond Roblin, writing in the November 1913 issue of *Dominion Magazine* about one of his favourite dreams, the Hudson Bay Railroad. In this quote we get a hint of the ringing phrases of his great speeches, but we also catch a glimpse of Roblin the promoter, the booster, who, like so many Winnipeggers of his generation, never really stopped selling the dream of a bright tomorrow.

> I would like to live long enough to see what this country will be like 25 or 40 years from now, to witness the glories of the future. I believe it will have cities of five million on Hudson's Bay. You see all we have to do is build a road from Gypsumville to The Pas and we will connect with the Hudson Bay Rail Road and establish a direct route to Scotland three days shorter than any other.

On a quiet summer afternoon, I drove into St. John's Cathedral graveyard. I wanted to visit the people who had created the Winnipeg of 1912, the people who made it the third city in the Dominion, a city with a shot at real greatness. So many of them are there, you see, buried within a few paces of one another. In the first path over from the cathedral is the grave of Sir William Whyte, of the CPR. Under a high, white stone monument with his wife, he lies facing the church. On one side of him lies his neighbour, Fred Heubach, who laid out the garden suburb of Tuxedo but died in July 1914, far too soon to see it become reality. Walk toward the river to the next path and there, under a beautiful Celtic cross, lies Sir Augustus Nanton, who encompassed all that was best about his city: charitable, serious, honest, but yet a dreamer too. He wore himself out during the war, raising money and looking after the families of men who were overseas. In 1923 the death of his partner forced him to leave his home of forty years and return to Toronto to take up one last burden and become president of the Dominion Bank. He died in Toronto a year later but was brought home to Winnipeg to be buried here among the trees in St. John's churchyard.

Less than seven metres away, closer to the river still, we find the grave of Sir Douglas Cameron, Nanton's friend, whose son married the Nantons' daughter. Cameron continued to serve as the Lieutenant-Governor until 1916, when he had the unpleasant task of bringing the political impasse over the Legislative Building scandal to an end by convincing Rodmond Roblin to resign. Cameron died shortly after, in 1921, and was buried here under a magnificent brown monument. Nearby can be found his successor, Lieutenant-Governor J.A.M. Aikins, and Colin Campbell, Roblin's Attorney General, who died in 1914. Standing alone in a circular spot in the path is the monument to James Ashdown, who came to Red River in the 1860s with his tinsmithing tools and died a millionaire in 1924. The monument is surmounted by a statue and proclaims the worldly success of this hard-working Methodist for all to see. How many young men took heart from the career of plucky little James Ashdown, Winnipeg's Dick Whittington.

We will leave them in peace in the beautiful cemetery and make our way back out into the streets of the city that, in many ways, was their creation and remains as their real monument.

Endnotes

Introduction
1. *Dominion Magazine* (November 1911): 243.
2. Marilyn Baker, *Symbol in Stone* (Winnipeg: Hyperion Press, 1988), 25.
3. Editorial, *Dominion Magazine* (January 1912).
4. George Schull, *100 Years of Banking: A History of the Toronto Dominion Bank* (Toronto: Copp Clark, 1958), 87.
5. James Gray, *Red Lights on the Prairies* (Saskatoon: Fifth House, 1995), 59.
6. Michael Mancharuk, *The Ukrainian Canadians: A History* (Winnipeg: Ukrainian Free Academy of Sciences, 1970), 67.
7. Victor Turek, *Poles in Manitoba* (Toronto: Polish Alliance Press, 1967), 71.

January
1. Catherine Donzel, *Grand Hotels of North America* (Toronto: McClelland and Stewart, 1989), 204.
2. Marion Harland, *Everyday Etiquette* (Indianapolis: Bobbs-Merrill, 1907), Introduction.
3. Lillian Gibbons, *Stories Houses Tell* (Winnipeg: Hyperion Press, 1980), 122.
4. Alice Weiss, *A Little Girl Remembers* (n.p., 1983), 40.
5. Emily Holt, *Encyclopedia of Etiquette* (Toronto: Musson Book Co., 1916), 26.
6. Anne Springsteed, *The Expert Waitress* (New York: Harper & Brothers, 1912), 58.
7. J.W. Chafe, *An Apple for the Teacher* (Winnipeg: Winnipeg School Division No. 1, 1967), 68.
8. Peter Morris, *Embattled Shadows: A History of Canadian Cinema 1985–1939* (Montreal: McGill-Queen's University Press, 1992), 20.
9. Ruth Harvey, *Curtain Time* (Boston: Houghton Mifflin, 1949), 153.

February
1. Ella Sykes, *A Home Help in Canada* (London: G. Bell, 1912), 33–34.
2. Ibid., 33.
3. W.H.P. Jarvis, *The Letters of a Remittance Man to His Mother* (Toronto: Musson Book Company, 1909), 48.
4. *Dominion Magazine* (October 1911).
5. *The Work of Women and Girls in Department Stores in Winnipeg*, (Winnipeg: University Women's Club, 1914).
6. Ibid., 10.
7. Ibid., 11.
8. Jarvis, *Remittance Man*, 81.
9. *Labour Gazette* (1912): 631.
10. E.G. Ingham, *Sketches in Western Canada* (Toronto: Hoddart and Stoughton, 1913), 30–31.

11. Lt. Colonel J. D. Sinclair, *Westminister Church: 45th Year* (Winnipeg, 1937), 47.

12. Ibid., 51.

March

1. *Canadian Annual Review* (1912): 493.

2. Archives of Manitoba, Colin H. Campbell Papers, Correspondence, October-December 1913, Letter of November 10, 1913.

3. *Manitoba Free Press*, February 27, 1912.

4. E.A.Wharton Gill, *Love in Manitoba* (Toronto: Musson Book Company, 1911), 261.

5. Randy Rostecki, ed., "Personal Recollections: The Jewish Pioneer Past on the Prairies," *Jewish Life and Times*, vol. vi (Winnipeg: Jewish Historical Society of Western Canada, 1993), 80.

6. G. Paterson, *Report of the Royal Commission Constituted to Inquire into and Report on All Expenditures for Road Work during the Year 1914* (Winnipeg: King's Printer, 1917).

7. D.N. Irvine, "Reform War and Industrial Crisis in Manitoba: F.J. Dixon and the Framework of Consensus 1903–1920," MA thesis, University of Manitoba, 1981, p. 40.

8. Nellie McClung, *Black Creek Stopping House and Other Stories* (Toronto: William Briggs, 1912).

9. Arthur Grenke, *The German Community in Winnipeg, 1872–1919* (New York: AMS Press, 1991), 96.

10. Letter Book, Minister of Public Works, 1911–1913.

11. Ibid.

12. *Canadian Annual Review* (1912): 491.

13. K. Judson, *Selected Articles on Government Ownership of Telegraph and Telephone* (New York: HW Wilson, 1914), 29.

14. James Mavor, *Government Telephones: The Experience of Manitoba* (New York: Moffat Yard and Co., 1916), 76–77.

15. Ibid., 113.

16. For a detailed discussion of this issue, see J.E. Rae, "How Winnipeg Was Nearly Won," in A.R. McCormack, ed., *Cities in the West: Papers of the Canadian Urban History Conference, University of Winnipeg, October, 1974* (Ottawa: National Museums, 1975).

17. *Manitoba Free Press*, March 20, 1912.

April

1. Canada Sessional Papers, 1913, No. 6, "Shareholders in Chartered Banks."

2. Gibbons, *Stories Houses Tell*, 122.

3. Ibid.

4. J.W. Dafoe, "Early Winnipeg Newspapers," in *Transactions of the Manitoba Historical Society*, Series III, No. 3, 1947, p. 23.

5. *Annual Financial Review* (Toronto: Houston's Standard Publications, 1913), 224.

6. Henry Gadsby, "Retrospect of the Session," *University Magazine* 11 (April 1912): 184.

7. Archives of Manitoba, MJB Campbell Papers, P2495, Letter of April 23, 1912.

8. Gibbons, *Stories Houses Tell*, 122.

9 Sidney Low, *Egypt in Transition* (New York: Macmillan, 1914), 157.

10. "William Sloper," in Encyclopedia Titanica, http://www.encyclopedia-titanica.org/bio/p/1st/sloper_wt.shtml, accessed January 2004. The details about the Winnipeg passengers were taken from this source.

11. *Town Topics*, May 11, 1912.

May
1. *Royal Commission on the Municipal Finances and Administration of the City of Winnipeg* (Winnipeg: King's Printer, 1939), 335. For a complete account of the struggle to get the main line of the CPR to run through Winnipeg, see Alan Artibise, *Winnipeg: A Social History of Urban Growth* (Montreal: McGill-Queen's University Press, 1975), 66–67.

2. Reuben Bellan, *Winnipeg First Century: An Economic History* (Winnipeg: Queenston House Press, 1978), 61.

3. Harold Innis, *A History of the C.P.R.* (Toronto: McClelland and Stewart, 1923), 212, 221.

4. Joseph Adams, *Ten Thousand Miles Through Canada* (London: Methuen, 1912), 128.

5. Frederick Talbot, *The Making of a Great Canadian Railway* (London: Seeley Service and Company, 1912), 142.

6. Canada Sessional Papers, 1913, No. 37, Annual Report of the National Transcontinental Railway Commissioners.

7. *Canada Yearbook*, 1912, p. 315.

8. John Eagle, *The Canadian Pacific Railway and the Development of the Canadian West, 1896–1914* (Montreal: McGill-Queens University Press, 1989), 103.

9. Alfred Price, *Rail Life: A Book of Yarns* (Toronto: Thomas Allen, 1925), 67.

10. Ibid., 72.

11. Ibid., 256.

12. Doug Smith, *Let Us Rise: A History of the Manitoba Labour Movement* (Vancouver: New Star Books, 1985), 18.

13. *Labour Gazette* (1912): 1068.

14. Price, *Rail Life*, 235.

15. Ibid., 21.

16. Ibid., 251.

June
1. City of Winnipeg, Department of Health, *Annual Report,* 1912, p. 26.

2. *Town Topics*, November 9, 1912.

3. Winnipeg City Archives, City Council Document no. 9653, 4, December 2, 1912.

4. Ibid.

5. Conrad S. Riley, *C.S. Riley* (Winnipeg: self-published, 1955), 16.

6. P.D. Stevens, ed., *The 1911 Election: A Study in Politics* (Toronto: Copp Clark, 1970), 108.

7. Elizabeth Ewing, *History of Twentieth Century Fashion* (London: Batsford, 1992), 66.

July

1. *Canadian Annual Review* (1912): 94.

2. *Manitoba Free Press*, July 11, 1912.

3. W.L. Morton, *Manitoba: A History* (Toronto: University of Toronto Press, 1957), 315.

4. Erik Larson, *The Devil in the White City: Murder, Magic, and Madness at the Fair that Changed America* (New York: Crown Publishers, 2003), 319. See also Missouri Historical Society, "Overview of the Fair" in 1904: The World's Fair http://www.mohistory.org/content/fair/wf/html/overview/, accessed July 2005.

5. Monseigneur Jean d'Artigue, *Six Years in the Canadian Northwest* (Toronto: Hunter and Rose, 1882), 202–203.

6. *Report of the Superintendent of Indian Education*, 1911/12, House of Commons Canada, Sessional Paper No. 27, 1913, p. 352.

7. Ibid.

8. Ibid.

August

1. F.J. Billiarde, *Citizens in the Making: Annual Report of the Superintendent for the Province of Manitoba 1912* (Winnipeg: Attorney General's Department, 1912).

2. Canada Sessional Papers, 1912, No. 25, Report of the Minister of the Interior, p. xxiii.

3. *The Economist* (March 16, 1912): 573–74.

4. Michael Katz, *The People of Hamilton, Canada West: Family and Class in a Mid-Nineteenth-Century City* (Cambridge: Harvard University Press, 1975), 193.

5. Royal Commission on Impairment of University of Manitoba Trust Funds, *Report*, University of Manitoba Archives, p. 36.

6. Ibid., Testimony, 6814.

7. Randy Rostecki, *Pillars of the Community* (Winnipeg: Historic Buildings Committee, 1993), 5. The pillars still stand, although not always in their original location.

8. R.T. Riley, *Memoirs* (Winnipeg: n.p., 1928), 67.

9. Thomas Flanagan, *Metis Lands in Manitoba* (Calgary: University of Calgary Press, 1991), 61.

10. R.G. McBeth, *Sir Augustus Nanton: A Biography* (Toronto: Macmillan, 1931), 27.

11. Peter Low, "All Western Dollars," in *Transactions of the Manitoba Historical Society*, Series III, 1944/45, 13.

12. Archives of Manitoba, MG11C44, Correspondence Outward, A-K, 1911/12, March 4, 1912.

13. Ibid.

14. M. Bliss, *A Living Profit: Studies in the Social History of Canadian Business 1883–1911* (Toronto: McClelland and Stewart, 1974), 23.

15. Canadian Bank of Commerce Annual Report, 1912, p. xxvii.

16. George Schull, *100 Years of Banking in Canada: A History of the Toronto Dominion Bank* (Toronto: Copp Clark, 1958), 116.

17. Canadian Bank of Commerce Annual Report, 1914, p. xxv.

September

1. Randy Rostecki, ed., "Personal Recollections: The Jewish Pioneer Past on the Prairies," *Jewish Life and Times*, vol. vi (Winnipeg: Jewish Historical Society of Western Canada, 1993), 3.

2. Ibid., 2.

3. Arthur Chiel, *The Jews in Manitoba: A Social History* (Toronto: University of Toronto Press, 1961), 10.

4. *Labour Gazette* (March 1912): 914.

5. S. Hershfield, "Growing Up in North Winnipeg," *Second Annual Publication, Jewish Historical Society of Western Canada*, 1972, 22.

6. Quoted in Chiel, *The Jews in Manitoba*, 175.

7. Laura Rockow, "I Remember Winnipeg," *Jewish Life and Times* 4 (1985): 69.

8. Rostecki, "Personal Recollections," 42.

9. Information about individuals is taken from the Henderson Directory and from the *Biography Scrapbooks* in the Legislative Library of Manitoba.

10. Maranchuk, *The Ukrainian Canadians*, 234.

11. Daniel McIvor, "Work and the Working Men of Winnipeg," MA thesis, University of Manitoba, 1908, p. 7.

12. Billiarde, *Citizens in the Making*, 1137–138.

13. Hershfield, "Growing Up," 23.

14. Rostecki, "Personal Recollections," 43.

15. Harry Gutkin, *The Worst of Times and the Best of Times* (Toronto: Fitzhenry and Whiteside, 1987), 82.

16. James Gray, *The Boy from Winnipeg* (Toronto: Laurentian Library, 1977), 69.

17. Hershfield, "Growing Up," 21.

18. E. Wharton Gill, *A Manitoba Chore Boy* (London: Religious Tract Society, 1912), 7.

19. Rostecki, "Personal Recollections," 85.

20. Quoted in Sybil Shack, "The Education of the Immigrant Child in Manitoba Schools in the Early 20th Century," *Jewish Life and Times* 6 (1983): 93–94.

21. City of Winnipeg Archives, Council Document 9499, 1912.

22. Roz Usiskin, trans. and ed., *A Lifetime of Letters: The Wolodarksy Family, the Period of Separation, 1913–1927* (Winnipeg: The Editor, 1995), 22.

23. Michael Horn, *Academic Freedom in Canada: A History* (Toronto: University of Toronto Press, 1999), 33–34.

24. Rockow, "I Remember Winnipeg," 63.

October

1. Robert Ankli and Robert Litt, "The Growth of Prairie Agriculture," *Canadian Papers in Rural History* 1 (1978): 37.

2. A. Barker, *The British Corn Trade* (London: Sir Isaac Pitman and Sons, 1919), 84.

3. Clarence Piper, *Principles of the Grain Trade in Western Canada* (Winnipeg: Empire Elevator Company, 1915), 140.

4. Kathleen Strange, *Bill Little of the Grain Exchange*, reprinted from the *Canadian Countryman*, c. 1948, 3.

5. The battle to have the farmer-owned company established as a member of the Exchange was long and complex, described in Alan Levine, *The Exchange: 100 Years of Trading Grain in Winnipeg* (Winnipeg: Peguis Publishers, 1987).

6. H. Patton, *Grain Growers' Cooperation in Western Canada* (Harvard University Press, 1928), 34–35.

7. Public Archives of Canada, RG 80, v. 36.

November

1. *Labour Gazette* (November 1912): 536.

2. George Brandow, *The Real Home-Keeper* (Winnipeg: The Brandow Publishing Company, 1914), 50.

3. Public Archives of Manitoba, MG14 C85, Nanton Papers, Kilmorie, 1900 1935.

4. A.A. den Otter, *Civilizing the West: The Galts and the Development of Western Canada* (Edmonton: Hurtig, 1982), 232.

5. H.G.G. Herklots, *The First Winter: A Canadian Chronicle* (London: J.M. Dent, 1935), 8, 9.

6. Ibid. 10.

7. Emily Holt, *The Complete Housekeeper* (Garden City: Doubleday, Page, and Co., 1903, 1917), 318.

8. Herklots, *The First Winter*, 12.

9. Ibid. 13.

10. Robert Baden-Powell, "The Boy Scout Movement," in J. Catell-Hopkins ed. *Empire Club of Canada Speeches 1911-1912* (Toronto: Empire Club, 1912), 12.

11. Colonel A. B. Cunningham, "The Canadian Militia," *Queen's Quarterly* (Spring 1912): 381. Although Cunningham acknowledged the benefits of the reforms, he argued that much more was needed to bring the militia up to fighting trim.

12. Sykes, *Home Help*, 34.

December

1. Harvey, *Curtain Time*, 142 152.

2. Lyle Dick, "Historical Writing on 'Seven Oaks,'" in Robert Coutts, ed., *The Forks and the Battle of Seven Oaks in Manitoba History* (Winnipeg: Manitoba Historical Society, 1994), 69.

3. George Bryce, *The Life of Lord Selkirk, Colonizer of Western Canada* (Toronto: Musson Book company, 1912).

Selected Bibliography

1. Books

Annual Financial Review, 1913. Compiled by W.R. Houston. Toronto: Houston's Standard Publications.

Annual Report of the Canadian Bank of Commerce, 1912.

Artibise, Alan. "An Urban Environment: The Process of Growth in Winnipeg, 1874–1914." In Canadian Historical Society, *Historical Papers*, 1972.

____. *Winnipeg: A Social History of Urban Growth, 1874<3>1914*. Montreal: McGill-Queen's University Press, 1975.

d'Artigue, Monseigneur Jean. *Six Years in the Canadian Northwest*. Toronto: Hunter and Rose, 1882.

Barber, Marilyn. *Immigrant Domestic Servants in Canada*. Ottawa: Canadian Historical Association, 1991.

Bellan, Reuben. *Winnipeg First Century: An Economic History* Winnipeg: Queenston House Press, 1978.

Berger, Carl. *The Sense of Power: Studies in the Ideas of Canadian Imperialism 1867–1914*. Toronto: University of Toronto Press, 1970.

Billiarde, F.J. *Citizens in the Making: Annual Report of the Superintendent of Neglected Children for the Province of Manitoba 1912*. Winnipeg: Attorney General's Dept., 1912.

Blanchard, J.A. *History of the Canadian Grain Commission, 1912–1987*. Winnipeg: Canadian Grain Commission, 1987.

Bliss, Michael. *A Living Profit: Studies in the Social History of Canadian Business, 1883–1911*. Toronto: McClelland and Stewart, 1974.

Brandow, George. *The Real Home-Keeper*. Winnipeg: The Brandow Publishing Company, 1914.

A Brief History of the Social Planning Council of Winnipeg. Winnipeg: Social Planning Council, 1989.

Canadian Almanac, 1912.

Careless, J.M.S. "Aspects of Urban Life in the West, 1870–1914." In Stelter, G.A., and Alan Artibise, *The Canadian City: Essays in Urban History*. Ottawa: Carleton University Press, 1977.

Castell-Hopkins, J., ed. *The Canadian Annual Review of Public Affairs, 1912*. Toronto: Annual Review Publishers, 1912.

Chafe, J.W. *An Apple for the Teacher*. Winnipeg: Winnipeg School Division No. 1, 1967.

Chiel, Arthur. *The Jews in Manitoba: A Social History*. Toronto: University of Toronto Press, 1961.

Chipman, G.F. *The Siege of Ottawa*. Winnipeg: Grain Growers Guide, 1910.

Cowie, Isaac. *The Company of Adventurers: a Narrative of 7 Years in the Service of the H.B.Co. during 1868–1874*. Toronto: William Briggs, 1913.

Dempsey, Hugh. *The Best of Bob Edwards*. Edmonton: Hurtig Publishers, 1975.

den Otter, A.A. *Civilizing the West: The Galts and the Development of Western Canada*. Edmonton: University of Alberta Press, 1982.

Denison, George T. *The Struggle for Imperial Unity*. London: Macmillan and Co., 1909.

The Dickens Fellowship, Winnipeg Branch, Souvenir with Portraits and Illustrations. Winnipeg: The Fellowship, 1913.

Donnelly, Murray. *Dafoe of the Free Press*. Toronto: Macmillan of Canada, 1968.

Donzel, Catherine. *Grand Hotels of North America*. Toronto: McClelland and Stewart, 1989.

Eagle, John. *The CPR and the Development of Western Canada 1896-1914*. Montreal: McGill-Queen's University Press, 1989.

Ewanchuk, Michael. *Ukrainians in Canada*. Winnipeg: M. Ewanchuk, 1994.

Ewing, Elizabeth. *A History of Twentieth Century Fashion*. London: Batsford, 1992.

Flanagan, Thomas. *Metis Lands in Manitoba*. Calgary: University of Calgary Press, 1991.

Friesen, G. *The Canadian Prairies, A History*. Toronto: University of Toronto Press, 1984.

Galloway, Margaret. *I Lived in Paradise*. Winnipeg: Bullman Brothers, 1942.

Gill, E.A. Wharton. *A Manitoba Chore Boy*. London: Religious Tract Society, 1912.

_____. *Love in Manitoba*. Toronto: Musson Book Co. Ltd., 1911.

Gray, James. *The Boy from Winnipeg*. Toronto: Macmillan of Canada, 1970.

Grenke, Arthur. *The German Community in Winnipeg, 1872–1919*. New York: AMS Press, 1991.

Gutkin, Harry. *Journey Into Our Heritage*. Toronto: Lester Orpen and Denys, 1986.

_____. *The Worst of Times, the Best of Times*. Toronto: Fitzhenry and Whiteside, 1987.

Ham, George. *Reminiscences of a Raconteur*. Toronto: Musson, 1921.

A Handbook of Winnipeg and Province of Manitoba. Winnipeg: Executive Committee, 79th Meeting of the British Association for the Advancement of Science, 1909.

Harland, Marion. *Everyday Etiquette*. Indianapolis: Bobbs-Merrill, 1905, 1907.

Harvey, Ruth. *Curtain Time*. Boston: Houghton Mifflin, 1949.

Heaton, Ernest. *The Commercial Handbook of Canada, 1912*. Toronto: Heaton's Agency, 1912.

Henderson's Winnipeg Blue Book and Householders Directory: Private Address Directory, Ladies' Visiting and Shopping Guide and Club Lists. Winnipeg: Henderson Directories Ltd., 1907.

Herklots, H.G.G. *The First Winter: A Canadian Chronicle*. London: John Dent, 1935.

Herrick, Christine T. *The Expert Maid-Servant*. New York: Harper Brothers, 1904.

Holt, Emily. *The Complete Housekeeper*. Garden City: Doubleday, Page and Co., 1903,1917.

_____. *Encyclopedia of Etiquette*. Toronto: Musson Book Co., 1916.

Houston, W.R., comp. *Annual Financial Review, 1913*. Toronto: Houston's Standard Publications, 1913.

Howell, M.L., and R.A. Howell, eds. *History of Sport in Canada*. Champaign: Stipes Publishing Co., 1981.

Hudson Bay Company Autumn and Winter Catalogue, 1910–1911. Winnipeg: Watson and Dwyer, 1977.

Jarvis, W.H.P. *The Letters of a Remittance Man to His Mother*. Toronto: Musson Book Co., 1909.

Katz, Yossi, and John Lehr. *The Last Best West.* Jerusalem: Magnes Press, 1999.

Katz, Michael. *The People of Hamilton, Canada West: Family and Class in a Mid-Nineteenth Century City.* Cambridge: Harvard University Press, 1975.

Knysh, George. *Michael Sherbynin in Winnipeg: A Preliminary Study.* Winnipeg: Ukrainian Academy of Arts and Sciences Press, 1994.

Lacelle, Claudette. *Urban Domestic Servants in 19th Century Canada.* Ottawa: Research Publications, Environment Canada, Parks, 1987.

Legget, Robert E. *Railways of Canada.* Vancouver: Douglas and McIntyre, 1987.

Levine, Alan. *The Exchange: 100 Years of Trading Grain in Winnipeg.* Winnipeg: Peguis Publishers, 1987.

Low, Sidney. *Egypt in Transition.* New York: Macmillan and Co., 1914.

MacBeth, R.G. *Sir Augustus Nanton: A Biography.* Toronto: MacMillan, 1931.

McDonald, Donna. *Lord Strathcona: A Biography.* Toronto: Dundurn Press, 1996.

Macoun, J. *Manitoba and the Great North-West: The Field for Investment, the Home of the Emigrant.* Edinburgh: T.C. Jack, 1883.

Macvicar, Helena. *Margaret Scott: A Tribute and The Margaret Scott Nursing Mission.* Winnipeg: Margaret Scott Nursing Mission, 1939.

Maranchuk, Michael. *The Ukrainian Canadians: A History.* Winnipeg: Ukrainian Free Academy of Science, 1970.

Mavor, James. *Government Telephones: The Experience of Manitoba.* New York: Moffat Yard and Co., 1916.

Medovy, Harry. *A Vision Fulfilled: The Story of the Children's Hospital of Winnipeg 1909– 1973.* Winnipeg: Peguis Publishers, 1979.

Morris, Peter. *Embattled Shadows: A History of Canadian Cinema 1895–1939.* Montreal: McGill-Queen's University Press, 1992.

Patton, H. *Grain Growers' Cooperation in Western Canada.* Cambridge: Harvard University Press, 1928.

Piper, Clarence. *Principles of the Grain Trade in Western Canada.* Winnipeg: Empire Elevator Company, 1915.

Price, Alfred. *Rail Life: A Book of Yarns.* Toronto: Thomas Allen, 1925.

Riley, R.T. *Memoirs.* Winnipeg: Riley Family, 1947.

Ross, Victor. *A History of the Canadian Bank of Commerce.* Toronto: Oxford University Press, 1922.

Rostecki, R. *Crescentwood: A History.* Winnipeg: Crescentwood Homeowners Association, 1993.

_____. *Pillars of the Community: Roadside Markers in Winnipeg, 1911–1963.* Winnipeg: Historic Buildings Committee, 1993.

Salmon, Lucy. *Domestic Service.* New York: Macmillan, 1901.

Salverson, Laura. *Confessions of an Immigrant's Daughter.* Montreal: Reprint Society of Canada, 1949.

Shaw, Rose. *Proud Heritage: A History of the National Council of Women of Canada.* Toronto: Ryerson Press, 1957.

Sherwood, Mrs. *Manners and Social Usages.* New York: Harper Brothers, 1907.

Sinclair, J.D., ed. *Westminster Church: 45th Year, A History.* Winnipeg: Westminster Church, 1935.

Smith, Doug. *Let Us Rise: A History of the Manitoba Labour Movement.* Vancouver: New Star Books, 1985.

_____. *The Winnipeg Labour Council, 1894–1994.* Winnipeg: Manitoba Labour Education Centre, 1994.

Springsteed, Anne Francis. *The Expert Waitress.* New York: Harper Brothers, 1912.

Steen, J., and W. Bryce. *Manitoba and her Industries.* Chicago and Winnipeg: Steen & Boyce, 1882.

Strange, Kathleen. *Bill Little of the Grain Exchange.* Toronto: Reprinted from the *Canadian Countryman*, c. 1948.

Stubbs, Roy St. George. *Men in Khaki.* Toronto: Ryerson Press, 1941.

Sykes, Ella. *A Home Help in Canada.* London: G. Bell, 1912.

Talbot, Frederick. *The Making of a Great Canadian Railway.* London: Seeley Service and Company, 1912.

Tunnell, Arthur, ed. *Winnipeg Society Blue Book and Club List 1926/7.* Winnipeg: The Author, 1927.

Turek, Victor. *The Poles in Manitoba.* Toronto: Polish Alliance Press, 1967.

Usiskin, Roz, ed. and trans. *A Lifetime of Letters: The Wolodarsky Family, the Period of Separation, 1913–1927.* Winnipeg: The Author, 1995.

Veblen, T. *The Theory of the Leisure Class.* New York: Macmillan Co., 1902.

Vining, Charles. *Bigwigs: Canadians Wise and Otherwise.* Toronto: Macmillan, 1935.

Wade, F.C. *Experiments with the Single Tax in Western Canada.* Vancouver: Saturday Sunset Press, 1914.

Weiss, Alice. *A Little Girl Remembers.* Winnipeg: The Author, 1983.

Whates, H.R. *Canada the New Nation: A Book for the Settler, the Immigrant and the Politician.* London: J.M. Dent, 1906.

The Work of Women and Girls in Department Stores in Winnipeg. Winnipeg: University Women's Club, 1914.

Woodsworth, J.S. *My Neighbour.* Toronto: University of Toronto Press, 1972.

Yeigh, Frank. *Through the Heart of Canada.* Toronto: Henry Froude, 1911.

Zangwell, Israel. *The Melting Pot.* New York: Macmillan and Co., 1919.

2. Articles

The American Review of Reviews: an International Magazine. New York: Review of Reviews Company, Vol. 45, 1912.

Ames, Herbert P. "The Organization of Political Parties in Canada." *American Political Science Review* 6 (February 1912): 181–88.

Artibise, Alan. "Advertising Winnipeg: the Campaign for Immigration and Industry, 1874–1914. In *Transactions of the Historical and Scientific Society of Manitoba*, 1970–71, Series III, No. 27, pp. 75–106.

Atkinson, George. "In Canadian Prairie Lands." *The Public* (April 12, 1912): 345.

Beattie, Norman. "The Cab Trade in Winnipeg 1871–1910." *Urban History Review* 27, 1 (1998): 36–52.

Bladen, M.L. "Construction of Railways in Canada to the Year 1885." *Contributions to Canadian Economics* 5 (1932): 43–60.

_____. "Construction of Railways in Canada, 1885–1931." *Contributions to Canadian Economics* 7 (1934): 82–107.

"British Capital in Canada." *The Economist* (November 16, 1912): 1012–1013.

"Canada and the Navy." *The Round Table* 8 (September 1912): 627–57.

"Canada: The Census." *The Round Table* 5 (December 1911): 142–44.

"Canada: The Conservative Cabinet." *The Round Table* 5 (December 1911): 139–42.

"Canada: French in the Schools." *The Round Table* 9 (December 1912): 144–51.

"Canada: The General Election." *The Round Table* 5 (December 1911): 130–38.

"Canada: The Naval Proposals." *The Round Table* 9 (December 1912): 134–40.

"Canada: Railways in the West." *The Round Table* 9 (December 1912): 141–44.

"Canadian Finance." *The Economist* (January 6, 1912): 13–14.

"The Canadian Northern Report." *The Economist* (November 30, 1912): 1119.

"The Canadian Pacific." *The Economist* (August, 17, 1912): 316–17.

"Canadian Pacific New Issue." *The Economist* (October 5, 1912): 617.

"Canadian Railways." *The Economist* (February 24, 1912): 40–05.

Canadian Securities (letter). *The Economist* (November 23, 1912): 1082–83.

"Canadian Trade and the Increase of Public Liabilities." *The Economist* (June 8, 1912): 1300–01.

"The Canadian West: The Prices of Land in Manitoba." *The Economist* (March 16, 1912): 573–74.

Careless, J.M.S., "Aspects of Urban Life in the West, 1870-1914." In G.A. Stelter and Alan Artibise, *The Canadian City: Essays in Urban History*. Ottawa: Carleton University, 1984.

_____. "The Development of the Winnipeg Business Community, 1870-1890." *Transactions of the Royal Society of Canada*, Series 4, Vol. 8, 1970, pp. 239–54.

Carter, Sarah. "The Woman's Sphere: Domestic Life in Riel House and Dalnavert." *Manitoba History* 11 (1986): 55–61.

Chipman, G.F. "Winnipeg: The Melting Pot." *The Canadian Magazine* 33, 5 (1909): 409–16.

_____. "Winnipeg: The Refining Process." *The Canadian Magazine* 33, 6 (1909): 548–54.

_____. "The Voice from the Soil." *The Canadian Magazine* 36 (January 1911): 240–46.

"Christmas Cheer in Winnipeg." *Social Welfare* (December 1928): 61–62, 66.

Clemens, Paul. "Winnipeg Hydro." *The Public* (January 28, 1912): 78.

Creighton, D. "The Fate of the Empire." *The Canadian Magazine* 41 (August 1913): 363–66.

Cunningham, A.B. "The Canadian Militia." *Queens Quarterly* (April, May, June, 1912): 375–82.

Douglass, W.A. "Canadian Problems and Politics." *The Westminster Review* 177 (April 1912): 398–404.

Duckworth, H.T.F. "The New Britains and Old." *The Canadian Magazine* 41 (July 1913): 245–52.

Emery, G.N. "The Methodist Church and the 'European Foreigners' of Winnipeg: The All People's Mission 1889–1914." *Transactions of the Historical and Scientific Society of Manitoba*, Series III, No. 28, 1971–72, pp. 85–100.

Ewart, John. "Canadian Independence." *The Canadian Magazine* 37 (May 1911): 33–40.

Firth, J.B. "The Bubble in the Far West." *Fortnightly Review* 92 (December 1912): 1051–59.

Ford, Arthur R. "Western Political Dominance." *The Canadian Magazine* 34 (January 1910): 230–32.

Gadsby, Henry. "A Retrospect of the Session." *The University Magazine* (1912): 183.

Hamilton, Margaret. "The Servant Girl Problem." *Everywoman's World* (May 1914): 24.

Hiebert, Daniel, "Class, Ethnicity and Residential Structure: The Social Geography of Winnipeg, 1901–1921." *Journal of Historical Geography* 17, 1 (1991): 56–86.

Hinther, Rhonda. "The Oldest Profession in Winnipeg: The Culture of Prostitution in the Point Douglas Segregated Area, 1909–1912." *Manitoba History* (Spring/Summer 2001): 2–13.

Jarvis, W.H.P. "Streetcar Service in Winnipeg is an Eye Opener for Torontonian." *Toronto Saturday Night* (November 26, 1910): 23.

____. "Winnipeg—Where Town Lots Are Gold Mines and Everyone Is Welcome Save the Pessimist." *Toronto Saturday Night* (November 12, 1910): 23.

Jewish Life and Times. Winnipeg: Jewish Historical Society of Western Canada, 1983–.

"K.E." "Her At Home Day." *Town Topics*, April 6, 1912.

Lehr, John C., and D. Wayne Moodie "The Polemics of Pioneer Settlement: Ukrainian Immigration and the Winnipeg Press." *Canadian Ethnic Studies* 12, 2 (1980): 88–101.

Lenskyj, Helen. "Servant Problem or Servant Mistress Problem: Domestic Service in Canada, 1890–1930." *Atlantis* 7, 1 (1981): 3–11.

MacTavish, Newton. "East and West in Canada." *The Westminster Review* 179, 6 (June 1913): 597–603.

Mallett, J. "Railway Development in Canada." *The United Empire* 3 (1912): 960–69.

Norrie, K.H. "The Rate of Settlement on the Canadian Prairies." *Journal of Economic History* 35 (1975): 410–27.

"Playgrounds in Winnipeg." *The Playground* 7, 7 (October 1911): 244–48.

"Present Conditions in the Canadian West." *The Economist* (March 9, 1912): 514–15.

"The Price of Farm Lands in Alberta and Saskatchewan." *The Economist* (March 30, 1912): 685–86.

Rae, J.E. "How Winnipeg Was Nearly Won." In A.R. McCormack, ed., *Cities in the West: Papers of the Canadian Urban History Conference*, University of Winnipeg, October 1974. Ottawa: National Museums, 1975.

Schmidt, R. "Winnipeg as a Transportation Centre." In T. Kuz, ed., *Winnipeg 1874<&>1974: Progress and Prospects*. Winnipeg: Manitoba Department of Industry and Commerce, 1974.

"Some Notes on Winnipeg: About Mud and Other Matters." *Toronto Saturday Night* (April 7, 1906): 8.

Taylor, F. Williams. "Canadian Loans in London." *United Empire* 3 (1912): 985–97.

Titley, E. Brian. "Hayter Reed and the Indian Administration of the West." In *Swords and Ploughshares: War and Agriculture in Western Canada.* Edmonton: University of Alberta Press, 1993.

Wheeling, A. Lambert. "Opening Week at Ottawa." *The Canadian Magazine* 38 (February 1912): 379–85.

Wilton, Shauna. "Manitoba Women Nurturing the Nation: The Manitoba IODE and Maternal Nationalism, 1913–1920." *Journal of Canadian Studies* 35, 2 (2000): 149–65.

"Women Behind Winnipeg's Counters." *The Survey* (July 25, 1914): 428.

3. Theses and Student Papers

Bellan, R.C. "Relief in Winnipeg: The Economic Background." MA thesis, University of Toronto, 1941.

Dodds, Michelle. "'Strictly Private!!!'? A Focused Feminist Biographical Profile of Minnie Campbell." Undergraduate paper, University of Manitoba, 1983.

Henderson, David. "A Study of Housing and Environment in Winnipeg." MA thesis, University of Manitoba 1952.

Irvine, D.N. "Reform War and Industrial Crisis in Manitoba: F.J. Dixon and the Framework of Consensus 1903–1920." MA thesis, University of Manitoba, 1981.

McIvor, Daniel. "Labour in Manitoba." MA thesis, University of Manitoba, 1908.

Orilikow, L. "A Survey of the Reform Movement in Manitoba 1910–1920." MA thesis, University of Manitoba, 1958.

Acknowledgements

Many people have helped me in the creation of this book. I want to thank Randy Rostecki who was, as usual, always ready to answer my questions about Winnipeg history and to offer suggestions about sources. At the Provincial Archives Chris Kostecki has been extremely helpful in guiding me to sources and giving encouragement. I am grateful to Roz Usiskin for generously allowing me to use some of her unpublished writing. Rosemary Malaher alerted me to valuable source material for the book and I thank her. I owe a great deal to friends and family who have listened patiently to me over the years as I talked about this project and who encouraged me to complete it. Lastly, I want to thank David Carr and Pat Sanders of the University of Manitoba Press and Steven Rosenberg of Doowah Design Inc. for their work in turning my manuscript into a book.

Photo Credits

All photographs and illustrations are from the Archives of Manitoba except for the following:

Pages 7, 20, 23, 258 from *Winnipeg: The Gateway to the Golden West* (The Valentine's & Sons United Publishing Co. Ltd., ca. 1912)

Pages 15, 18, 126 from *Winnipeg Illustrated 1912* (Winnipeg Industrial Bureau, 1912)

Pages 36, 37, 102, 121, 124, 230, 252 from *Town Topics*, 1912.

Pages 67, 74, 115, 179, 206, 222 from *Manitobans As We See 'Em 1908-1909*, a book of caricatures by Winnipeg newspaper cartoonists

Page 100, from the Western Canada Pictorial Index

A Note on the Type

This book has been set in Cochin, with display type in Bernhard Modern Engraved.

Charles Malin cut Cochin in 1912 for the Paris foundry Deberny & Peignot, based on the design of Georges Peignot. This font is named after the French engraver Charles Nicolas Cochin (1715-1790), although its style had little to do with that of the copper artist's. It displays a curious mix of style elements and could be placed as a part of the typographical Neo-Renaissance movement. Cochin was especially popular at the beginning of the 20th century.

Bernhard Modern Engraved was designed in 1937, although its designer, Lucian Bernhard, created his first popular font, Bernhard Antiqua, in 1912.